The Big O

The Big O

My Life, My Times, My Game

Oscar Robertson

RODALE

Printed in the United States of America
Rodale Inc. makes every effort to use acid-free ∞, recycled paper ♻.

Except where otherwise credited, photographs appearing in this book are from the personal collection of Oscar Robertson.

Credit and additional permission information is located on page 333.

Book design by Christina Gaugler

Library of Congress Cataloging-in-Publication Data

Robertson, Oscar, date.
    The Big O : my life, my times, my game / by Oscar Robertson.
        p.   cm.
    Includes index.
    ISBN 1–57954–764–8 hardcover
    1. Robertson, Oscar, date.   2. Basketball players—United States—Biography.   I. Title.
    GV884.R6A3   2003
    796.323'092—dc22   2003016132

Distributed to the book trade by St. Martin's Press

2   4   6   8   10   9   7   5   3   1   hardcover

RODALE

WE **INSPIRE** AND **ENABLE** PEOPLE TO IMPROVE
THEIR LIVES AND THE WORLD AROUND THEM

FOR MORE OF OUR PRODUCTS
WWW.RODALESTORE.COM
(800) 848-4735

To the one true love of my life and my friend, my wife,
Yvonne, who has been a tremendous beacon for me
to grow culturally and intellectually.

To my daughters, Shana, Tia, and Mari.
I deeply appreciate being your father.

Contents

Acknowledgments

M Y THANKS TO Charles Bock, Jeremy Katz, and Rodale for ful-
filling this project. And special thanks to Zelda Spoelstra.

To my grandparents Early and Pearl Bell and all my Bellsburg, Tennessee, family. To my hardworking mother and father and my brothers,
Bailey and Henry, for providing an innocent, happy childhood.

To Crispus Attucks High School for those wonderful growing and
learning years—two state high school basketball championships, one undefeated—and for providing the catalyst for the black population of Indianapolis to be proud. My greatest teachers were from Crispus Attucks High
School, who showed me the great value of education. It certainly made it
easier for me to compete in college.

The success I enjoyed came from those teammates and those I
played against. Thank you, all those players from Colton Street, Lockefield
Gardens, and "Mr. Lockefield," James "Bruiser" Gaines.

Thank you, Coach Tom Sleet, Albert Spurlock, and especially Ray
Crowe for helping me achieve against odds that I had not even met yet.

To George Smith, my coach at the University of Cincinnati, for letting me use all my talents on a national level. I am grateful to the University of Cincinnati for an indispensable role in my educational growth. I

appreciate those talented professors who did not hinder me from achieving academic excellence.

I owe Jimmy and Para Lee Brown deep appreciation for providing a safe haven away from home. My heartfelt thanks to Austin and Gladys Tillotson for their love and many kindnesses, to Art Hull for his friendship, and to Dr. Odell Owens for his enthusiasm.

Thank you to Mrs. William C. Swatts Sr. for all your care; for producing my best friend, Dr. William C. Swatts Jr.; and for helping to shape my childhood.

To all those special friends . . .

To Walter Paul for his persistence in getting me to the University of Cincinnati. Thank you for being a sensitive, supportive, and wonderful friend. To J. W. Brown, my attorney and dear friend, who provided guidance, wise professional advice, and loyalty. Jake understood people and made our personal talks so very enjoyable. I sincerely miss his presence. To his son, Robert, my attorney now, my profound indebtedness for writing the Milwaukee Bucks contract and for being a steadfast supporter and lifelong friend. And special thanks to Larry Fleisher.

Thank you, Michael O'Daniel, Ira Berkow, Leonard Lewin, and Tom Collins—the elite of sportswriters. A special thanks to another special writer, Milt Gross, for his wisdom and advice starting when I was a shy, young player and continuing on to the end of my career.

Preface

I'VE ALWAYS THOUGHT that a wonderful thing about sports is that they give everyone a chance. A child doesn't have to be the best. He or she doesn't have to make the team in high school or college. A child can decide if he or she doesn't want to play, doesn't like the sport, or doesn't want to do the work it takes to improve. But all people should be given the opportunity to go out and compete and see what they can do in comparison to others. That's one of the wonderful things about America as well. This country promises everyone a chance. It is a promise that has not always been kept. A promise many of us had to fight for, even die for. But the promise has always been here, a shining beacon down the road.

And when some shy, small boy somewhere gets a chance and picks up a ball—say, a basketball—who knows what can happen, what heights to which he might rise? If he is dedicated enough, talented enough, strong enough, he just might do things on the basketball court that no one has ever seen before. Things no one has done since. He might wind up changing how the game of basketball is played.

Maybe, just maybe, if he works hard enough and is strong enough, he could be called the best who ever lived.

And maybe this would be just the beginning.

CHAPTER ONE

The Crossroads of America
1938–1951

THE WORLD OF MY CHILDHOOD has as many ties to the Civil War as it does to today. My great-grandfather Marshall Collier was born in 1838, less than two years after Davy Crockett died at the Alamo. Marshall was raised in slavery, in rural Dickson County, smack-dab in the center of Tennessee's western highland rim, some thirty miles outside Nashville. Collier was the surname of the estate's landowner, and I don't know what Marshall's family name might have been. Family lore has it that Marshall ran off a lot when he was a slave. He would usually get no further than the Cumberland River. Marshall was always caught, but he was never beaten, or so I'm told. Whenever my father told me this story, he said that Marshall wasn't beaten because he was the master's son. He said that this was one of the small ways in which Marshall's parentage was acknowledged.

Some accounts have set his height at seven feet two inches. I don't remember him being that tall, but he certainly was a long, lanky man, with light skin and high cheekbones. Marshall had keen features and mixed blood, no doubt about it: part Cherokee, West African, and white. As a boy, he heard of Nat Turner's rebellion and as a young man saw his unacknowledged father and brothers go away to fight in gray. He saw Union troops in blue, manning nearby Fort Donelson. He lived through Reconstruction, the infestation of carpetbaggers, and later still, the Klan nights.

With the end of the war and emancipation, Marshall received a stretch of land. Like all my other Tennessee relatives, my great-grandfather spent his life as a farmer, a genuine man of the land. He went out into the fields every day of his life, planting and harvesting crops. He worked those fields right up until the day his eyesight failed him and he could no longer recognize his own hand in front of his face. Daddy Marshall lived to be 116. When he passed from the earth, he was the oldest man in the United States, and he had never traveled above the Mason-Dixon line.

My father came from the little nearby community of Bellsburg, a town of just a few hundred residents in the north end of Dickson County. I once did some research and discovered that the town was named after a settler named Shadrach Bell during the early 1800s. Supposedly, Shadrach founded the territory while selling slaves, many of whom also ended up taking the Bell surname. Meanwhile, one of the area's first white settlers was a man named James Robertson. In 1799, this particular Robertson undertook a minerals survey in the area. On that first expedition, James Robertson brought a Negro man with him. Soon after, he returned with a number of slaves to build a fort on the bluffs of the Cumberland. Not long after this, James Robertson started the first iron furnace in that area. To this day, the names of Robertson, Bell, and Collier—names that white settlers and farmers brought with them to Tennessee—can still be found there, carried by their descendants, whether acknowledged or not.

One of Daddy Marshall's daughters, Lonnie Collier, married a former slave from Virginia named Ed Robertson. Ed wound up in Tennessee because the man who owned him died. Not long after that, the man's widow had to take a mule to Tennessee. My grandfather helped her, and when they got to Tennessee, she freed him. Ed Robertson became a minister at the Mount Zion African Methodist Episcopal Church. He and his brother, Herschel, often took to the road, driving around in an old rumble-seat car, preaching the word of the Lord, often running into members of the Klan. But everyone knew Ed Robertson was doing holy work. "That's just Ed," someone would say, and they'd let him go. Later, he married Lonnie. Their son, Bailey Robertson Sr., is my father.

Ed Robertson and Lonnie Collier split up after their children were born. For a time, Ed and his children kept traveling the road with Herschel, preaching, until Ed passed away. I was never told what did him in. My dad was raised by his aunt, Ever Robertson. Dad called her Aunt Ever. For a long time, my father thought Ever was his mother. When he graduated from sixth grade, Dad joined the rest of his family, friends, and pretty much everyone else in Bellsburg, working full-time, farming tobacco and corn out in the fields. The work was honorable, Dad used to tell me, and the white farm-owners treated him pretty well. Dad wasn't especially tall, five feet eleven inches or so. If you look at a picture of him as a young man, you can see my cheeks and build. I could easily be mistaken for his brother.

Among whites, Mom's parents went by the nicknames of Uncle Early and Aunt Pearl. Pearl worked as a domestic in white homes, even breastfed white children. The whites refused to call my grandparents Mr. and Mrs. Bell. Nobody in my family—or the rest of the black community, really—called them Aunt and Uncle. Papa and Mama Pearl were the names we knew them by.

As a young man, Papa worked on the Ohio River as a sharecropper. He read the Bible every night, and he worked hard in the fields all day, walking behind a mule and a plow. A white man, Blake Span, and my grandfather worked together in the bottomland. Though they were good friends in the fields, it ended there. Other white people who lived nearby also thought highly of my grandfather, but outside of certain accepted places, such as the fields, socializing between races simply was not accepted.

My grandfather worked the fields and over a stretch of years saved up enough money for a down payment. He bought a plot of land from the white farmer who lived across the road from him. His three hundred dollars, quite a bit of money back then, bought him less than twenty acres.

Papa dug his own 187-foot well on the property. He worked his own mills and milked his own cow; he raised hogs and a kitchen garden—one he kept in the wintertime as well as the summertime. He grew crops of corn, black-eyed peas, hay, and tobacco, using a horse and mules even when most other people got tractors. Papa also worked twenty acres along the Cumberland River for a white man named Lightfoot.

Papa wasn't a complex man. What he did with his life was raise the crops that kept his family and the animals fed, make a little money, and pay off his farm so that his family had something that belonged to them. He read the Bible every night, sang church songs, and talked about the Bible. I have distant memories of him leaving the house before sunrise and returning after dark. He used to sit on his porch all night and rock in his favorite chair, shelling peas and singing hymns.

I wish I could provide a romantic story about how my parents met. But the truth is, I don't know. Bellsburg, as well as the other bottomlands outside Charlotte, Tennessee, was and remains farming country. Its people are farm people. There aren't too many ways to meet folks out there, and, when you get down to it, not too many folks to meet. But my paternal grandfather, Ed, had been the minister at Mount Zion; my mother's side of the family was numerous and spread throughout Dickson County, with the church a center of their social lives. So if I had to guess, I'd say there's a good chance that my parents met at church.

They were young when they met. My mom, Mazell, was less than twenty, and Dad was somewhere around the same age. Once they were married, they lived with Mama Pearl and Papa Bell in their small farmhouse on State Highway 29 in northern Dickson County.

My older brothers, Bailey Robertson Jr. and Henry, were born in that farmhouse. And on a snowy Thanksgiving Day, 1938, exactly one hundred years to the day after Daddy Marshall's birth, I was born there too. It was a tough birth, and I was a frail, sickly infant. According to my mother, nobody thought I would survive. If I did somehow make it, then it looked like my left foot would be deformed. Mom and my grandfather took turns massaging that foot during the first weeks of my life, telling each other that I had to pull through.

My childhood memories of Tennessee are of stretching fields of grass and corn, with trees and mountains lining the distance, and a blue sky thick with clouds. We lived what I imagine was, back then, the typical life of a Negro family in the rural South. The Klan was active in Tennessee, but we never saw them, and no one talked about our conditions. We were simply happy to be around our families, see our relatives, go to church, work in the fields, and get together on Sundays and socialize. There were cakes and chickens and other food. My memories of those days are wonderful ones, and it's not crazy to imagine that my family could have stayed on that patch of land forever, passing the farmhouse and the chores down from generation to generation, with nothing changing except the names on the birth certificates and the names on the gravestones.

But the 1930s were a brutal decade for American farmers—harsh on whites, and you know that only deepened the hardship for blacks. As the decade came to a close, farming throughout the South was in the middle of something of a revolution. Tractors and harvesters were replacing mules and manual labor, and mechanization was in the process of making black tenant farmers and sharecroppers expendable. Though Daddy Marshall and Papa Bell kept working their land, my father started traveling twenty-five miles a day to Nashville to work. Over time, Dad came to understand that no black man had a realistic chance of getting the money necessary to purchase any of the expensive machinery now needed to make a go of farming. He had a wife and three kids, and we were growing. Bailey Jr. was about ready to finish grade school, and Henry and I were not that far behind. I was too young to be attending classes, but rules or not, I'd started going to school with my brothers at nearby Mount Zion, where I was taught by Lizzie Gleaves. She had to be god-sent. I knew the alphabet, could count to a hundred, and listened to a lot of the Bible.

No nearby white high school admitted black children, and none of the black high schools were close enough for us to attend. My father was intent on making sure his children had more chances at an education and a better living than he'd had.

Dad had an aunt named Inez who lived in Indianapolis. She constantly encouraged him to try his luck up north in Indiana, the self-proclaimed Crossroads of America. This was 1942. The attack on Pearl Harbor had the draft board busy issuing letters to every available white male. Logic followed that someone was going to have to stay at home and manufacture those tanks, bombers, and battleships. President Roosevelt had issued executive orders barring discrimination in defense-industry hiring, so all of a sudden, something of a duplication of the chain of events from World War I was underway, and all sorts of jobs were available for black folks in most of the big cities. Inez made sure that my father knew that there were jobs to be had in Indianapolis, and after a cursory stint in Nashville, trying to find work, Dad listened to Inez and ventured over to Indianapolis.

He worked in a defense plant for a time, then got lonely for Mom, came back, and then left again, this time to look for a permanent job. About four months later, my mother, brothers, and I gathered up our meager possessions. We sat in the back of the bus, and became part of history—this nation's second great Negro migration to the North—making the all-day trip, three hundred miles, through Tennessee and Kentucky. Along the way we ate from the basket of bologna sandwiches that Mom had packed. When the bus stopped, we weren't allowed in the restaurants on the side of the road. And like every other black person on the bus, we marched around behind the restaurant in order to relieve ourselves.

Aunt's house didn't have a phone; that luxury was simply out of the question, so my mom had no way of communicating with my father in Indianapolis. When we arrived at the bus station, nobody was there to greet us, and we had no way of getting in touch with my dad. So my mom, my brothers, and I gathered up our belongings and walked the twenty-four long blocks from the station near the old Claypool Hotel all the way to Aunt Inez's house on the city's west side.

Dad answered the door, surprised. He'd had no idea we were coming. I was four years old.

I DON'T KNOW if anyone told my dad how racist a state Indiana was. Or, coming from the South, if he just figured every state was segregated by race. The truth was, we weren't headed to any kind of heaven. In Indiana's not too distant past, the Ku Klux Klan had openly financed the campaign of the governor, Ed Jackson, as well as a number of pro-Klan judges, mayors, and state legislators. Signs—NIGGER, DON'T LET THE SUN SET ON YOU HERE!—dotted the state's rural landscapes and fields, and in almost any town, white robes and peaked hats were readily available at six dollars apiece. In Indianapolis, the state's capital city, things weren't much better. Yes, the National Association for the Advancement of Colored People had successfully fought against a city zoning ordinance officially segregating black and white neighborhoods. But as a response, white landowners had constructed what were known as "spite fences" around some properties. Civic leagues had been founded with the sole purpose of keeping whites from leasing to blacks. Handbills frequently circulated asking, DO YOU WANT A NIGGER FOR A NEIGHBOR? Curfews existed for black folks but not for whites. Simply put, if you were black, you could not move freely through the city.

We lived with Aunt Inez for a while, but that wasn't going to work out. So Dad found a little shotgun house on Colton Street in an area that was your basic black ghetto. Everyone called it Naptown, or sometimes Frog Island. With Century Canal to the east, the White River on its south and west, and Fall Creek to the north, Naptown was a low-lying area surrounded by water, prone to flooding. There was no indoor plumbing, and the city came around just once a year to empty out all the waste, so the air was perpetually full of bad smells and festering diseases.

Colton Street wasn't much of a street—maybe two blocks long; it wasn't paved, just surfaced with a mix of gravel and oil that had been packed down over time. We found a small house at 1005 Colton, adjacent to the Lockefield Gardens housing developments. The place was your standard shotgun shack. Its rooms joined in a straight line that you could look through, and the roof was made of tar paper—just strong enough to protect us from rain, but too flimsy to shelter us from cold, windy nights or flies and mosquitoes. There was running water, but the toilet was outside. A big potbelly stove sat smack-dab in the middle of the house, and there was a bin outside, underneath the house's frame, to hold the coal. The house had four rooms: one for Mom and Dad, one for the potbelly stove, one for me and my brothers, and one room for cooking and eating.

Even with the potbelly stove, there was no heat in the wintertime. You would get under all the covers you could, but the wind would come right through the windows. You would hear people across the street arguing and fighting all the time. And gunshots at night. Later, my father got a toilet put in, a commode, but no bathtub. You bathed in a foot tub. Standing up.

Being black in America at that time was not the greatest thing in the world, let me tell you. At the time I did not know we were poor. I did not know we were being discriminated against. The only time I even saw white people was at a very early age, back in Tennessee—those farmers that my dad worked for. Otherwise I never had any contact with white people. I never thought about them. There were places my parents said we could go and places that we knew not to go, and that was fine with me. My brothers and I had a roof over our heads. We had enough to eat. Yes, there were craps games floating through the neighborhood. Yes, the streets could be rough. Yes, there were druggies, drunks, and people doing all sorts of wrong things. But we were happy in our new home.

Dad's plans went awry when all the factory jobs had been filled. He ended up landing a job as a meat cutter at Kingan and Company, a meat-packing plant on the White River. It wasn't what he wanted, and over the years he moved through a variety of different jobs. Dad was a quiet man. He was strict with us, but I do remember him coming home from work at night sometimes with the smell of meat and blood still on him.

Mom was also very strict and stern, very bossy, a strong country woman. She sang gospel in the church, was always quick with an opinion, and was a very good cook. When Dad came home, she'd have dinner ready. Since we couldn't afford too much beef, we usually had a one-dish meal, without any sides or extras. Just cabbage, beans, or cornbread. But no matter what we had or did not have to eat, our parents never made us feel like we were poor.

I know that it galled my father that he was not allowed to go into the restaurants whose food he helped pack. I know that Mom had her hands full with the four of us and her housework, and soon she'd be working part-time jobs as well. My parents had real problems making ends meet, and Mom was always telling Dad about things our family needed. But they never talked about race. They did not lecture us about what we could not do. Rather, they simply worked hard and did what they could. I can vividly remember my father preaching to us about education and being a good student, dead tired after a day's work and still making sure to check that we had finished our homework. For me, they embodied the idea that integrity depends on inner dignity, and from their example, I learned that inner dignity is one thing that should never be compromised.

I can remember my mother reciting scripture to us, especially Isaiah and Jeremiah. She would take complicated Bible verses and break them down for us, reducing them to basic elements so that we could understand them. Matthew 25:15, for example, a very complicated passage, she explained this way:

> God gave three men a talent. The first one threw it away and the birds ate it. The second man put his in the sun and it melted. The third man took care of his. The Lord will give you more if you take care of what he gave you.

MY BROTHERS AND I had a lot of time to ourselves. We couldn't go into the south side of town because it was all white. The east side was very, very tough, so we stayed away from there too. We weren't wanted downtown and didn't have money to spend there anyway, so that was out. And while some blacks lived on the north side of town, we didn't have either the money or the transportation to get there. My brothers and I didn't roam around Naptown either. Indiana Avenue, long a mecca of African-American commerce in Indianapolis—comparable to Harlem in New York City, Beale Street in Memphis, Walnut Street in Louisville, or Twelfth and

Vine in Kansas City—had begun its slow decline. Storefronts were boarded up and residential houses abandoned. Most of the businesses there had turned into nightclubs, and then bars. Two major theaters, the Lido and the Walker, remained on the avenue, but the Lido was a basic, no-frills theater, and at times it could be dangerous. As for the Walker, there were occasional fights there too, and the place was a lot more snobbish—I never liked going there either. Douglas Park had the only African-American swimming pool in the city, but it was also a place where fights were common. Riverside Amusement Park was along the northern edge of Naptown, but its roller coasters and roller skating rink had scores of "whites only" signs, so that was out too. Every once in a while they designated "Colored Frolic Days." But so what? Me, my brothers, and all our friends from the neighborhood, we stayed put.

When you are growing up in the ghetto and don't have any money, sports are king. Everyone plays. If it's football season, guys tell each other, "Run down six cars and turn left by that green Ford." During baseball season, fire hydrants and stoops serve as bases, the middle of the street as the field. In Indianapolis, basketball was the emperor of them all. Guys played sunup to sundown. There was a vacant lot a few blocks from our house. Some enterprising guys put up a pole, a backboard, and a basketball hoop on the lot. Soon all the dribbling and running would send dirt, clay, and dust flying everywhere. People started calling the courts the Dust Bowl. Neighborhood kids and even some of the high school players from nearby Crispus Attucks High School would stop by, joining in a pickup game. I used to pretend there was a hoop set up on a tree by our home. Since we didn't have the money for a real ball, I used a dingy rag ball I'd fashioned, held together by elastic, or else I'd use rolled-up socks, tied together with string. That's really how it began: me playing make-believe in front of the house, shooting at an imaginary basket with a ball of rags.

When we were old enough for my mom to get us membership cards, I'd follow Bailey and Henry around to the YMCA on Senate Avenue. I should say right now that Bailey was one hell of a basketball player. He had a great nickname: *Flap*. Flap was a talker. Talked *all* the time. Talking, irritating opposing players, as they irritated him, doing whatever he could to get an edge, anything to win. Flap got his name because of his shot. He could shoot—much better than I ever could. And his shooting style was very dramatic—all wrist, with this exaggerated forward extension, like he was waving at the ball as it left for the hoop. Even as he ran back down court afterwards, Bailey's hand kept flapping.

My brothers and I lived an outdoor life, playing basketball and baseball, going to the Y and the Dust Bowl and the courts over at Lockefield Gardens. When the sun went down, we'd come home, do our chores and our homework. On Friday nights we'd gather around the radio and listen to the Pabst Blue Ribbon Friday Night Fights. I don't remember watching television or listening to the radio all that much growing up, but I do remember listening to boxing. Whenever a black person, a Joe Louis, Sugar Ray Robinson, or Kid Gavilan, had an opportunity to fight, it would be great for the black community, a real source of pride and interest. I can remember cheering when Joe Louis knocked out Billy Conn in the eighth round of a championship fight, and listening when the "Brown Bomber" defeated Jersey Joe Walcott in successive brawls.

Basketball and boxing, church and school comprised my young social life. But the day summer came and school let out, Mom got busy, packing up some of our clothes, wrapping a day's worth of fried chicken in paper bags. The next day, soon as morning broke, she'd walk me and my brothers onto the bus that went back to Nashville. Eight hours and three hundred miles later, my grandmother would be crushing us in her bosom with massive hugs. Aunts, uncles, cousins, half-cousins, grandparents, great-grandparents, great-great-grandparents. We'd make the family rounds on foot, along lengthy dirt roads and well-beaten paths that rose and fell across the hot and rolling land. Whenever we got to my great-grandfather's house, Daddy Marshall would be sitting on the front porch. He would say hello and whatnot, then we would leave. You couldn't be around him very long because he would get irritated. I guess when you get to be his age, you don't want to be bothered by a whole lot. I imagine you sort of live in your own world.

One of his children, my Aunt Nelly, was really fair-skinned, and some of her sisters looked almost white. On that side of the family, you could see the entire range of colors. My mother's side was filled with dark, handsome men. Every Sunday, the entire extended family met up at the Mount Zion AME church—the women heading inside to listen to a preacher with a big rolling voice, the men lingering outside, sipping whisky, talking, and laughing. I loved those summers, that place, and that time.

Every year on the third Friday in August, there was a huge family outing called the Charlotte Picnic, a huge gathering of relatives and friends from all over. The Charlotte Picnics continue to this day, and I still go every year, but back then white politicians used to attend, stumping, trying to win votes. And they'd always bring liquor with them. Most of the men were country folk, guys who spent all day working the fields and didn't drink all that often. They'd spend the day drinking all that free liquor, and by the end of the night a lot of them were drunk. Guys would question one another's manhood, and that's when the fighting would start. I never participated.

In those days, you could walk for miles in the fields, maybe fall in creeks, and nobody worried about you. I was free to explore the whole wide world. There was this huge gorge near my grandparents' house, and my grandmother would tell me, "Don't go fiddlin' in that gorge." But that forbidden gorge was so tantalizing, and I wanted to swing across the gorge, wanted to see if I could do it. So I cut this huge tree vine. I swung across it. Didn't tell my grandmother. I loved the danger of it. We'd pull on a vine, and if it didn't come down, it must be all right. We'd be out there, just sailing over the danger.

By the time I was thirteen years old, it was assumed I could put in a man's day of work, but even as a child I spent some time in the field. The day after arriving back in Dickson County, I went out in those fields with my brothers and cousins and picked tobacco or shucked corn. Any other chores Papa Bell told me to do, I did. My grandparents and everyone else on the farm got to working before sunup and stayed at it until past sundown. Papa worked the fields; Mama Pearl cooked all day long. I emulated my grandfather in every way I could. I tried to work like him and talk like him. Once I even made a wagon that was a replica of his wagon, and I used to pull it around, pile it full of rocks, toiling just like he toiled. Unlike my little wagon, however, Papa's was horse-drawn and full-sized. Though it couldn't have been crawling along at more than two or three miles an hour in those fields, to me it seemed like it was going twenty times that. As it moved along the fields, we had to pick up the bales, throw them in, and stack them.

I didn't mind the work. I never even thought about questioning what I was doing. The only thing I didn't care for down there were the snakes. There were water snakes in the bottomland, rattlesnakes wedged between the rocks of wooden areas, and copperheads all over the place—especially in the shade under bushes and tobacco plants. It got to where I'd be stripping tobacco suckers from the plants, and I'd be able to sense a lurking copperhead. I could smell them—like cucumbers. People thought I was crazy when I told them, but it was true. There was also this big rat snake in the barn—I couldn't smell it, but a lot of times I'd be working in the loft, all of a sudden I'd discover that big king snake, coiling up, getting ready to strike. Whenever I told my grandfather about it, he used to say I better not kill that snake. It was a good snake. Killed the rats.

Down in Dickson County, the rule was that you let the good snakes alone, so whenever I was in that loft, I just had to be careful. Another county rule stated that you should keep a mean snake dog around to take care of any bad snakes. I didn't know the difference between a good and a bad snake, but Papa Bell had himself one hell of a snake dog. I guess it must have known how to separate the good from the bad.

Whenever I tried to befriend that dog, it bared its teeth and gave me a snarl. If I complained, my grandfather told me to leave it alone. One day I asked why I wasn't allowed to feed the dog, why the dog stayed under the house and was supposed to be left alone. Papa told me he fed the dog only once a week because he didn't want that dog depending on him. "You know," he said, "that dog's got to take care of himself. I might not always be around."

I thought about this for a while and soon enough understood. Instead of waiting for table scraps, that dog had learned to forage for itself. It went and killed what it could, then dragged the kill off somewhere and ate it. It was just an extension of farm mentality. That was a big lesson for me. Everybody had to pull his own weight. Dog included.

I was eleven years old when my parents divorced. It's a sensitive topic for me even now, all these years later. But I think all the financial pressures may have had something to do with it. Even after the divorce, money was so tight that my father kept living in our house, sleeping in the same room as my mom. He'd get up and leave for work before me or my brothers were out of bed, or while we were getting ready for school. Then at the end of the night, he'd come home from whichever of the three jobs he might have been working. Mom and Dad didn't talk to each other. And they never told us about the divorce. We just kept living our lives. Me and my brothers wouldn't find out they'd been divorced until years later, when I was in high school.

By now, mom was working too. Although she was trained to be a beautician, she got a part-time job as a domestic, cooking for a white family. I don't remember their name, but I'll never forget the street. It was the 5500 block of Broadway. Every day she arrived at the home of the rich white family she worked for and would walk around back, to the servants' entrance. She even had to eat her meals on the back porch.

That Christmas, in the middle of all this hardship, she brought home what turned out to be the best and most important present of my life.

It seems one of the boys in that family had discarded a basketball.

It was sort of scarred up. Old. Didn't have the greatest trim on it. But then again, the tread wasn't lopsided, and the ball was regulation size.

It was my ball.

LOCATED IN THE HEART of Naptown, Crispus Attucks was a source of pride for the black community of Indianapolis. Named after the African-American who had been shot by British troops in the 1770 Boston Massacre, the school was a lumbering, three-story red brick building. The foul-smelling canal was close to its front doors, and Fall Creek was just a few blocks away. The building didn't have a regular-size fieldhouse or a regular-size track. It was overcrowded, with almost double the number of students it had been constructed to hold. And yet it was a miraculous place.

The principal was black, and the majority of teachers were black Ph.D.'s who weren't allowed to teach in white schools.

Legend has it that the week that Attucks opened, the Klan had a parade and celebrated the separation of black and white students. That was before my time, so I can't verify the story any more than I can dismiss it. What I can say is that when I was a child, seeing the school's green, gold, and white colors on a tee shirt commanded my attention. Players from Attucks dominated at the Dust Bowl and the Y.

In those days, if you were black, you were told you weren't smart. You were bad. You were inferior. Black people needed something to look up to, something to give us hope. This was why my brothers and I listened to Joe Louis and Sugar Ray Robinson on the Friday night fights, and this, I think, is why the Crispus Attucks basketball team was so important to the black population of Indianapolis, why the African-American newspaper, *The Indianapolis Recorder*, covered the team so fervently. They won games.

Well, imagine how important to our family it was when, in 1950, Flap made it onto the varsity squad at Crispus Attucks.

Standing five feet nine, Flap was just a sophomore. He filled in as a reserve guard on a team loaded with talent. There was Hallie Bryant, the team's leading scorer, who would go on to become one of the first black players to enroll in the University of Indiana. And Willie Gardner, a tall, thin, six-foot-eight forward, would be recruited by various colleges, but because his family was dirt-poor, he ended up signing on directly with the Harlem Globetrotters. As for Flap, after his high school career, he went to Indiana Central College (now the University of Indianapolis) and set a state collegiate scoring record, with 2,268 points in four years—a record that, as I write this, still stands for small colleges. Flap would also spend a short stretch with the Harlem Globetrotters. But that was later. In 1950 to 1951, the Crispus Attucks Tigers, coached by Ray Crowe, was the first all-black basketball team that played in the state finals of the Indiana High School Basketball Tournament.

I vividly remember watching the regionals and the game that got them into the state finals. The state tournament was broadcast on television, and we watched the regional finals in our home. It was really something—

that game was the first Crispus Attucks basketball game I ever watched, as well as the first sporting event I ever saw on television. Even if I didn't understand that it was the state high school tournament, I knew something important was happening.

With four and a half minutes to play in the 1951 regional finals, the Crispus Attucks Tigers trailed the all-white Anderson Indians by ten points. John "Noon" Davis, the Tigers' fine forward, was called for his fifth and eliminating foul. My mother's fist curled around a napkin as she watched a five-foot-nine sophomore checking into the game to replace Davis. Bailey "Flap" Robertson.

A smattering of polite applause came from the sea of black faces stuffed behind the Attucks bench. There were shouts of encouragement from the black fans way up in the corner of the back bleachers, where all the police were on watch, ready to prevent any problems.

Coach Ray Crowe had left Flap's name off the roster during the sectional tournament for reasons he never fully explained. So this was Flap's first action in the playoffs. He later told me and Henry that when he got a chance to play, he wanted to make sure the coach would remember him. And he did. The first time Flap touched the ball, he shot. Fifteen-foot jumper. Nothing but net. Anderson's lead went down to eight.

The Indianapolis Recorder's Jim Cummings would report that this shot "rekindled a spark of hope in Attucks hearts. If sophomore Bailey Robertson—who didn't even play in the sectional games—could score so easily, so can we."

Two quick baskets by Willie Gardner. A free throw by Bob Jewell. Within ninety seconds, the lead had been cut to three.

Fifteen thousand fans were going wild in the Butler Fieldhouse. The Attucks supporters were stomping their feet and shouting. Across the floor, the Anderson fans were just as crazy.

Hallie Bryant hit a turnaround jumper to cut the lead to 74–72. Now the Attucks corner broke into their legendary "Crazy Song."

Oh, Anderson is rough
And Anderson is tough

They can beat everybody
But they can't beat us
Hi-de-hi-de, hi-de-hi
Hi-de-hi-de, hi-de-ho
That's the skip, bob, beat-um
That's the crazy song

Twenty-three seconds left. Anderson ahead by one. We brought the ball up court. A newspaper account of the game says there was light back-court pressure. And that the Attucks coaching staff was trying to get the attention of his players, or the referee. Ray Crowe wanted to call time-out and set up a last shot. Nobody paid attention.

Twelve seconds left. The ball was in the hands of Charlie West, a substitute Attucks guard. He drove and pulled up and attempted an acrobatic scoop. Missed. Ball out-of-bounds. Referees signal Attucks's possession.

Seven seconds left.

Center Bob Jewell held up two fingers to set up an out-of-bounds play. The first two options were covered. Flap was not. My brother caught the ball on the baseline far in the corner. He did not look for Hallie Bryant. Did not worry about the called play. Flap jumped, cocked his wrist in its usual style.

"I just grabbed the ball, shot, and prayed," he told a reporter later.

Some would remember the shot as flat and arcless, striking the side of the rim and bouncing straight up, as high as eight feet. Others offered the opinion that the ball bounced only a foot or so above the rim. Attucks's coach Ray Crowe would always say that the shot floated with a lovely, high arc. One thing for sure, it hung high enough above the rim for some suspense.

Straight down. Through the hoop.

Final score: Crispus Attucks 81, Anderson 80.

You could hear horns honking on the street and people cheering in the homes up and down Colton Street. Attucks players and fans started hugging in the middle of the court. All of a sudden, the world of black Indianapolis had somehow, magically expanded.

"People told me their relatives died of heart attacks," Flap would recall. "One lady said when the ball went through that hoop, she started to go into labor."

My mom and Henry were elated; I was overwhelmed with joy and happiness. I stayed up that night, anxious, waiting for Flap to come home. I did not realize that he had to deal with reporters (*Indianapolis Recorder*: "Without a doubt one of the most thrilling high school basketball games ever played in Indiana—or the world."), or that the team would take a victory ride down Indiana Avenue, that the head of the police traffic division would—in the name of caution and security—send extra patrolmen to the west side and tour the area himself, in a squad car, or that the team and coaching staff would stop at Seldon's Café for a late dinner of ham and sweet potatoes. I did not realize that there would be a celebratory walk back to Crispus Attucks, a bonfire, even a snake dance.

There was no way for me, or anyone else, to know that Attucks would lose its next game, in the state semifinals, to Evansville Reitz. And there was no way of imagining the way basketball would infuse my life, the long, strange, and sometimes heartbreaking journey the game would take me on, the highs of championships and ceremonies, the lows of hardball politics and being blackballed from the sport that I so loved. No. All I knew that night was that things had changed. It was almost as if Sugar Ray Robinson had knocked out his mightiest opponent in the first round, except that on this night my brother was Sugar Ray; on that night the rest of the world was the opponent. I did not know how, could not have explained it for a million dollars. But after Flap's shot, things would never be the same again for me. I knew it. For the first time, a candle of hope flickered inside my heart.

It was early in the morning when Flap finally made it home. By then I was in bed, dreaming.

CHAPTER TWO

Li'l Flap
1951–1954

INDIANAPOLIS'S FIRST public-housing project was known as the Lockefield Gardens. The Gardens rose adjacent to Colton Street, not far from my house, and were built with asphalt basketball courts out in front. Eventually, as many of the players from the lot on Colton shifted to playing at Lockefield, the asphalt courts absorbed the "Dust Bowl" name. The day after Flap hit that shot in the finals, I pretty much started living at the Lockefield courts. If it was a school day, I'd go there straight from school and stay until it was time to go home to do my chores and homework. If it was a weekend, I'd leave as soon as I got up, or right after changing out of my church clothes. Me and my trashed, secondhand basketball would head down Colton.

That year, during Attucks's run in the state tournament and on through the spring and summer, the Dust Bowl seemed especially crowded.

The neighborhood echoed with the hard reverberations of basketballs getting pounded into the dirt, clay, and asphalt, and a film of dust was ever present, wafting through Naptown's shanties and apartment complexes. There might be fifty or sixty guys on the side of the court—adults, high school cats, you name it—all of them sitting and waiting for their turn to run. If your team lost, you weren't going to play anymore that day, so players had to put out, really compete. There wasn't spare time to look around, pose, and see who was watching.

Since I was too young to run with the best players, I had to show up early if I wanted to play and get on a team when games were just forming, before the big guns had taken over the courts. Lots of times I ended up off to the side, on my own, working on something basic: free throws, crossover dribbles, or dribbling with my weaker left hand. The basics were about all I could achieve back then, but I always liked counting down the seconds on an imaginary game clock. Then, with the score tied and time running out, I'd take the same shot Flap took, for all the money.

Whether it was at the Dust Bowl, the Senate Avenue Y, or during Police Athletic League games a bit later, I took any chance I got to get in a game with older players, like Hallie Bryant, Willie Gardner, Henry, and of course, Flap. The younger group of guys I ran around with and I were always trying to get in those playground games, but there was a pecking order, and the older guys wouldn't let us on the court. In order to play against the older guys, you had to have the size and strength necessary to win your way through the day. Eventually, though, we became the dominant team. The tough guys.

Basketball players—even good ones—don't become smart all at once; it takes years and years of playing the game. In my case being a smart player and a good player were wrapped up in one another. Getting a chance meant you had to make the most of it. Nobody out there was running a charity. If I wanted to stay on the court, I had to be good enough to keep myself on it. Guys were bigger and older and stronger than me, and they tried to overpower me, pushing and holding me, playing rough. Guys would try and set up down low against me all the time, getting position near the basket. Then, once they had the ball, they'd back me in, muscling their way toward the basket, protecting the ball with their bodies and clubbing me out of the way, or simply jump over me. In basketball terms, it's known as posting up. And I had to learn how to deal with it. I had to figure out how to hold my ground, learn when to sneak around from the weak side for a steal, or box out a charging, flying body and get the rebound.

When I was bringing the ball up court, a guy might leave his man and rush me, double-teaming me, trying to steal the ball. So I had to be aware of where the other players were in relation to me, had to learn to recognize when a double-team was coming and what to do about it. If someone crowded me, I had to know how to blow past him. In every game, it seemed I would pick up something worth practicing. Then, the second that I got even passable at a certain move, I would try it out in a game. Something didn't work? More practice. A different move. Now could I use that to better advantage?

There's a saying about the Lord helping those who help themselves, and it's true in basketball as well. The guys noticed me improving, saw how serious I was about the game. Soon they started giving me pointers. *Hey, Oscar, you know, if you use your foot to jab . . .*

Maybe it was because of all the basketball beatings I'd taken at the hands of my elders, the gauntlets I'd been put through just to be able to shoot at the back of the house with my brothers, let alone to stay in a game at the Dust Bowl, but after a while, whenever I played, I felt at ease. I had skills nobody else had, understood things in a way that they did not, did things they could not. As I played, I was hearing whoops of approval and getting high-fives from other guys—both on and off the court. And rather than bask in a good play or win, I was the kind of kid who got greedy from success. It made me want to do better, work harder. Without knowing it, I started becoming a better player, someone who knew how to react and adjust to a situation without having to think about it, a player who understood that huge effort had to be his routine. Throughout my adult life, I've been described as one of the most fundamentally sound players in the history of basketball. But so much of what I know I learned on the playground. I didn't learn much basketball in high school, or even in college, but rather from playing outside in the park.

It was Tom Sleet—my coach in seventh, eighth, and ninth grades—who started it, and then other people began to call me Li'l Flap. I was a different kind of kid than Bailey. I didn't have Flap's personality or style. I didn't play a lot of ball against Flap; he generally wouldn't play against me, his little brother. On a rare occasion, we did get on the court at the same time. He might be rough on me, but never mean. I just played and practiced, kept my mouth shut, then dribbled my ball home when the sun went down.

Bailey was a flashy player, an aggressive and vocal player. There's a lot of talk that flashes on the court, and Bailey was a big part of that. Coach Crowe used to get mad at him for talking during high school games, but believe me, all that talk came out in the playgrounds. He would have fit in the modern NBA very well; he had that fiery style and brashness, and the guy could shoot the living daylights out of the ball. Me, I might give you a single look or make a slight gesture to a teammate, but I was very polite. Now, I'll say what I have to say.

I don't know exactly how long it was before the paved courts over at the Lockefield Gardens took over the Dust Bowl name, but I know that it was sometime during my adolescence. The Indianapolis Police Athletic League sponsored basketball and football leagues at the "new Dust Bowl." All the credit for discipline and fair play at Lockefield Gardens goes to James "Bruiser" Gaines. He made sure that there wasn't any trouble on those courts and provided some guidance and order. Local coaches used to make the rounds, checking out league games and pickup games alike. They'd come from the nearby middle schools, Public Schools 17 and 19 and 24, with one eye looking to future teams.

When I started seventh grade, I had skills as a player, but they were street skills. I was rawboned and lanky and really didn't have any knowledge or experience with organized basketball. But that year I got my first real coaching. At P.S. 17, Tom Sleet was in charge of working with the seventh and eighth graders. He also coached the Crispus Attucks freshman squad. I didn't have any expectations, but I was excited to go to practice each day, where Coach Sleet taught me the basics, things like how to pivot, how to pass. "Throw it as close to your man's head as you can," he told me, showing a pragmatic ruthlessness that one day I'd become famous for. "It'll get by—your man will have to blink." Tom Sleet started me in the right direction.

Back in the old days, they really didn't teach you but one thing: to pass and cut off the pivot. The principles of offensive basketball taught back then revolved around the idea of catching the ball, pivoting, passing to an open man, and then taking off, or cutting, in the opposite direction. Catch, pivot, pass, and cut. It's known as a motion offense, because at its best and most flowing, it looks as if everyone is in perpetual motion.

In those days, the pivot was a passing pivot. The center—the tallest player on the court—handled the ball a lot. He'd come out from close to the basket and stand at the free-throw line and look for cutting players. You hit the high post pivot and then cut, like I said, away from the ball. Everyone was in motion, passing and cutting. You would move and then run toward another designated offensive player or area, at which point you would come to a stop, setting what is known as a pick (think of a picket or a post). A guy on your team would then run closely past you and try to "bump" or lose his man by running him into your pick. This was perpetual: moving, then setting a pick, and then cutting again, creating advantages for offensive players while confusing, tiring, and impeding the defense. Eventually, when an offensive player got the ball back, he would have an advantage over his defender, which the offensive player would use—either taking an open shot, driving, or somehow creating an opportunity. Pivots, picks, and cuts are fundamental concepts of basketball, although they have a hard time getting kids to do them nowadays. As far as defense went, Coach Sleet had us learn how to play man-to-man.

After practices, with Coach Sleet encouraging me, I started giving myself daily assignments: layups and tip-ins with either hand, free throws, crossover dribbles, dribbling with my left hand. I just liked to play. The game helped sustain me and gave me a sense of identity. I never thought about being better than anyone else. I did not spend much time thinking about how good I was, or how I stacked up in comparison to other players— any of that stuff. It's true that if I had played nowadays, someone would have noticed me. Tout sheets these days can declare sixth graders to be future Hall of Famers; high school kids are on magazine covers and cable tele-vision. But I was just a kid who liked to play.

I'll always be grateful to Tom Sleet for providing me with guidance. He supported my desire to escape what seemed to be my fate and helped me refine and develop the skills that would help me accomplish my dreams. Basically, the man worked with a bunch of inner-city kids who took life one day at a time and had no dreams for the future, he helped mold us into good citizens, and he gave us self-confidence, a winning attitude, and the en-couragement to believe we would succeed on the court and in other facets of life. This encouragement probably proved to be the most important thing of all.

My eighth-grade team played in the Capitol City's first junior high school tournament. Reports have it that during the last minute of every quarter, guys would pass the ball around the perimeter, until it reached me. Then, with the clock running out, I would shoot. I don't remember this happening. But I do know that long before that tournament, when our team from P.S. 17 swept through the competition and took the Indianapolis city championship, Ray "the Razor" Crowe was in the stands. The future was watching, making its own plans.

Playing other teams from throughout the city provided my first ex-posure to organized games. And more. Aside from my visits to Tennessee, when I'd see my grandfather's neighbors and say hi, this was my first real exposure to white people. Certainly, it was the first time I'd ever been on the same basketball court as any of them.

The funny thing about racism is that when you're young and growing up and you go to an all-black school and have friends all around you, you don't think about race. Oh sure, racism was present in my life, but it was sort of like polluted air. I inhaled it and did not realize the damage it was doing.

IN INDIANAPOLIS, about eight hundred black students attended integrated schools until the early 1920s, when a wave of fear-mongering, racial hatred, and opportunism swept the state. The Indianapolis school board was dominated by members of the Ku Klux Klan, and throughout the 1920s, 1930s, and 1940s, they passed zoning ordinances for the express reason of keeping blacks out of white high schools. And while integrated high schools and varsity athletics came to rural Indiana fairly early—with Muncie's championship squads featuring black players as far back as 1930 and 1931—in the capital city, voters approved the building of a segregated high school. (In due time, other Indiana cities followed suit, opening Lincoln High in Evansville and Roosevelt High in Gary.) Originally, the Indianapolis school was going to be named after Thomas Jefferson, but wiser heads prevailed, and Crispus Attucks became its given name.

According to some historians, Crispus Attucks was little more than a waterfront worker. Called "the Mulatto," Attucks was a black man with liberal doses of Indian blood. He was born in 1723, and late in his teen years slipped loose from slavery, to become a sea tough prowling lower Boston's waterfront, where he acquired a reputation for brutality. This man became a central figure and hero on the night of March 5, 1770, when British soldiers fought with three groups of Boston street fighters. The evening ended with Attucks and three others bleeding to death in the snow in what history now labels the "Boston Massacre." Daniel Webster, the famous patriot, and John Adams, the second president of the United States, both singled out this night as a pivotal moment in the American Revolution.

In 1930, at the age of thirty-two, a black man named Dr. Russell A. Lane left his position on the faculty of Wilberforce University in Xenia, Ohio, and took over as Crispus Attucks's principal. Lane had a law degree from the University of Dayton and a doctorate in education from Indiana University, and he insisted that his teachers have at least a master's degree if they wanted to stay at Attucks. These were teachers who, solely because of their skin color, could not teach at white colleges, who had gone through trials and tribulations to become educated. They suffered and were discriminated against, and yet for all their suffering were still educated and dignified—men and women who knew that it was education that would help you improve your life, would get you out of the ghetto. That was the imperative at Attucks. Getting kids educated.

I think that Principal Lane and the other school administrators believed in using sports as a corollary to their concept of black education and dignity. Their idea was to grow smart, polite, educated citizens, while also showing the white community that these citizens were good, decent young men who could compete on athletic fields without any problem. Along these lines, Principal Lane and the other administrators believed that Attucks's sports teams were best used to help build relationships with the white community. So basketball coach Fitzhugh Lyons selected his players more for their manners than their athleticism. Then he taught them polite basketball. "Keep your feet on the floor when you shoot and pass," he told them. "Don't get too close to your man on defense." Lyons even gave speeches before games about how losing now might give way to winning in the long run. Still, seeing how the state high school athletic association wouldn't admit black schools to its membership, the mandates of politesse did not help much. The school didn't have a regulation gymnasium, or even a decent track or football field. All basketball games were played on the road, very few of them against white competition except for the occasional small rural school or Catholic academy (the Klan had also made sure to ban Catholics).

Finally, in 1942, the wartime effort began a shift in the state's political mood. Some city schools, like Howe High, started winking at the Klan's zoning laws and accepted black students. Soon after, a meeting of the Council of the Indiana High School Athletic Association allowed for white schools to play black schools and share revenues from games. Attucks may not have had a gym, but the Tigers started playing a few home games nonetheless—at Tech High School, a cross-town integrated school that would become our rival, and at Butler University.

Ray Crowe was hired as an assistant basketball coach in 1948. The eldest of ten children, Ray had a younger brother, George, who had played pro baseball on the New York Renaissance with Jackie Robinson. Eventually, George would go on to a ten-year career with the Braves, Reds, and Cardinals, and was involved in a minor scandal when the baseball commissioner ordered that Stan Musial start the all-star game ahead of him. As an assistant, Ray Crowe was influenced by Lyons's approach of capitulating and making sure not to make waves. And in 1950, when Lyons stepped down and Crowe became Attucks's head coach, he continued that nonaggressive style.

Looking back to the year Flap hit his big shot, I think this tendency toward capitulation and nonaggressiveness probably played a large role in Attucks's loss to Evansville Reitz in the state title game, in which Bailey Robertson would not play. Evansville Reitz's starters also started on their team's state championship football team, so they were big and physical and athletic enough to win on their own. But I know that in the days before the game, the mayor of Indianapolis met with Principal Lane and Coach Crowe, worried about blacks starting a riot in the streets in the event of an Attucks victory. I also know that Ray Crowe told people that he didn't like Bailey's attitude, and Bailey was kept out of the state finals for reasons that never were publicly explained. (Bailey didn't even dress for that final game.)

It does seem that a lot of factors came into play that night that all added up to an Attucks loss. For instance: With two minutes left, our star forward, Willie Gardner, jumped between two players and double-clutched and hit a reverse layup. The official called charge. Evansville made the foul shot, then stole Attucks's inbounds pass and scored a layup. This was the key moment in Evansville's 66–59 win. The next day, an editorial signed by the five-man sports staff of the *Indianapolis News,* the highest circulation newspaper in the state, termed it a "highly questionable and challengeable call." For a week after that, a bitter debate ensued. And while Coach Crowe never uttered one word of criticism—he wasn't about to let himself be called an uppity nigger—in later years, he told people the charge was "the worst call I ever saw in a lifetime of sports."

Look at the box score from that night. You'll see that referees had called fourteen personals on Crispus Attucks, seven on Evansville. To me it all adds up.

I know Ray sees things differently. Later on, he looked back on the loss and said it was his own fault. "It was my first year of varsity coaching. Here we were, suddenly in the final four with a shot at it all. It was unreal. I didn't know how to get the team up for such a test. Evansville had scouted us real well, and they picked our little, simple zone defense to tatters. That's all we had, because that's all I taught them. If I had gained the experience to vary the defense a little on the week before, we might have won it. It was my fault, but I learned a lot."

One of the big lessons the loss must have taught Crowe was that incompetent and malicious refs could cost you a close ball game; the alternative was to play over and beyond their calls, to try to keep things from getting so close that the refs could determine the outcome. I say this because it's one of the things Coach passed down to me. And it would be easy to take this lesson and say, well, lesson learned, all's well that ends well, and let it go at that. The only problem is that things don't necessarily end here.

Understand, all this was not happening in a vacuum. No black man suited up for a Big Ten basketball team until 1949. When it finally happened, it was because a white booster and part-time referee named Nate Kaufman was on the board of trustees at Indiana University. Kaufman basically told the university he would withdraw his financial support if the school did not offer a scholarship to a kid named Bill Garrett, a black star from Kaufman's hometown of Shelbyville. That's how Garrett got offered a scholarship to the state school supported in part by his parents' annual tax money. And while Garrett ended up being a star at Indiana, that didn't mean that blacks were necessarily accepted, or even wanted, at that university. I say this for a reason. If you grow up in Indiana, you live basketball and dream of playing for the Hoosiers. But the coach at Indiana back then, Branch "the Sheriff" McCracken, had his own priorities. He might recruit four or five black kids for a team, but he'd only play one at a time.

McCracken was riding the crest of his second national championship, so he was a winner as a coach, there's no denying that. And when McCracken passed away in 1970, his funeral was attended by dozens of former players, both white and black, including Walt Bellamy, Bobby "Slick" Leonard, and the Van Arsdale twins. But there's also no denying some of the bull he pulled, or that the way he coached was part of the reason for the old joke about blacks—*Put one in the game when you are at home, two when you are on the road, and all five when you're down fourteen at the half.*

There wasn't a dime's worth of difference between Bailey's talents and those of Attucks's star center, Hallie Bryant. And both of them wanted desperately to go to Indiana University and play for the Hoosiers. Mc-Cracken signed Bryant. But he did not so much as recruit Bailey. Now, maybe he didn't have a place for Bailey, maybe he simply had enough guards. Could be. But it's just as possible that McCracken decided that Hallie Bryant could assimilate better into a predominantly white college than Bailey. His sitting on the bench for the championship game couldn't have helped things.

I know that Bailey was shut out from both the Indiana all-star team and Indiana University. Instead, he went to Indiana Central College, a small school on Indianapolis's south side, where he was one of nine black students. By 1957 Bailey would help the Greyhounds vault into the top ten of the small college rankings. He'd consistently rank among the top five in the nation in scoring. I would watch him score forty-five points one night. I know that Butler University consistently refused to play their cross-town rival while Bailey was at Indiana Central.

I also know that Bailey never got a real chance at the pros. Although he was drafted by Syracuse's NBA franchise, they still had a quota system back then. Instead, Bailey opted first to play with the Harlem Ambassadors, then with the Harlem Globetrotters, touring Europe and South America with Abe Saperstein's crew. Later he played ball with a Special Services Army unit in Germany, then settled in Cincinnati and worked for the city. My brother died a few years ago, and I know all the trouble I had trying to get him into the Indiana Basketball Hall of Fame, let alone gain any consideration from the National Hall of Fame in Springfield, Massachusetts. I know that it's not absurd to look back and wonder if my older brother could have had a career like mine.

I also know that this was nothing exceptional at the time. Ten million other guys were coming up the same way at the same time, having the same shit happen to them.

IN THE SUMMER OF 1953, I was thanking my lucky stars because puberty had kicked in. I'd ended my freshman season of high school standing about five feet eight inches and looking younger than my fourteen years. By the time my sophomore year started and basketball tryouts came around, I had grown almost seven inches after a summer on the farm. I still looked young, but I wasn't lanky anymore. All that farm work had put some breadth in my chest and some meat on my arms. All summer I'd picked tobacco and put up hay, shucked corn and worked in the gardens. I'd followed that hay wagon and tossed up those bales and gotten myself one brutal workout, one day after another, one bale after another.

When I left Tennessee, went back to the city, and showed up again at the Dust Bowl and the Y, I was almost six feet three—stronger, taller, and faster than guys who used to push me around. Now I was the size of a post player—large enough to play down low, with my back to the basket—with all the coordination and ball-handling skills that had kept me on the courts back when I was physically overmatched. Guys were looking at me like, "What happened? You really grew a lot."

On the first day of tryouts for the high school team after my freshman year, the players were divided into two groups on the court. The first group was thirty or forty juniors and seniors trying out for the varsity team. The second group had about as many guys, but they were younger, sophomores mostly, plus a few juniors who didn't have a shot at varsity, but figured they could play on the junior varsity squad. I sat with the other sophomores. After all, Attucks was establishing itself as an emerging athletic power—even without Bailey and Hallie Bryant, the varsity squad had a bunch of returning players, and, forty guys trying out or not, you pretty much knew which guys were going to make the team. Besides, everyone knew varsity Coach Crowe and his cuts. That's why people called him Razor.

But Bill Mason kept gesturing to me from the varsity group. Bill was a senior, a returning letterman, and a friend of mine from the courts. "Come on over here," he said, and I'll always be grateful to him for that.

If I'd opted for junior varsity, it would have probably been my show to run. But who knows? The experience might have hurt me later on, made me less prepared to deal with competition.

I went over to the varsity side of the court.

Coach Crowe hadn't said a word to me about trying out. That was strange. In fact, I don't think he'd said a word to me, period. Just the other day I found out that during the tryouts, Coach Crowe told his seniors to work me over and see what I could do. I couldn't believe it. Crowe later said in interviews that he liked the way I didn't try to do too much, but just played the game naturally. It wasn't my basketball ability which impressed him during those tryouts, he would say, but my leadership ability, that it was as if I knew things about the game that the other kids out there would never know enough to even think about. I remember that he put me with a group of second stringers; we were matched in a pickup game against the regulars. But I'd been playing against most of those varsity guys on the playgrounds. This was a competitive situation and I liked to compete. I figured, why not now?

When the Razor made his final cuts that day, I was still on the squad. I walked home in a daze and about burst with pride when I told Bill Swatts, my friend.

Every morning, I'd get up before seven, wash and get dressed, and walk to school. Classes started at eight, and every kid who played on any basketball team, from ninth grade to twelfth, met in Coach Crowe's homeroom. We talked about our studies, how we were going to get the night's work done. I think back then he still thought of me as Li'l Flap, Bailey's little brother. He wasn't alone; I was shy enough that I wouldn't say anything to anybody I did not know.

At the same time, little by little, I was starting to come into my own. Around friends, I could let loose some, talk without questioning myself. In the hallways and at lunchtime, I'd be natural and crack jokes. Honestly—and it may not be fashionable or politically correct to say this—I don't think I would have done nearly as well or been nearly as comfortable at an integrated school, not when I'd grown up in such a rigidly segregated world, anyway. But the halls and classrooms at Attucks were natural to me; they were like home.

Coach was about average height, a strong-built guy. He used to style his hair in an ordered fashion, kind of a box cut. He always wore pressed suits and bow ties, and basically presented himself as the stern but fair principal type. Every now and then, Coach and his wife would prepare picnics and outings for the program members.

Coach also had an unusual habit. In practice and in games, his cheeks would protrude sometimes, like he was clenching his teeth. Looking back, it's easy to see that he was controlling his impulses and natural reactions, then thinking through how to address a problem. He had a pair of assistants in my eighth-grade coach, Tom Sleet, and Al Spurlock, an industrial arts teacher who had coached my freshman team and later would coach me in track as well. The two of them used to walk around the edges of the court during practice, acting as second and third pairs of eyes and ears, helping out on drills and fundamentals. In direct contrast to all stereotypes about black players, our team played a disciplined offense, with three or four passes around the perimeter before anyone could shoot.

With Hallie Bryant at Indiana University, Willie Gardner playing for the Harlem Globetrotters, and Flap spending his freshman year at Indiana Central, the team that I joined had neither height nor a consistent scorer—our tallest player was six feet three and a half inches—so Coach Crowe had me playing forward, down low, in the post pivot. When I'd played in the park, I'd played outside. Seventh grade, eighth grade, ninth grade, all I'd played was guard. I didn't know anything else. Didn't matter. I was about six three, and we needed someone to be able to rebound, score from the post, and defend inside. I was going to be that man.

When he handed out uniforms, Coach Crowe didn't make a big deal of it, and I took Flap's old number, forty-three.

It was supposed to be a down year. Before we'd played our first game, *The Indianapolis Recorder*—usually optimistic about Attucks's chances to the point of boosterism—had doubts, writing, "If there's a Hallie Bryant on the squad, he is as yet undiscovered." When their reporter asked an Attucks student for a word on the team, he was answered, "Oh, they say they won't get anywhere."

Our first game of the season was against Fort Wayne North and was played at Arsenal Technical High School's gym. Coach told us when to arrive for the game, but not how to get there. I knew where the gym was and decided to take a cross-town bus to the game. Damned bus seemed like it took forever, and it went through one neighborhood after the next. Some dude pulled a knife on me. Why? Just life on the streets. I was so worried about missing the game I just looked at the knife and got off the bus.

What was later to be voted the greatest high school career in the history of Indiana started with me riding pine. For all of three minutes.

Then Crowe sent me in, to play a forward spot. Since I was Bailey's brother and wore his number, people in the audience were calling me "Li'l Flap" all over again. I did okay, scored about fifteen points, and we won. I was too shy to talk to reporters, so I showered and left before they even made it into the locker room. The next day, *The Indianapolis Star* said I displayed "poise unexpected of a sophomore." From that point on, I was in the starting five.

We played three games that first week, going on the road to win two games. Road trips were quite an experience for me. Our principal used to get onto the team bus before we'd hit the road and tell us we were representing our school and to act accordingly, and there was good reason. In the same way that the Globetrotters were a much hotter draw than any NBA teams back then, out-of-town schools regarded games against us as big-money games. Our visits became the focal point of these guys' seasons. We'd arrive in these matchbox towns, and folks would be waiting for our buses to arrive. Like we were from outer space, they'd follow us into the gym. Really. It's comical in retrospect, the long gawking stares they'd give us.

I heard the word nigger yelled a few times during those trips. But being raised in the South, I'd been taught to not let that crap get to me; the taunts made me play harder. The Indiana Officials Association excluded all blacks from membership, so we played a lot of those games with a bunch of white, hometown refs making calls. Coach Crowe used it to motivate us. At least once a trip he'd say, "Get a big lead and keep it. Then the referees and crowds won't have anything to do with it."

We started the season on a hot streak, and this built up interest for our first game against our cross-town rival, Arsenal Tech. Our schools hadn't played each other in two years, since an Attucks win in the state tournament. Part of the rivalry had to do with geography: one strong team on the west side, the other on the east. Naturally, they're going to eye each other. On top of that, we used their gym for our home games. And of course race played a part. Arsenal had two black kids in their starting lineup, but still there were a lot of people who looked at them as the "great white hope."

On December 8, 1953, eight days before the rematch, things took an ugly turn, which made the rivalry more intense. According to published reports, Arsenal guard David Huff, age seventeen, was walking home after basketball practice when he noticed a parked, mud-splattered automobile. As Huff moved past the car, three black men in their mid- to late twenties supposedly leaped out and surrounded him. One grabbed his collar. The other two poked him with knives.

"You're Huff? You better not play too good. If you make one single point, we'll come back and cut you wide open."

The threats plastered the front pages of the Indianapolis newspapers. Anonymous school board officials questioned the wisdom of having the game. The city turned on edge, everyone scared of what the blacks were fixing to do to the nice white boys. But it never made much sense to me. Huff was okay, but he wasn't Tech's best player. Going over box scores from the Indianapolis newspapers back then show him to be a steady role player, that's about it. If you're going to threaten somebody, why not target a player who has some impact on the game?

One threat led to reports of more. Huff's mom and Tech coach Charles Maas supposedly received telephone calls with the same message: If David Huff played, he would regret it. Notes penciled on toilet paper arrived not only at Huff's home, but also Maas's: "Keep Huff and [Don] Sexton out of the ball game," the notes read. "We mean it." Police came up with detailed strategies to keep the races separated at the game. Soon Coach Crowe started receiving some threats too. The most interesting was unsigned and misspelled, a rough note written on scratch paper. "Do not play Winford O'Neal or William Mason if you value their lives. I have all my possessions bet on the game, including my car and house, and I want to see Tech win."

A few nights before the game, I got a call. If I played, the guy said, he was going to shoot me. I told him to go to hell. My father didn't like that, but I didn't worry. It was probably just some gambler who wanted to give me something to think about. With the Tech game approaching, we beat South Bend Riley pretty good, then beat this other cross-town team, Broad Ripple, finally losing a pretty rough game to the state's top-ranked team, Terre Haute Gerstmeyer.

By the time Crispus Attucks hit the court against Arsenal Tech, five different players had been threatened, and the newspapers were covering every crank counterthreat and stray boast. About ten thousand fans crowded into the long bleachers of Butler Fieldhouse, a new attendance record for a regular-season game in Indianapolis. Police patrolled outside both dressing rooms and followed our teams when we went to warm up, and then back into our locker rooms before the game. Uniformed and plain-clothes police and a few FBI agents were crawling around the arena, because the death threats had been sent through the mail. David Huff wasn't out there for Arsenal. Later, I heard that his parents and coach wouldn't let him play—the story goes that his coach had to give the news to him, and when David he heard it, he broke down.

It was a tense, sloppy game. Both teams shot terribly, and there were lots of turnovers. Winford O'Neal, our leading scorer, made two of fifteen shots. Harold Crenshaw was one for ten. Same thing on the other side of the court. The pressure and drama and press coverage of the whole thing really got to everyone. I scored the first basket of the game, and we got an early lead, extending it to fourteen in the second half. After a late Tech rally, we held on, 43–38. I ended up with fourteen points, I think. Afterwards, I showered and, just like the last time, got out of there before any reporters could talk to me.

After that game, reporters never called me "Li'l Flap" again, but I wasn't anywhere close to being my own man. I had a spotty sophomore season, filled with the typical peaks and valleys of a developing player. A twenty-point game might be followed by four points. But we had a balanced, strong team, with lots of athletic ability. Winford O'Neal was undersized at center, and while he could really play, he was injured and missed the first half of the season. Harold Crenshaw took up for him inside, along with Sheddrick Mitchell and me as forwards. I got most of my points driving and drawing fouls or hitting short jumpers. Like I said, we were a good, smart team. We could have out-jumped and outrun all of the white kids, but we played team basketball, slowed things up when we had to, ran when we had to, knew who to milk and where to attack. In a re-match with Arsenal Tech at a holiday tournament, we couldn't come back from a fifteen-point fourth-quarter deficit, and there were a few other bumpy roads. But I think if we'd been completely healthy through the whole season, nobody could have touched us.

"If" may be a powerful word, but usually it has nothing to do with what really does happen. When O'Neal got back, Willie Merriweather promptly messed up his shoulder; he was out for the second half of the season. Then Sheddrick Mitchell tore his knee ligaments playing football. As if this wasn't enough, three weeks before the playoffs started, O'Neal hurt himself again, this time during a game against Indianapolis Sacred Heart. Three starters, done for the year. The sports page of the *Indianapolis News* proclaimed: "Attucks's Long Reign of Supremacy Is Over."

If we wanted to make any noise in the playoffs, something had to happen. So Coach Crowe switched our lineup. He didn't do it to affect some sort of chain of events that would eventually change the game, or be-cause he had a vision of the future that included long, tall athletes han-dling the ball while they sprinted up and down the court, or because he saw me as some kind of prototype. I don't think he had any idea of the revolu-tion he set in motion. He put me in the backcourt for the same reasons that most people do things, out of a combination of convenience and necessity, insight and desperation. He saw that I had ball-handling skills. He saw that while I may not have been forceful off the court, I knew how to run a team and I had real potential as a leader. He also knew that with our frontcourt basically out of commission, we needed to be able to run and slash and do things that would speed up the game and emphasize our perimeter skills. It simply made sense to have me handle the ball more. Though I still re-bounded and defended on defense, now I assumed the role of a guard when we had the ball, helping against full-court pressure, driving and penetrating and dishing the ball, attacking defenses more, and finding the open man when teams decided to double-team me. This was the stuff I'd grown up doing, and of course my comfort level jumped several notches.

Practices started running longer, with Coach Crowe driving us harder than ever, working to turn us into a frenetic team, pressing on defense, attacking on offense. It took awhile to adjust to our new team— not only to playing without our starting frontcourt, but to our new style as well. We lost a pair of games, came away with close victories in three others. Slowly, however, during the first weeks of February, the team began to play with more confidence. By the end of the regular season, we routed Indianapolis Cathedral and finished the season on a roll, with a 17–4 record.

The state tourney always marked the official end of winter along Indiana Avenue. *The Indianapolis Recorder* was filled with advertisements. "One Two Three Four, Who Are We For? . . . Attucks," said the ad paid for by the Twenty-Second Street Cigar Store. "Roll! You Tigers, Roll!" read the copy paid for by Jack's Upholstery. "Come on Attucks! Load 'em Up, Haul 'em Away, We're Pulling For You All The Way"—Spurling Trucking Co. "Attucks! Attucks! All the Way!"—Dave's Market. Liquor stores. Furniture stores. Mattress companies and moving companies, pharmacies, bars, bakeries, beauty shops: ads filled the back pages of the *Recorder,* even as the front pages filled with stories of police raids, investigations that resulted in a crackdown on citywide gambling and shut down a bunch of cigar stores, smoke shops, and nightclubs. Rumors drifted down the Avenue like jazz— the gambling raid was a matter of political convenience; it was a way of keeping blacks in their place; it was one of the end results of what had begun with Arsenal Tech and David Huff.

We were ranked as one of the top ten teams in the state and were one of the sixteen teams that, with our fans, crowded into the Butler Fieldhouse in Indianapolis for the Indianapolis sectionals. The first round was on a Wednesday, the second on a Friday, and the semifinals and finals were on the same Saturday, with the survivor emerging and moving forward into the state's version of a final four.

Most of the teams playing in the sectionals stayed on the Butler campus. Not us. Win or lose, we went home for the night. We were also treated differently in some other ways. Beneath the fieldhouse bleachers was a room with several baskets, where teams could warm up before their games. We played in that fieldhouse every year during the regular season. I played three years of playoff games there. I didn't find out about that room until I was in the NBA. On Saturday we beat Broad Ripple in the early game and set up a rubber match against Arsenal Tech, this time for the sectional championship. We wanted a rematch. We'd made up our minds that if we played them again, we would beat them, and even spent those first two days we had to wait before the sectional championships rooting for our rival to win their bracket.

Before the game, Coach drew upon everything we'd been through in all our road games. Once again he stressed the importance of taking the referees out of the game. This time we followed his words to the letter, blanking Arsenal in the first five minutes and building a 12–0 lead. Tech didn't score a field goal in the first quarter, and from there we played deliberately and made sure not to turn the ball over, milking the clock until it ran out.

So on we moved, advancing to the semifinal round on Saturday. In the first game, two tiny schools were matched up, Montezuma High School and Milan. Montezuma had something like seventy-nine students in their school—just thirty-six boys—and no home gym. Milan wasn't much bigger. Nestled in the rolling farmlands just northwest of Cincinnati, Milan had roughly eleven hundred people, and most of their time was spent worrying about their hogs and chickens and crops. The high school had all of 161 students, just seventy-three boys—fewer than tried out for Attucks's varsity squad. They were a bunch of farm boys who were unfamiliar with stoplights, let alone neon. But they'd made it to the state finals the previous year and had eight returning players, including schoolboy heartthrob Bobby Plump.

Indiana basketball had been increasingly dominated by larger, more urban schools from Evansville, Anderson, Lafayette, Indianapolis, and South Bend, so you just know that reporters loved the small school, David versus David matchup, and covered the hell out of the game. Milan beat Montezuma by ten or so, and afterwards their coach, Marvin Wood, let his players sit in the stands and watch part of the next game before he bused them off to a postgame meal, then to their hotel, for whatever rest and recovery time they could get.

We were in the late game, matched up against another large school, Columbus High. Some people looked at being in the late game as a compliment—you were the team chosen to play in the main event. But on the other hand, there were only a few hours between the end of that game and the nightcap, where you came back and went at it for the championship. Truth is, I didn't consider either opinion. The whole thing was such a new, wild experience for me that I didn't really know what to think; it was too busy happening for me to have many thoughts about it.

Well, we went out there and stunk up the place. Columbus scored twenty-three points in the third quarter and toward the end of the quarter had a fourteen-point lead. But we chipped at the lead, point by point. I kept driving, going to the basket, hitting Bill Mason with passes for open jumpers, and halfway through the fourth quarter, it was a game again. I drove and drew a fifth and eliminating foul on the Columbus center. Then I did the same thing to their leading scorer. There were about four and a half minutes left and, leading by three, Columbus tried to stall and turned the ball over twice. I started bringing the ball up from the backcourt, running and calling the plays, emerging through the gauntlet, stepping into the player I would become.

We took the lead, then gave it up, then took it back. With a minute left, and the score tied, I took my man off the dribble, drove, got fouled, and made both free throws. Columbus came down and hit a jumper. I drove again, got fouled, and hit one of two. Five seconds left. We led by one. They got a final shot and missed. What was the highest scoring game in the history of Indianapolis semifinals was over, 69–68, an Attucks win.

There wasn't much time to celebrate, only a few hours. Then we went back out there again, to play Milan for the sectional. I can't honestly tell you that exhaustion had anything to do with what happened next. Milan had a strong team. They started fast and shot sixty percent in the first half and captured a comfortable lead. Bobby Plump shot the hell out of the ball and ended up leading all scoring with twenty-eight. I played okay, with twenty-two. We had another forward who would be critical to our winning our first championship. His name was Willie Merriweather. But he was out with an injury. We were outmanned. If we'd had Winford O'Neal and Merriweather, I would have liked our chances. As it was, Milan won by eight or ten and advanced to the state finals. It was a rough loss, and afterwards our locker room was quiet. I remember that one guy, a reserve, sat in the dressing room and stared at the doors, waiting for the stream of visitors and reporters. "They'll all come in now," he said, and he didn't say it bitterly, but with a certain resignation. There were a lot of people happy to see us lose, probably even more who were happy to see a bunch of small town white farm boys beat us.

In the state finals, Milan defeated powerful Muncie Central when Plump hit a last-second jumper. You may have heard about the shot and the game; they became immortalized in the 1986 movie *Hoosiers*. Maybe you remember the film: the rusted car driving down country roads, the golden morning light and grain elevators, cornfields and barns with weathered paint and churches with large, white steeples. A coach heads toward the town of Hickory. At each bend in the road, there is a basketball hoop, and more hoops beside grain elevators, nailed to barns, at a crossroad. Coach Norman Dale instructs his players to always throw at least four passes before taking a shot, reinforces the timeless notions of discipline and patience and teamwork. Men gather on frosty nights to talk about what kind of defense the town should play. There are town meetings to decide on the future of the coach. Before the state championship game, the schoolboy hero looks at his teammates and says, "Let's win one for all the small schools that never had a chance to get here."

I ask you this: when the fictional version of Milan—a team named the Hickory Huskers—reaches the championship game in *Hoosiers*, what does it mean that the filmmakers twisted the truth? Instead of having Milan defeat Muncie Central and an integrated team with two black guys on it, which is what happened in real life, Hickory defeated a fictional team of black players, coached exclusively by black men, whose rooting section consists of black men, women, boys, and girls. Is the proverbial race card being played?

Bailey and Ray Crowe both had small parts in the film. You can see them sitting on the South Bend bench, coaching. Obviously, they disagree with me on this point. They're entitled.

The night Bobby Plump's shot gave Milan the real state title, a convoy of Cadillacs hauled the players around Indianapolis's Monument Circle. The next day the caravan headed south, down back roads toward Milan. Thousands of people turned out along the way, waving flags. Children were perched in the boughs of sycamores. Women stood on porches, with freshly baked pies and peach cobbler for the conquering heroes.

At the Senate Avenue Y in Indianapolis, good-natured banter and laughter filled one end of the basketball court. The other end was empty except for a lone player, who was in his own world, dribbling, faking, shooting, lost in the sport's subtle rhythms.

CHAPTER THREE

"They Don't Want Us"
1954–1955

T HE SUMMER BEFORE MY JUNIOR year, the city took the land on Colton Street to build a hospital, and we had to move. Dad married Ivora Helms. Mom and the rest of us moved into a nearby home at 3945 Boulevard Place. But Mom could not make the payments on that place, and soon we moved down the street to 3453 Boulevard Place. My brothers and I did not get much of an explanation for the split. We just had to move. Dad wasn't coming with us. That's just how things went. Honestly, it wasn't that strange to me at the time. My parents had in fact been divorced for three, maybe five years by this point, and if Bailey and Henry and I did not know about the actual divorce, we knew enough to understand that our parents were living separate lives underneath the same roof. Still, we were black people from the country, raised with a deep religious background, and we never heard of divorce, let alone knew about it happening to people like us. It wouldn't be until I was in college and started to see a bigger world that I learned that people got divorced all the time.

Our new neighborhood on the west side was known as the city's Black Gold Coast. Our house at 3453 Boulevard Place had three full bedrooms, a living room where we could watch television, and indoor plumbing. In all ways it was a huge improvement. Strange thing, my dad lived a couple blocks away, on Kenwood Boulevard. I'm sure he contributed something, but it was not enough to take care of everything. Bailey was at Indiana Central on scholarship, so there weren't as many expenses, but my mom still worked two full-time jobs—by day as a licensed beautician, then at night cooking for the family on Broadway. At the same time she made sure our house was clean and there was food on the dinner table, mostly cabbage and green beans and cornbread, with some sort of meat dish— maybe pork chops or fried chicken—showing up once a week or so. My mother didn't have much spare time, but with what little she had, she joined the Beck Jubilee Singers, a traveling choral group. She used to tell us there were two reasons to sing: You sing because you're depressed, or you sing because you're happy.

Instead of spending the whole summer in Tennessee, I worked with a construction crew, then got a job paving asphalt. That freed up my father from giving me money, which he didn't have anyway. The work hardened my body. I built a hoop up at Dad's house with two-by-fours. It had a plywood backboard built on a triangle base, and was held down with sandbags. There was an alley behind Dad's house, and a little driveway off the alley. I'd roll the basket out there. I spent hours upon hours in that driveway, working on my shot. For instance, I used to shoot from the spots where I had difficulty—bank shots from every conceivable angle, side shots, hooks, running jumpers, layups and tip-ins with either hand. Hugo Green was a local player whose style of play I admired, and I tried to copy it. I'd stand out there when the wind drove other players inside, to figure out the angle of the wind, how to best control my dribble in the rain. When Bailey came back from school for summer vacation, every now and then we'd go back there and get after it. Bailey was still a better shot than I was, but I'd grown a couple of inches taller—and a bit stronger than him. We wouldn't play one-on-one too often, but whenever we did, Bailey would tease me that I played harder against him than anyone else.

Maybe I did. To a certain extent, basketball in Indianapolis meant a certain power. I could go all over the city and get in a pickup game. If you were not an athlete, people in other neighborhoods might try to beat you up. But I could go places. I played ball, and everybody in black Indianapolis knew it. I'd show up, and immediately guys wanted me on their team. If the guys had already made their team, or if there was a bunch of people waiting to play, it didn't matter. I was going to be chosen. I'd run with the next squad, because the guys on that squad wanted to win. As long as a team won, they were staying on that court and guys wanted to stay out there. Which meant I was playing. I'd get out there and would hold a court all day long.

This neighborhood court time might have something to do with why I never dunked during a regulation game. It wasn't that I couldn't dunk. I competed in the high and long jumps in track. I could jump with anyone, and I could dunk. But the Dust Bowl backboards were held up by wooden posts set right on the other side of the out-of-bounds line. During one game, I had a lane to the basket and went to dunk. Some guy knocked me right into the post. It hurt enough that I never dunked again. Instead I did what I was taught, making sure to put my body in between any defenders and the ball. If someone flew into me, I scored the layup and then went to the line.

I think one of the big benefits of playing organized sports is that it teaches you about loss. The fact is, if you play a game, you are going to lose sometimes. In life you are going to lose sometimes. But how do you respond to losing? Do you blame the world? Throw a fit and sulk and shy away from trying again? Coaches have remarked that I practiced as hard as any player they'd ever seen. Former teammates have said that I had great control, not just in how I handled the basketball, but in how I controlled myself and controlled the game. I think a big part of my game had to do with responding the right way. When you get down to it, this is just a matter of having answers and being smart. All I ever wanted was to have the same chance to compete as anyone else.

I always believed that if you gave me a chance, I would figure out the rest. For instance, if you played me to go to my left, or off, hand. In that case, I had practiced enough with my left hand to be able to beat you. But I also knew enough about the game to be able to see whether it was a trap. So I might start left and then spin back the other direction. I might go left and draw the double-team and make sure to hit the open man. The next time down the court, I'd build off what I'd just done. Anything you did, I knew how to react. It was important to be a smart player on the floor, but it was just as key to be unpredictable, to have the guy guarding you wondering what you were going to do to him *this time*.

My newfound status as one of the city's prep elites occasionally had perks as well. Like getting to know the Harlem Globetrotters. Willie Gardner—the star on Bailey's team—had signed with the Globetrotters straight out of high school. Through him, I ended up meeting and getting to know the Globetrotters' ace ball-handler, Marques Haynes. I also saw the team's clown ringmaster, Goose Tatum, play a lot of baseball with Indianapolis's triple-A baseball team, the Indianapolis Indians.

The first time I saw the Globetrotters play, I think Willie Gardner invited me. At halftime someone took me down into the locker room. Everyone was playing cards. I couldn't believe it, I literally said it to the locker room, "Man, they're playing cards!"

Someone explained to me what was going on. The Trotters played something like 250 games a year. Every one of them had a halftime show, which lasted for about a half an hour. The guys played cards to pass the time.

Doors to halftime locker rooms weren't the only ones that opened. By the time my junior year started, administrators, coaches, and students at Shortridge High School would have been thrilled to have me attending their school. Mostly white in its student body, Shortridge High was only a few blocks east of Mom's new house. Among their student body and supporters, the thinking went that with me on their basketball team, they'd have the best squad in the city, maybe even the state. I wasn't interested, though. I'd much rather walk the twenty-four blocks to Attucks on foot or thumb a ride, often with one of the teachers headed to work.

I loved my time at Attucks. The city fathers may have instituted a roll call in the middle of the day so they could keep track of where the black teenagers were, but aside from on the basketball court, there was no place I would rather have been. It sounds corny, but sitting in class, having teachers who you knew cared—cared not just about me as a player, but as a person—that made me feel good. Special. I pretty much went through the equivalent of a Black Studies program, reading DuBois, Ellison, and Wright. My best grades were in English, Spanish, and math, and I was better than average in chemistry.

A picture was taken for an article about me in *The Indianapolis Star*. I am in the school cafeteria at lunchtime, sitting at the end of a long, rectangular table. The table is jammed with students and covered with plates and food—you can read the label on a near bottle of A1 steak sauce. Three or four other students are looking at the camera, everybody neat and groomed. I am closest to the camera. Wearing a collared shirt with thin stripes on it, I look skinny. You wouldn't know I am an athlete. My eyes are focused on the camera, composed, with a hint of uncertainty to them. I am smiling warmly.

As much as I can't help but be taken aback by how young I look—how young we all look, how long ago that was—what really comes through in that photo is a sense of optimism, a sense of life and joy.

Often that year, I'd finish with practice and would head over to my friend Don Brown's house. His dad worked in the sheriff's department, and his mom worked for the school system. I'd go over there and unwind, listening to the blues on his record player. Para Lee and Jimmy Brown, Don's parents, were like parents to me.

In 1955, not one school in the city of Indianapolis had won in the forty-five-year history of the state tournament. But with Willie Merriweather, Bill Hampton, Sheddrick Mitchell, and Bill Scott among our seven returning veterans, our Attucks team was the clear favorite. I was labeled the best player in the city, with Charles Preston of *The Indianapolis Recorder* writing: "Willie Merriweather has grown an inch and a half, Oscar Robertson is shooting goals all day long in an alley behind his house—and away we go!"

I think Coach Crowe had enough of capitulation and close finishes and refs getting their shots at us, because he finally unleashed our offense and let us run a lot more. We started the season on fire, winning our first fourteen games. Our only regular-season loss came on the road, near the end of the season, against a small-town team named Connersville High. The school's swimming pool was directly underneath the basketball court. It was an unbearably warm night and the gym was packed, and this made the place hotter and more stifling, so the windows and doors were open wide to try and cool off things. But right in the middle of the game, one of those low-pressure fields—the kind that Indiana weathermen still like to talk about—moved in. By the time the second half started, the temperature had dropped thirty degrees, and the Connersville floor had turned into a skating rink. To top this off, we had played some complacent ball in the first half, and Connersville was tough anyway—they'd opened up a good lead, and there was simply no way we were going to catch them while trying to run around that basketball court without skates on.

The only other close game we had all year was also something of a fluke and came in the city holiday tournament, against Shortridge High. In that one, Coach Crowe permitted us to load up on food before the game. Naturally, we went out there and were sluggish. The game went to overtime, then double overtime. I decided to jump the center tip to start each overtime period. I'd win the tap, get the ball back, and start running the offense. I had grown to six feet four inches and would play every game, alternately bringing the ball up court, finishing fast breaks, and posting up like a center. We took the game in double overtime, and I learned a good lesson. I never ate less than four hours before tip-off again. I would take long walks during the junior varsity contest and think things through for myself, rolling my shoulders, getting loose.

When the playoffs started, we had a 21–1 record and were clearly the best team in the state. Willie Merriweather shot .705 for the season and averaged a state record twenty-one rebounds a game, but a lot of attention was being thrown my way, with different papers naming me the best player in the tournament. We cruised through our first four games, winning by an average of something like twenty-eight points per contest. In the state semifinals, we played a highly anticipated game against Muncie Central, a power from up north. That program had won two state titles in the early

1950s and was considered the other favorite to win this year's title. If there was a glamour game in the tournament so far, this was it.

Radio station WOWO in Fort Wayne made sure to broadcast it, its signal carrying the details through the night, all the way from California to Virginia: the berth in the state finals on the line. Attucks leading by six with a minute left; Willie Merriweather fouling out and turning his back to the court, disgusted with himself, taking his time in putting on his jacket and then slouching down at the end of the bench; a one-point game, eleven seconds left, Muncie taking the ball out-of-bounds; their guard noticing that I seemed about three steps behind my man, not realizing it was a trap. When he threw the pass, I intercepted the ball, ending the game, putting us in the state finals . . .

There was a week break before the final games and throughout it, our team was loose and confident and more than a little giddy. At Butler Fieldhouse, we had to wade through lines of photographers and reporters who had gathered from all over the state. We joked and posed for pictures. We weren't exactly overconfident, but we'd lost only one game all year. We'd just finished defeating the only other team anyone thought had a chance to take the whole show, and now we were exactly where we wanted to be. For the first time in our lives, there was some serious attention focused on us. It was fun. It was novel. Plus, this year we were scheduled for the first game of the semifinals match, so if we won, we'd have some recovery time before the finals.

On Saturday, March 19, 1955, the temperature climbed into the low forties. There was a light drizzle and a gray sky. Traffic from the city's west side began to snake north toward Butler long before tip-off time, inching over Fall Creek and near my mom's new home on Boulevard, past the Crown Hill Cemetery, toward the barnlike arena just off Forty-ninth Street. The line of automobiles, decked out in Attucks' green, gold, and white displayed signs of support and honked their horns, like some sort of circus riding into town.

Almost fifteen thousand spectators jammed the Butler Fieldhouse that afternoon. The air was electric. And when the ball was tossed to start our game against New Albany, we weren't ready. We went out there and made lazy passes, threw the ball away. We had two-on-one fast breaks and didn't convert. Not once or twice, now. *Seven times.* If New Albany had possessed half of our talent, we would have been in serious trouble. As it was, the game went back and forth. We'd build a lead, Jim Henry would score and bring New Albany back. Gradually, like it seems we always did, we wore them down. We were just too quick, too large, too determined. In the fourth quarter, with six and half minutes left, they cut the lead to 65–58. Then I took over, scoring two baskets and two more free throws in thirty seconds. And there you had it. The game was out of their reach.

With a 79–67 victory, we not only accomplished something none of my brother's teams had been able to do, but also made up for the previous year's disappointment in the state semis. Moreover, for the first time in school history, for the first time in the history of Indianapolis, an all-black team was in the state finals. For the first time, Crispus Attucks would be playing for the championship.

Nobody on our team celebrated. We showered, then went up in the stands to watch the first half of the next game. Fort Wayne North against Gary Roosevelt was an even match. Like Crispus Attucks, Gary Roosevelt was an all-black team and was loaded with players. Their center, Wilson Eison, was six feet six and about the finest big player in the state—he went on to win Mr. Basketball in the state of Indiana and received all Big Ten honors at Purdue University. And I'd see their forward, Dick Barnett, for more than a decade in the NBA. The rumor was that after they'd won their sectional, the players on Gary Roosevelt had gone wild in their dressing room, yelling and chanting, "Naptown, here we come." So of course we were curious to see what they'd brought.

Against Fort Wayne—another one of those small and smart teams that shot the hell out of the ball—it looked like a cakewalk. Roosevelt led by sixteen midway through the fourth quarter and tried to run out the clock. But Fort Wayne countered with a full-court press, took Eison out of the game, and rallied to outscore Roosevelt 16–2 over the last four minutes. Roosevelt survived, but just. They were decidedly worn down.

In any case, that night, the Butler Fieldhouse was cleared, cleaned, and then reopened. The stands and bleachers once again filled, and a statewide audience turned on their television sets, this time to watch real history in the making.

It was the strangest thing: While the teams were warming up, I remember the crowd being silent. Could it have been because there were no white players on either team? Because Indiana's legendary cultured and diehard basketball fans were not all that excited about sitting there and watching black players, black coaches, and black student managers? Because maybe they were worried about us racial interlopers kidnapping their beloved game? They weren't sitting on their hands because of a lack of cheerleaders. Squads from white schools in Indianapolis and Gary made a point of showing city and racial unity, coming out to join in with both teams' cheer lines. That touched me back then. Even now it's one of the little details in my life that helps me, when I look back.

We won the opening tip, and I immediately took a pass at the top of the key, gave my quick fake, and took that one hard dribble—a move I'd been making since I was a child, a move I'd practiced tens of thousands of times.

The game was nine seconds old. I pulled up for a sixteen-foot jump shot. The ball dropped through the bottom of the net.

We picked up their guards in the backcourt and applied pressure for all ninety-four feet of hardwood, going after them from the moment we scored, trying to prevent them from getting the ball inbounds, then from dribbling it, jumping right to them, putting hands in their faces, getting right into their jerseys. Pressure was our game. They weren't going to get to walk the ball up and easily, naturally start their plays. They weren't going to be able to make their natural four or five passes as they looked for a good shot. We'd seen from the Fort Wayne game that they couldn't handle pressure. That game had been a war, and those players had to be tired. Our backcourt of Bill Scott and Bill Hampton jumped all over them. Sheddrick Mitchell and Willie Merriweather constantly beat their big men down the court.

And me, I was not going to be stopped. I worked my move to death that night, putting together every possible combination I could think of off it, using every variation: that one move serving as the building block for others. First a jump shot without a fake. Then fake the jumper, take a dribble, and shoot. Now I'd fake, take two dribbles and drive. Now no fake, straight drive. I'd fake left and drive right, fake right and pull up for a short shot. They started double-teaming me. Then triple-teaming me.

We were ahead 24–15 at the end of the first quarter. Eison was hitting shots and trying to keep his team in the game, but in the second quarter we hit nine out of twelve shots, led 51–30 at halftime, and pretty much put the game out of reach. On television, the announcers stopped discussing the game, and started on whether Attucks would score a hundred points, and whether I'd break the scoring record for most individual points scored in the semifinals and finals.

We approached the century mark. What cheers there were grew louder. I scored thirty, bringing my three-game total to ninety-seven, breaking the record by four points. To his credit, Eison also broke the record, scoring thirty-two, for a three-game total of ninety-nine. With time running out, I had a chance to tie him, but passed up a running jump shot. Willie Burnley was a senior who hadn't played much all year—he was in the game, getting some mop-up time. He was wide open under the basket and took the pass and got himself a championship bucket, which mattered more to me than the record.

The final horn rang, and pandemonium broke loose.

We whooped and hollered and embraced, and it was the best, most pure feeling I've had in my life, all of us celebrating, the court filling and then overflowing with students and fans. I don't know how long the party lasted, don't have words to describe it. When we cut down the nets from each hoop, a picture was taken of me standing on the ladder with clippers, wearing my green, gold, and white warmup jersey. I am posed, about to cut down a strand, wearing about the biggest smile I've ever had; my eyes are shining, and you can see the absolute glee on my face.

There was a small awards ceremony, and, finally, we showered and dressed. Leaving the Butler Fieldhouse, our team was loaded on top of a red fire truck. It was a cold, brisk night, and I remember the chill against my still-overheated body, the stinging sensation of being alive like that. The fire truck followed Mayor Clark's limousine and a reinforced detail of police motorcycles. There was a line of buses and cars behind us, everyone honking and whooping, people singing the "Crazy Song" from windows, screaming out our chant, "Ba-ad, ba-a-ad Tigers."

Our motorcade moved east on Forty-ninth Street, and south onto Meridian, each street lined with people cheering to congratulate us. At Monument Circle, we made a victory lap around the fountains and statues and the shaft dedicated to all of Indiana's veterans of the Civil War. We passed all of the limestone soldiers, and then the crowning figure—known for more than half a century as simply Miss Indiana—and finally all the memorials of bronze and stone. Published reports have said there was a quick stop at the circle. Supposedly there was a raucous crowd, and the mayor presented Coach Crowe with the key to the city. That's not how I remember it. In my recollection we *did not* stop at the circle. The motorcade completed the circle and headed up along Indiana, and then north on West Street. Something was wrong. I knew the traditional parade route. I'd seen other champions go south, take a route that led downtown and through the heart of the city.

Instead, we were moving into territory I knew all too well. Into the heart of Naptown. Past the brick walls of Crispus Attucks.

Later I would talk about what happened with Bill Swatts, my best friend. I'd go over the evening with Willie. All of us would recall the large bonfire that lit up Northwestern Park, the sea of what seemed like thousands of people cheering as our truck stopped, the friends who embraced us as we climbed down, the familiar faces all around us, ecstatic.

Bill remembered this night as pure joy and told me about how nice it was to celebrate with *his* people, in *his* neighborhood.

"There was no place I would have rather been that night," he said, "no people I would have rather been with. I was just so happy."

I understand why he felt that way. I felt the same way. It was one of the greatest feelings in the world.

On that chilly night, I stood and stared at the bonfire and all the celebrating faces, all black, and I could not help but think about little Milan High—hadn't even been from the city, but their team got to ride through downtown around the squares of Indy. I knew all those stories about their long ride back to Milan, women coming out of houses with fresh pies for them, men standing on the lawn with flags. Why was that honor denied us?

For thirty years, the Indiana High School Athletic Association had refused to officially admit black schools into their organization or let black referees officiate games. Instead, a white-run government had empowered an all-white school district to decide that blacks were not good enough to attend schools with white children. This government had built an over-crowded all-black high school without a gymnasium, had underfunded this school and made us play all our home games across town at the Butler Fieldhouse. And then, during the playoffs, the same morons had complained, saying we had an unfair advantage because we played regular season games at the playoff site.

In the years to come, I would also learn about a meeting that took place the week before the state finals.

I would find out that the same mayor who was leading this motorcade had met with Coach Crowe and Attucks's principal.

The same mayor who would pay public lip service to our victory being for the entire city? Behind closed doors he had talked about the importance of proper security at the game. He worried about the possibility of rioting.

He and the other city fathers had decided it was too much of a threat to allow us to congregate around Monument Circle.

They sent us back to our neighborhood and made sure we had a police escort to guide our way.

Even now I wonder: Did they think we'd riot because we were primitive animals, beasts who could do nothing but destroy, or maybe, just maybe, did they worry because they knew we had good cause and were entitled to our rage?

It is hard to forgive them for this. I try, but I can't. We weren't savages. We were a group of civilized, intelligent young people who through the grace of God had happened to get together and win some basketball

games. We'd just won the biggest game in the history of Indianapolis basketball.

They took our innocence away from us.

How can I forgive them for doing that?

I eventually left the bonfire and the celebrating. I saw someone
leaving and caught a ride back to the house my dad lived in with his new
wife. I got to the house, and my dad greeted me, excited, hugging me. Then
he saw that something was wrong. I told him I was tired of all that noise. I
went into the kitchen and made myself a sandwich. Stretching out on the
living-room floor, I turned on the television. My dad stood behind me, not
asking questions, but concerned.

"Dad," I said. "They don't want us."

CHAPTER FOUR

"Talk Is Cheap"
1955–1956

ALTHOUGH I AM NOT WRITING this book to relate every injustice I've suffered, it's simply impossible to tell my story without talking about race. As much as I am an American, I am a black American. And to tell you about growing up in the Jim Crow South, and a segregated, Klan-infested Midwest, I must acknowledge the influence of race. Similarly, it's impossible to discuss my experiences with basketball without mentioning race, black and white. Otherwise, you might as well think about America's history during the second half of the twentieth century without acknowledging the civil rights movement. Or consider the Civil War without mentioning slavery. The subjects are all intertwined.

It wasn't until Attucks won our initial state title in my junior year that I had my first meal in a restaurant. I was seventeen years old, and before that, I hadn't so much as set foot in downtown Indianapolis, much less eaten there, except to catch the bus to Tennessee. Being a champion basketball player opened the restaurants' doors to me. Maybe there were some white high school basketball champs who had never been in a restaurant until they won it all, rural kids out on a farm or whatever. But they at least would have been welcome.

That first trip downtown filled me with a strange mixture of excitement and disappointment. I still felt the fresh glow of the win, an enormous pride in our achievement, a sense of giddy lightness inside. At the same time, it was a shadowed happiness, weighed down. When Ray Crowe shepherded our spiffed-up Attucks Tigers into a restaurant called La Fendricks, my smile had long faded. I don't remember being overly impressed by the place. I can't remember what I ate. But I do remember the camaraderie, the novelty, and the sense of a hushed excitement. We were on our best behavior, and we were treated like champions.

Besides the trip downtown and the restaurant meal, there were many other firsts as a result of being the state champs. Different civic organizations around the city invited the team to special ceremonies in order to celebrate our victory. The mayor called us "Indianapolis's Crispus Attucks" in public, whatever he might have said privately. People's willingness to honor us showed me that winning might not completely eclipse race, but it did rebalance the equation some. Our athleticism had always elevated our status in our own neighborhood, but now we had a chance to experience what it felt like to be welcomed and treated special *outside* our home turf.

While I was thrilled to be state champ, and while many of the experiences that came with victory were wonderful, I wasn't about to get complacent. I kept visiting the Dust Bowl and the Y, working on my shots, improving any weaknesses I could discover, doing what I had always done. I wasn't a little kid practicing with a worn-out basketball anymore. Now I was on the threshold of adulthood, and I had experienced what it felt like to win, both the sweet and the bitter. And if winning titles carried a tinge of disappointment, I sure didn't want to come close to losing.

My senior year, I was the sole returning senior player. But up from the eighth- and ninth-grade teams came Sam Milton, Bill Brown, and James Enoch, as well as a player I called "my defense," Al Maxey. I moved to a guard position. We won every regular-season game and extended our winning streak to forty-five games, a record for Indiana high schools. Nothing and no one could stop Crispus Attucks. Remember that Indiana is the basketball-craziest state in the nation, and there is a major college basketball prospect on just about every high school team. Even so, we completed the first undefeated season in the state's history.

The state playoffs were as easy as the season, and our average margin of victory was more than twenty points. I still have a copy of the telecast of the title game. The label on the tape reads, "Silent Film, Final, 1956 Basketball, Crispus Attucks vs. Jefferson Lafayette." Watching it, there is our team, a group of black boys in white uniforms. We appear about equal in height. We are fast and agile. Lafayette is a team comprised of white youths wearing dark jerseys. They play an antiquated half-court game that seems to have been dusted out of mothballs. Their players usually take one or two dribbles before passing, then throw the ball around the perimeter before someone launches a twenty-five-foot set shot. As the game proceeds, our defense becomes more aggressive, our two-three zone pushing their offense out farther and farther from the basket. Meanwhile, we claim defensive rebounds and take off. Our attack includes running hooks and thirty-foot jumpers. There aren't as many offensive sets; we crash the boards repeatedly, our 20–11 lead growing, turning into a rout.

On the videotape I am wide shouldered and muscular. I seem to play every position, bringing the ball up court early, and then posting up like a center at select moments. I make a string of long jumpers from a range that seems farther than I ever remember shooting from. If three-point shots had existed back then, who knows how much higher our score would have been?

Midway through the first quarter, I take a pass just over half-court and slow the ball up, letting the defenders catch up and pass me by. Before they are set, I put a move on my man, stutter stepping to get him out of position. A quick crossover dribble and I am past him, moving into traffic, cutting at the top of the key. I crouch and dribble low and slide by a defender who tries to take the ball. Then I spring, gliding toward the basket and throwing in a running hook.

When the final buzzer sounds, the scoreboard reads Crispus Attucks 79, Jefferson Lafayette 57. Crispus Attucks has become the first school in Indiana history to take an undefeated record into the tournament and win it all.

After we cut the nets down and celebrated in the locker room, the team once again piled into the back of a fire truck. Our motorcade followed the exact same route as the year before. I had a strange sense of déjà vu as we moved past the cheering crowds on Meridian, heading down to Monument Circle, around all the statues and memorials there, and then up West Street. I knew the outcome of this, realized exactly what was going to happen. Maybe we'd eat downtown again the next day, but on the night of our victory, the parade once again bypassed the heart of Indianapolis and headed back to Northwestern Park.

After the state championship game, I was named Indiana's Mr. Basketball. That made me officially the best player in the state. I was honored, but I didn't have much to say. And when they asked me for a comment, I think I became self-conscious, my shyness taking over once again. The only thing I could think to say was, "Thanks."

WHEN ATTUCKS WON its second consecutive state title, it had much more far-reaching consequences than introducing my team to the joys of restaurant meals and public ceremonies. The Attucks-Lafayette game was broadcast across the entire state, meaning that people had just seen an all-black school take home the title for the second consecutive year. I think this made people afraid that maybe Attucks would be unbeatable in athletics if all of Indianapolis's black students were concentrated there. In Indianapolis as well as other areas with a concentration of black students, white schools started encouraging black students, mostly athletes, to attend. Yes, legal integration of Indianapolis had already started, but until Attucks proved unstoppable, it was just a trickle. By the late 1950s, the school systems in Indianapolis were much more open. Other schools simply grew weary of trying to stay on the same court with Ray Crowe. Crispus Attucks played a huge role in that change, and I'm proud to have been a part of that.

AFTER WINNING THE state title, we had one more tournament to play: the Indiana-Kentucky series. I can't adequately relate how important this series is to the basketball fans in each state. Both states claim the game of basketball as their own and follow high school and college games with a fanaticism that borders on religious. In 1940, they started playing a series, matching the best Indiana high school seniors against Kentucky's finest, with all revenues going to the Blind Fund. During the first fourteen years, they played just one game a year, in the Butler Fieldhouse. Indiana won all but one, and of course Kentucky fans raised holy hell, citing a home-court advantage as the cause of the lopsided record. To this day the series is still going, one game played in each state, and each contest is sold out and played before a totally partisan audience. As it happens, in 1955, the same year the series went to two games, Kentucky also started naming black players to the squad.

In 1956, my senior year, the series was being billed by reporters as a battle between opposites—me and "King" Kelly Coleman, a braggadocious white boy from the Kentucky hills. Coleman had broken all Kentucky state scoring records, and he told reporters that the real contest might not be between him and me, but whether he'd score fifty in each game. He wasn't shy about telling them that he had averaged more than forty-six a game during his senior year at Wayland, and he was certain that a bunch of Indiana players could not guard him. When he showed up late for practice, he told reporters, "I didn't think I needed any practice against Indiana."

I didn't say anything to the press, but certainly read his comments. Before the first game, which was in Indiana, our team had steaks at a restaurant called the 500 Club and discussed strategy. Our coach was a man named Angus Nicolson, my brother Bailey's old college coach. When he asked who wanted to guard Coleman, about half the team raised their hands. Angus looked at all of them, then at me. "Oscar, you've got him."

Butler Fieldhouse was again packed for the first game. The papers say it was humid in the arena, and I knew from memory that when the place was packed like that, it didn't take much for your shirt to stick to your back. Coleman and I both wore the traditional number one, which is awarded to each state's Mr. Basketball. Before the opening tap, I shook hands with him. "Talk is cheap," I said.

Kentucky continued the tradition of teams getting off to comically fast starts against me. Their squad came out onto our home court and scored the first seven points. We regrouped enough to tie the score at 10, then took a 12–10 lead. Throughout, I worked pretty hard on defense, crowding Coleman and denying him the ball. He ended up with three points in the first half, and we stretched our lead. During the second half, whenever Kentucky threatened, I either drove and hit someone for an assist, nailed a jump shot, or finished a play myself. We took the first game going away, 92–78. I ended up with thirty-four points, breaking the single-game scoring record by six.

Coleman finished with seventeen, most of them coming during the fourth quarter.

The second game was more of the same, only this time it was played in Louisville, Kentucky. We scored thirty points in the third quarter and blew their doors off, 102–77. This time, Coleman ended up with all of four points, from one of nine shooting. I broke my new record, scoring my fortieth and forty-first points, when our coach reinserted me into the game with seconds left, for a shot at the buzzer.

After that second game, Coleman said he was out of shape and had a bad leg and, considering his condition, would never have made those kinds of predictions. But the coach for the Kentucky all-star team thought Coleman's performance had less to do with his leg than with me. He told reporters that I was "a pro playing with a bunch of high school boys. He's the best high school basketball player I ever saw." *Indianapolis Star* columnist Bob Collins wrote, "If there's anyone who doubts now that Oscar Robertson is the best high school player in the world, he's speaking in very faint tones." Most of his colleagues agreed. Of the 108 sportswriters voting for the Star of Stars in 1956, 106 voted for me.

By the time I graduated from high school, seventy-five colleges had recruited me, in one form or another, with at least forty schools contacting me directly. Only Wilt Chamberlain, who had signed the previous season to play at Kansas, had received more attention. Colleges had been in touch with me since my sophomore season, but during my senior year things got crazy. Calls came to my home and school on a daily basis. Indiana, Purdue, Notre Dame, Illinois, Duquesne, Kansas, New York University, Duke, Connecticut, Marquette, UCLA, Arizona State, Kansas, Nebraska, Cincinnati: All these, and more besides, were calling.

Maybe other athletes have enjoyed the recruitment process. There's a lot to enjoy: the attention, the constant praise, the promises. To some degree, everyone likes being romanced. Make that almost everybody. I wasn't at ease with the process. In fact, I was extremely cautious about it, wary of all these people I didn't know. I saw them as part of the other world, the white world, a world that had made very few sincere overtures to me. Moreover, I had heard of situations where other black players felt awkward simply because of their unfamiliarity with the way things worked. There was the story of a player who took a recruiting trip to Nebraska. On the plane he asked the stewardess how much it would cost him to have a sandwich. Well, the sandwiches were complimentary, they were the in-flight meal, but he'd never been on a plane. He didn't know. And he came back from a recruiting trip with money in his pockets to pay for his trip back home. His mom thought they were buying him like a slave and made him send all the cash back. Then there were the stories of black players, like Bill Scott, who went to white schools and excelled, only to be run from the team by their teammates who thought they were being shown up.

I was by no means afraid of the future, but I also wasn't in any hurry to commit to anything. I started planning. I realized that where I attended college was a huge decision, and I wanted to make it carefully, on my own terms. I was going to play college ball somewhere, that was for sure, and wherever it was going to be, I allowed myself to believe that the school I would choose would celebrate greatness in the same way for everyone, regardless of skin color. Maybe I was looking through rose-colored glasses, to believe there was such a place. But that's how I thought. If there were a college where merit mattered more than skin color, I'd find it. That would be where I would attend college.

NCAA rules were that colleges couldn't legally talk to me until after the Kentucky-Indiana all-star game, when my eligibility to play high school ball expired. So that bought me some time. And once basketball ended, I was busy all spring with the track squad—I qualified for the state championships in the high jump. I also played around with the baseball team (in one game, they let me pitch, and I went the distance for the win, striking out ten, allowing only five hits). So long as I was involved with high school sports, recruiters weren't supposed to contact me. Of course, they still did. My dad disconnected his phone three times. Guess all those recruiting folks didn't realize how little pull my dad had with me. Those recruiters could have become his best friends, and it wouldn't have affected my decision.

A publicity guy named Haskell Cohen, who worked for the NBA, wanted me to go to Duquesne. But that school turned me off when they suggested I be a bellhop at Kutsher's in the Catskills and play basketball all summer. They said it was the way to become an All-American. I told them I would like to develop into an All-American, but I had to work in the summer, and not as a bellhop. Cohen didn't care. He spread rumors that I was virtually pledged to Duquesne. There was even a rumor that our house on Boulevard Place was part of a deal made so that I would play ball at Duquesne. I heard that I had been given a $250 watch and a wardrobe of clothes. I used to look at my wrist to see if it was true, but there was never any watch. I used to stare down at my clothes, shirts that I'd had for years and years, and laugh at my stunning wardrobe. One rumor, spread during the height of the recruiting competition, had a FOR SALE sign appearing in our yard. Absurd.

When my friend Don Brown got in some trouble with his father and couldn't drive, I drove us to school in Don's car; of course that sparked rumors that I'd been given a car. The truth is, I didn't get my first car until after I graduated from high school, after I had made my decision, once recruiting was over. I got my first real job working for a businessman named Swanson that summer. I called him Swanney. He had a car wash and a construction crew. I worked on the crew, putting in asphalt all day long. It wasn't any harder than throwing hay into a moving wagon all day, so I didn't mind it. Swanney told me if I worked to make my money, at the end of the summer he'd help me get a car. At the end of the summer, I had maybe three or four hundred dollars. I found a used Mercury for sale, two-tone brown, for about five hundred dollars. He made up the difference, and boom, I had my first automobile.

Imagine going through your senior year of high school, trying to live a normal life while all these rumors that you're for sale to the highest bidder are flying around. Meanwhile, you're about to spend the summer putting in pavement and saving up money for a used, two-tone Mercury. Yes, people were trying to wine and dine me. But I wasn't on the take, so there wasn't much they could give me.

———————

INDIANA UNIVERSITY'S coach, Branch McCracken, was famous for recruiting Indiana high school players through a statewide network of clinics. High school coaches took the clinics, where they learned how to run fast-break plays using something called the McCracken System. Then the coaches would take that system back to their schools and teach their teams how to play that way. The best players were then funneled into Indiana University. Just about anybody who grew up in Indiana and played nothing more than recreational basketball had a dream, at one time or another, of playing for Indiana University. I was no different. Sure, I had reservations because of the way McCracken had refused to recruit my brother Bailey and then had wasted Hallie Bryant's talents by having him sit on the bench. I also knew that although Indiana had five black players on the team, they did not play more than one or two at a time. If they had all those guys on the bench, it followed someone wasn't going to play. I knew a lot of guys who had their careers ruined because of that, and it wasn't going to happen to me. So, yes, there were all kinds of potential problems. I knew that. They didn't eclipse the mystique that being a Hoosier held for me. I wanted to go to Indiana University.

My senior year of high school, Branch McCracken was nursing a heartache about losing Wilt Chamberlain. In 1954 to 1955, the seven-footer came out of Overbrook High in Philadelphia and set off what was then the largest recruiting war in college basketball history. More than two

hundred schools approached him. Indiana was one of the three or four fi-
nalists. In his first autobiography, *Wilt*, Chamberlain said that when he was
making his decision, rumors reached him that McCracken wasn't all that
fond of blacks. Chamberlain went on to write that although Indiana recruiters later told him they would double whatever any other school offered
to pay him, he signed with Forrest "Phog" Allen and Kansas. McCracken's
version of events was different. He would tell at least one reporter that
Chamberlain had been offered to him for five thousand dollars, up front.
In McCracken's version of the story, he refused to pay Wilt, and lost him
for that reason. "We thought we had Wilt. He announced he was coming
here. Phog Allen stole him away from us."

Well, I was the most hyped recruit since Chamberlain. Maybe that
made McCracken distrustful of me.

When track season ended, I became free of varsity obligations and
could legally make home visits to universities. The first place I wanted to
go was Bloomington. One cloudless spring day, Coach Crowe drove me
there. I got to McCracken's office expecting a certain warmth; after all,
they were one of the schools sending me information and saying they
wanted me to play for their team, and I *was* the state's Mr. Basketball.

McCracken's secretary said he was busy. Could I please have a seat
and wait?

Well, after I sat there for thirty minutes or so, McCracken's door finally opened. He invited me into his office, and I sat down. He was quiet for
a moment, looking at me, sizing me up. Finally he said: "I hope you're not the
kind of kid who wants money to go to school." I did not know that kids got
money to play at schools. I grew up religious and was taught to do the right
and honest thing. I didn't want money to go to college, I just wanted to go.

I didn't answer him and just walked out of his office, back to the car,
seriously insulted.

If that man had said, "Oscar, we would like you to come to Indiana
and play for us," I would have taken a pen from my own pocket and signed
with him right there. Instead I came away thinking that I wouldn't play for
Indiana University if it were the last place on earth.

"I got to leave," I told Ray.

My first choice was off the list, so I started going down the rest of them. I thought hard about Purdue. Willie Merriweather was there, but it was not to be.

John Wooden at UCLA had sent me one of his "Pyramids of Success," but he hadn't really started winning his titles yet. And when I thought of being out in Los Angeles, so far away from my family, I felt my heart drop somewhere underneath my stomach. I decided to stay close enough to home so I could ride a bus back home if I needed to. That helped narrow my choices some.

The University of Michigan was far enough away to necessitate an airplane ride, but also close enough that I could ride home on a bus if the situation demanded it. I decided to visit and rode in an airplane for the very first time. I was more nervous about the plane ride than meeting the coaching staff. The plane touched the ground in Detroit, and I felt like the rest of the visit would be a piece of cake. I got to the terminal and looked for someone to come forward and introduce themselves. I watched the rest of the passengers meet their parties and wander toward the baggage claim. I kept waiting, unsure of what to do or where to go. After half an hour, I called the coach. They'd forgotten I was coming. I got on the next plane for home.

A NOVELTY SALESMAN working out of Cincinnati by the name of Al Hutchinson was a major fan of the University of Cincinnati's basketball team. By chance he also had seen me play during my sophomore year at Crispus Attucks. Al was the first man to tell Cincinnati coach George Smith that he had to see the Attucks team. Smith went down to see what Willie Merriweather could do on a court, but he left interested in me. During my senior year, I was at the top of his list of students to recruit, but somehow Cincinnati's pitch hadn't made such a huge impression on me.

It was late March, awfully late to be thinking about recruiting for September enrollment, when a conversation took place in George Smith's office. Dick Forbes, a sports columnist for *The Cincinnati Enquirer*, was

talking with Tom Eicher, UC's sports publicity man. Walter Paul, an executive for Queen City Barrel and Astro Container of Cincinnati, was also
there. Paul recruited for the University of Cincinnati's basketball program,
partly as a hobby, and partly because they had such a limited coaching staff.
Walter Paul sat in the office, listening, as the reporter and the sports publicity man talked back and forth about me. One of them said, "I bet this
guy couldn't be had for less than ten thousand dollars."

This was the first time Walter Paul ever heard of me. Years later he
told me, "That comment triggered me. You know, you sustain a certain motivation all through life. But there are some things you want worse than
anything else. That—and convincing the woman I married—were the two
things that I worked hardest at in my lifetime over a short period of time."

Without George Smith knowing a thing about it, Walter Paul went
out on his own, trying to find out how to learn about me.

He started out by talking to the black truck drivers who worked for
him and then going into Kingan's, the meat-packing plant where my dad
used to work in Indianapolis. The workers there told him that my father
would have very little influence on me. Then he found a meat inspector
who said he knew my minister. That too was a blind alley. Finally, via the
process of elimination, he determined that the key people in my life were
Ray Crowe and my mom. (It's amusing, thinking of him working so hard
to find out who could influence me.) Later, both Ray and my mom told me
that neither one of them felt they had a hold on me. Each suspected that
the other one had control. George Smith thought it was my mom who was
the major factor in my decision as to where to attend college, and said,
"Nobody else in his life even came close." But in the end, as Smith and
Paul found out, I was my own man.

Paul's first approach to Ray Crowe didn't get him anywhere. Then,
he happened to meet a Wilson Sporting Goods distributor who called on
Crispus Attucks. Paul complained to the distributor that he couldn't get
next to this guy Ray Crowe. The distributor mentioned that Ray Crowe
liked to play golf, so they arranged a match one afternoon. That brought
forth a warm letter of thanks from Ray and led to the two of them and their
wives going out socially a couple of times.

Next, Paul contacted my mother. "We had long discussions about the poverty, the holes in the roof, the tacky linoleum, no showers for the kids, and all that. I listened, no comments. Just listened. Then she played me some spiritual numbers that she wrote in hopes of recording. They had a great beat to them."

My mom told Walter Paul that she wanted two things. One, she wanted to get on the 50-50 Club—a midday variety show piped out of Cincinnati WLW-TV into Indianapolis, Columbus, and Dayton. Two, she wanted to get somebody with some clout to listen to that music. She wanted to try and have it published.

My mom told Paul that the apartment owner next door to us had been authorized by a wealthy Indiana University alumnus to offer the family five thousand dollars for my enrollment at Bloomington. But she also said that Bailey had been cold-shouldered by IU, and there was no way I would go there. Furthermore, she said that I wasn't for sale. That stuff had gone out ninety years ago. She also told him about Haskell Cohen, that publicist for the NBA who also seemed to be scouting for Duquesne, bothering the devil out of her and trying to get me to a Catskills basketball retreat. So Paul told her all kinds of stories about how the Catskills was a terrible place, filled with gamblers and who knows what else.

Next, Paul, with Bearcats coach George Smith in tow, visited Crispus Attucks. They wanted to talk with Principal Lane, but he was out of town, so they had a long chat with the assistant principal. Not only did Paul and Coach Smith come away impressed with the cleanliness and the atmosphere of the school, but the assistant principal gave me high marks on character, scholarship, and moral fiber. He told them that my desire to be a great player kept me out of trouble; I avoided anything off the straight and narrow, and even stayed away from teammates who were headed the wrong way.

After they got the tour of Attucks, they met me. Two or three months of intense work had gone into the project at this point. Walter Paul's dad was furious at him, claiming that his son had neglected the family business to run around chasing a basketball player. But finally, Paul laid eyes on me.

It was my first time in a hotel suite. Of course I was shy, didn't say two words to the man.

Paul and Coach Smith made their presentation. They said, "Look. You are the most-sought-after basketball player in the United States. No matter where you go, you will be looked upon skeptically. At the University of Cincinnati we have a co-op program in the business administration school. We have arranged a double-section version of our regular co-op program, where you can actually go to school for fourteen weeks and then work for fourteen weeks and legally be paid for it and not made ineligible as an athlete. You will work at Cincinnati Gas and Electric on a regular wage scale."

I sat still, stayed quiet.

When Paul got back to Cincinnati, he contacted Professor Newman in the English Department at UC. Newman's wife was Ruth Lyons of the 50-50 Club at WLW. Soon enough, my mom appeared on the 50-50 Club. Paul also arranged for her to cut an audition tape at King Record Company, which was big in country and western at the time. My mother never breathed a word of any of this to me; I had no idea it was going on. In fact, it wasn't until years later that I learned about all these plans and machinations. In any case, the morning after Mom's audition, Ray Crowe called Paul and asked, "What in the world did you do with that woman yesterday?" Paul told Ray about the studio visits and also how he gave my mom a tour of his plant. He had introduced her to several of his longtime black employees who had grown up with him and were almost like family.

"Well," Ray said, "She just called me and told me, 'Look, I know you control my son, but I want to tell you that he just *has* to go to the University of Cincinnati.'"

As if this wasn't enough, Walter Paul then set up a visit. I went to Cincinnati and met Jack Twyman, a forward who was the leading scorer on the Rochester Royals and an NBA all-star. We worked out together, one-on-one, at an old school gym. Afterwards, Twyman told Paul that I was the greatest player he'd ever seen. That night the Twymans, the Smiths, and the Pauls took me to dinner. They dropped me off at the Cincinnati Y after dinner. Apparently, Twyman told Paul, "If I were George Smith, I'd go to bed with that boy, keep an eye on him, and let Mrs. Smith go on home by herself."

The next day Walter Paul took me to Crosley Field to watch a Reds game. There, I met his old friend Jake Brown. He was a UC booster who had gone through its undergraduate and law programs. When I met him, he was the senior partner in his law firm of Brown and Gettler. All I knew at the time was that he was kind to me without seeming fake or overly deferential, but later I found out that he was a major power broker in Cincinnati and had quite a reputation throughout the Midwest as a civil libertarian. He told me to call him J. W. We watched the ball game for a while, and I didn't say much, as usual. Jake's son Robert, who was about thirteen or so, was there, and I chatted mostly with him.

I know that the bleachers at Crosley Field were segregated—I had taken a few trips to Cincinnati to see Jackie Robinson and the Brooklyn Dodgers play—and I can't exactly account for how we all sat in the same section, except to wonder if it was a private box. But I remember being surrounded by friendly faces. I remember feeling that if Jackie Robinson could play in Cincinnati, with the whole Negro population turning out to greet him, then maybe I had a shot of playing there without problems.

Maybe it was another rose-colored vision. A lot of people who sat in those same bleachers had memories from years before of shouted obscenities and a threat of violence in the air. Many people remember that in 1952, death threats had brought armed bodyguards to Crosley when Robinson and the Dodgers had visited. But to me, being at a major-league game had been such a kick that, as naïve as it makes me sound, I didn't really notice any warning signs that day.

Near the end of the game, J. W. started talking to me as if just the two of us were at the game. "Oscar," he said, "I want you to know that if you come to Cincinnati, I will not just see you through college. I will give you business assistance. I will see you into your pro career. Help you handle your finances. Give you business advice. Be a friend of some importance to you, even after you leave the university."

Something about Jake's demeanor told me that I could trust what he said. With some people, you don't have to spend much time with them to know that you can take them for their word. And that promise for the future seemed to offer me something that no one else had: respect for me beyond my basketball abilities and a real concern for what was best for me as a person regardless of what I could do for them.

I hadn't actually investigated the university itself. Cincinnati was two hours or so south of Indianapolis on Highway 52. I knew the city was about the same size as Indianapolis and had about the same demographics. The Bearcats had an all-white team and a white coaching staff, and they weren't exactly basketball legends, so I hadn't placed them high on my list. At the same time, my choices were really narrowing. If I wanted to stay close to home, there weren't too many choices. These people seemed to be honest and sincere. Plus, there was the matter of the coach, George Smith.

George had grown up on an Ohio farm and had a style that put people at ease. Recruiting was one of the things he was good at. He was a charmer, but in an easygoing way that didn't make you feel like you were being charmed. When we sat down for our first interview together, I was prepared. He asked me the question that everyone asks, "What do you want out of college?" I answered him promptly: "One, naturally I want a good education. Two, I want the opportunity to play major-league basketball for exposure in the large cities. Three, I want no black problem. Four, I want to be close to my family and friends in Indianapolis. Five, I want to play in Madison Square Garden. They say that's the mecca of basketball, and that's where I want to play."

I wasn't trying to make a good impression. I was just answering honestly and being myself. I had thought plenty about what I wanted out of college, and I knew that none of it was negotiable. My friends always said, even way back then, that I was driven. A friend once told me, "At seventeen you knew exactly what you wanted by twenty-seven. At twenty-seven, you were getting right on target for thirty-seven." I might not have phrased it that way, but I couldn't disagree.

Coach Smith seemed impressed by the clarity of my list and the lack of hesitation I showed before giving it to him. He smiled at me, nodded, maybe gave a little laugh.

My trip had other memorable parts. Ted Berry, who later became

Cincinnati's first black mayor, had a reception for me. I will never forget how nice he was to me. On another recruiting visit, Ross Hastie, a wealthy university supporter, led a private tour around his home for me and a teammate, Al Maxey. The house had a pool and tennis and basketball courts. As they showed me around, I kept shooting Al looks, *Can you believe this?* I keenly felt how little I knew about finance or culture or international relations. I couldn't add much to any conversations, so I stayed quiet.

At some point, while I was sitting by the pool, Ross Hastie's young son, who must have been six or seven years old, turned to me and said, "Gee, you sure are black."

Well, it got quiet. *Really* quiet.

I smiled at him and calmly explained that my ancestors came from another continent. It was very hot there, and dark skin was the norm. That answer was probably more words than I'd said all day, and after it came out of my mouth, it felt like the whole room exhaled.

On June 8, 1956, I wore my cap and gown along with 170 other seniors graduating from Crispus Attucks. I was sixteenth in my class, which put me in the ninety-first percentile, and a member of the National Honor Society. The next day, I announced my intention to enter the University of Cincinnati.

CHAPTER FIVE

Collegiate Life
1956–1958

N OWADAYS, SOME GUYS jump straight from high school into the NBA. The time when Moses Malone, Bill Willoughby, and Darryl Dawkins defied convention and logic is long past. The individual and collective success of Kevin Garnett, Kobe Bryant, and Tracy McGrady burst open the floodgates. When Kwame Brown went straight from his high school graduation to the number one pick in the draft, it solidified the trend, turned what was once a rarity into a rite of passage. This past year, anyone with cable television and even a moderate interest in sports watched LeBron James become a SportsCenter celebrity, with special segments about the Hummer his mom got him and the replica jerseys that the boy was given, with announcers all the while lecturing and pontificating about exploitation, even as their network was broadcasting his games.

Coming from the kind of poverty I did, I certainly can understand someone making the leap right into the professional ranks, especially when there are millions of dollars involved. Hell, if someone had offered me a Jackie Robinson jersey when I was in high school, rules or not, I would have taken it.

Having said this, I also know that there's a difference between being physically capable of doing something and being mature enough to understand everything that comes with what you are doing. The NBA draft has become something of a futures market, with teams taking young, raw players and relying on the idea that they will develop gradually, blossoming into stars three or four years down the line. Kids are being put in a situation and a life they aren't prepared for. Part of playing basketball is having the game experience, maturity, and smarts to know what to do. But every year, there are more guys running up and down NBA courts with no idea how to play or handle themselves professionally. On the one hand, good for them; they made it into the big time. But the flip side is, once you get enough guys on the court who don't know how to play or conduct themselves, who throw tantrums and scream at their coaches and get into trouble and are generally too young and self-centered to know what they're doing, the end result is that quality of the game gets diluted. The state of professional basketball is adversely affected.

But my experience wasn't a textbook example on the way things should be either. In 1956, when I enrolled in the University of Cincinnati's School of Business Administration, freshmen weren't eligible to play varsity basketball in college. Schools had freshman teams. The idea was to give incoming student-athletes a year to adjust to college life, at the same time allowing them to assimilate gradually into their athletic program, mature physically, and get ready for varsity competition. That was the idea, anyway.

If you had told me then that I'd spend the great majority of my adult life living in Cincinnati, I probably would have laughed at you. Yet I have spent forty-three of the past forty-seven years living here. Shortly after I graduated from Crispus Attucks, I packed up what few shirts I had, two pairs of pants, my sneakers, and moved to Cincinnati for the summer. Walter Paul helped set me up at the Cincinnati YMCA and got me a job in the shipping department of Queen City Barrel. Walter's brother ran the production line at the plant, and he had me working down on the line, in the factory's bowels. Someone had put up a basketball hoop at the end of the line. One day I started shooting during lunch. Soon enough Walter's brother called him long-distance. Wanted to know who I was. Everybody was stopping work to watch me pop them in from all over the lot. He told Walter I was disrupting production. He wanted to fire me.

"For God's sake," Walter screamed, "don't do that."

Soon enough he called the supervisor, and disaster was averted.

But things were far from perfect. The summer was less than a month old when I'd tired of living at the Y. My room was hot and terrible. I didn't know too many people in Cincinnati, the campus was pretty much closed up, and the people that I did see walking around there weren't anything like me. So I quit the job on the production line and spent the rest of the summer working for Swanney on his construction crew.

When I was being recruited, people from the university may have taken me into their homes, George Smith may have walked me through the Cincinnati Armory Fieldhouse, where the basketball team played, but the one place I didn't spend much time was the campus. Turns out, there was a reason for this. The University of Cincinnati had a small campus, for the school was a private institution, only accepting the cream of applicants, the top ten percent or so. I had no idea of the difference between a private and public school or how something like a high-end admission policy would affect the racial composition of the student body. Maybe I sound naïve. But when I sat in the stands at Crosley Field and watched the Reds play against Jackie Robinson, I saw all those black faces. I figured that if this was how things were in the stands, this was how things were in the city of Cincinnati.

I had told George Smith that I did not want any racial problems at the school I attended. He had agreed, as did all the other people I talked to. I'd figured that this meant there was some sort of balance, that problems were already dealt with. I'm not saying I expected some sort of utopia—however naïve I was, I wasn't *that* naïve. I am sure that, somewhere in my mind, I understood that I was still the exception, not the rule. Bradley University had a few black players back then, NYU had three or so, and a few other teams had black players. But Louisville was all white, for example—*Louisville*. Mississippi State's basketball team had to sneak out of the state just to play against a team with black kids on it. When you got down to it, the recruitment of any African-American player by a white college at that time was a clear statement against segregation. And while I may not have known all the numbers and details involved, I certainly understood that this was the case. I was aware of the lay of the landscape.

Having said this, I certainly did not expect to be one of the five black athletes who, basically, desegregated the school, nor to bear the brunt of that action. I did not expect that a graduate student named William Flax would write letters to the campus newspaper saying it was degrading to import black student-athletes, that it was insulting to the campus community. I could not know that during my time at the University of Cincinnati, I would be discouraged from entering a bar-and-grill where other players hung out, and I definitely did not expect that I would be attending a school where—though the majority of the professors were honorable, dedicated people who graded students on the quality of their work—it seemed a few professors did whatever they could to *prevent* black students from graduating.

School started in fall, and as I put away my misgivings about my summer job, I moved into an all-male athletic dormitory. I'd always loved school and was eager for classes to start, excited to be starting out for myself on my own two feet at a place that had gone to such lengths to welcome me. But when I walked into certain classrooms, immediately I sensed a reaction. I saw that a lot of people were uncomfortable with my presence. I had been comfortable at Crispus Attucks and felt at home, but now I was a walking anomaly. The only students I knew were my teammates and Ralph Davis and Ron Dykes. I wasn't going out of my way to meet people. I didn't know how to handle this new world and backed away from it, keeping to myself, relying on the cautious introverted habits that made me feel safe. It was a confusing, lonely time.

I'd met Austin Tillotson at the theater one evening with some teammates. Austin introduced himself. He was an older man. He'd played pro basketball in the 1930s, had heard about me from friends in Indianapolis, and went out of his way to help me. Austin and Gladys Tillotson's home turned out to be a blessing for me throughout college—a sanctuary and a refuge. I can't tell you how many Sunday mornings I went over there, had a morning meal, and joined the family for services over at Zion Baptist Church.

I remember going over to the Tillotson house once, really frustrated. Blacks just caught hell in class, and I couldn't take it anymore. It wasn't only me, I told Austin. There was one other black guy, a guy named George Welch, who was in a lot of my classes. We took a lot of abuse, and nobody did anything about it. An economics professor told me that I wouldn't pass. So I had to take an economics exam from a professor at another college, just to prove to the university that I knew the work. I was sitting there explaining all this bull to Austin. He gave me a look and laughed, a kind of bitter laugh. "Man. Black people don't go to school here."

Austin was one of few to sit me down and be completely honest with me. That day he explained the real deal with blacks and the university I had enrolled in, and I sat there, listened, and thought about it.

I already knew there were certain things I couldn't do. I knew that in high school, I had to watch where I went, who I was with, what I said. I knew that anyway, because that's the world of an athlete. But I also knew that being black meant there always would be extra burdens on your shoulders. Being black meant you had to be better than someone else to get by.

It's been written I never smiled in games. Never smiled during practice, never during a scrimmage. That's not strictly true, although, yes, I was an intense competitor. One Saturday morning, we were in a pickup game. Some money was riding on it. A college football player hit a wild shot and danced back up the floor. I told him to sit down in the bleachers, that I could get some kid watching on the sideline who would not pull that kind of junk to play instead of him.

"It's only a game, Oscar."

"Game, hell, I've got my money riding on this game."

"Ten cents. A lousy dime. If we lose, I'll buy the beer."

"You're missing the point. Any time I get out here at nine o'clock on Saturday morning to play basketball, I'm playing to improve. And I'm playing to win. If you don't want to play, go over and sit down."

I was driven, moved by something more powerful than I am. I think that's why when another exam—this one in marketing—came around, and everyone on the basketball team had a tutor available to him, I did better on the exam than my tutor. I remember that the head of the department called Coach Smith, and I was called into the athletic office. Coach asked how I could do better than the guy tutoring me. "Man," I said, " I just went and let him do all the talking. The guy taught me everything he knew, but I didn't tell him everything I knew."

I made no apologies.

When Austin Tillotson sat me down and explained to me that black people did not go to the University of Cincinnati, I could have left. I was a shy country boy, and the last role I was ready for was a barrier-breaker. I was the most-sought-after player in the nation, and schools would have been falling over themselves to take me. The easy thing would have been to walk away, transfer schools.

But I thought about what Austin said, swallowed, and said, "Okay."

In retrospect, I'm glad I did. Glad they picked me and glad I hung in there. I'm proud that I was successful both in the classroom and on the court.

I didn't do it alone, of course. Art Hull, a good friend, also helped me with the transition. Early in my freshman year, Jake Brown came to see me on a visit that helped me sort things out quite a bit. It had been a few months since we'd gone to that baseball game, and we met for lunch or something. I guess he heard that I was having problems adjusting and still feeling the sting of not being allowed into those off-campus theaters and restaurants. Immediately he welcomed me, greeting me with open arms, and before I knew it, he'd invited me to his home. Other than maybe in the South when I was a boy, it was the first time I'd ever been invited, by myself, to any white person's house. About all I could do in response was nod yes to the invite.

His home was in the Cincinnati suburb of Avondale. Jake—I'd

learn to call him J. W.—and his wife Shirley met me at the door and introduced me to their three daughters, Barbara, Penny, and Debbie. Penny and Debbie—the youngest daughters—put on a skit for me before we ate, and then J. W.'s son, Robert, about fourteen then, joined us.

During my time at the University of Cincinnati, J. W. Brown, Austin Tillotson, Walter Paul, and Art Hull acted as a support system, a second family. They let me pick their brains, bounce ideas off them, and presented me with different ways of looking at things. They provided me with a generous share of help and guidance.

For instance, as part of the school's co-op program, I worked forty hours a week, counting conduit cable in the treasury department of Cincinnati Gas and Electric. On Walter's advice, I took every dime I made from the treasury department job and invested it in U.S. Savings Bonds, as well as stock in Kroger and Cincinnati Bell. Walter helped me on certain other financial matters, things that might require a delicate touch. Nothing immoral or illegal, mind you; I didn't get free cars or anything. But when I was having problems at the cafeteria—the food was bland and uninteresting—I called Walter, and he figured out a solution. He also was there for me on other matters and taught me lessons I needed to learn, even those I did not want to learn.

One night I'd taken the train back to Indianapolis to visit my parents. I came back to town, didn't have cab fare, and needed a way back to the dorm. I called Walter, and he came with his wife to get me. He was dead tired and, I think, was wearing his bathrobe. I did not have the heart to tell them that my older brother took my taxi money from the top of the dresser. Much later, Walter Paul told an interviewer that I was hungry that night and asked if they could get me a burger and a shake. I don't remember that. But do remember that when I got in the car, Ms. Paul snapped. "Look, Oscar, I don't know who you think you are. I wouldn't take this from my own child. I don't intend to take it from you. From here on when you make a phone call at some unearthly hour of the night, stop and consider other people."

Another night, two years later. I was standing with Walter and his wife. We were in front of the fieldhouse. There were a few boosters present. Walter told them he wanted to introduce his son.

Then he motioned toward me. "Oscar."

BEFORE GEORGE SMITH took over the University of Cincinnati's basketball program in 1952, the Bearcats were an awful team with a losing record. George was six feet two inches, a good-size man. Reporters liked to call him Big George. He had been an assistant football coach for eight years, coached the freshman squad, and been a physical education instructor before that. If he wasn't exactly a basketball guy, he wasn't an awful coach either. Parents really liked him, and he made players feel safe and comfortable, like he was on your side. When he got you on the court, he was strict, a disciplinarian. It took George about two years to recruit some real players and turn things around. From 1954 until my enrollment two years later, there may not have been tremendous fan interest in the program, but the Bearcats showed a definite improvement, playing a fast and loose style of ball and winning seventy percent of their games.

Having said this, when I got to Cincinnati, I wasn't sure how things would go on the court. Time was important. College coaches used all their practice time installing offensive and defensive sets. They didn't have time for working on footwork and stuff like that. Once you get out of high school, you had to work on those things yourself. That was fine with me. I put in my hours and ignored the myths swirling around campus. I was embarrassed by the circulating word that my workout with Jack Twyman during the recruiting period was actually a game of one-on-one.

Basketball season was always inaugurated by the freshman squad's game against the varsity. On a blustery winter night, more than six thousand fans turned out to watch the varsity double-team me the whole game. Although I did manage to find enough openings for thirty-seven points, seventeen rebounds, and eight assists, the varsity won, 87–83. However, during that season, it wasn't uncommon for fans to show up at the Cincinnati Gardens to watch our game and then leave before the varsity squad took the floor. I guess they weren't particularly compelling that year. Until I twisted my ankle and missed the last two games, I averaged thirty-three points a game, and our freshman squad finished an uneventful year with a 13–2 record.

College basketball wasn't the same game back then. No three-point shots, no forty-five- or thirty-five-second shot clocks. No cable television with games on twenty-four hours a day. No coaches trying to make themselves bigger than the game for the sake of endorsement deals. Only sixteen teams went to the NCAA tournament at the end of the season, so if you did not win your conference championship, you were done for the year.

In my sophomore year, the games really mattered. Ralph Davis, Spud Hornsby, and Larry Willey were among the sophomores who came with me from the freshman squad. Connie Dierking was the top returning player on a Bearcats squad that had a 13–12 record and averaged a shade less than a hundred points a game. We didn't have any size, so whenever possible we ran, pushing the ball up the court after fast breaks, making baskets off out-of-bounds plays, you name it. It was a good bunch of guys; I got along with every one of them. That's important, because one of the binding principles of a locker room is that we're all in the same boat, that a team is united. Corny as it sounds, a locker room of tightly connected teammates who like one another is a special place. Almost anyone who played college or pro sports will tell you that once their playing days were finished, they missed locker room camaraderie as much as anything.

Before my first varsity game, the story goes that Coach Smith held a special team meeting, one at which I was not present. Supposedly he said, "I want you fellows to understand something, and I don't want Oscar to hear what I have to say. You were a good team before, but with Robertson you can become a much better one, maybe a great one. He'll get all the headlines and all the publicity. You might as well make up your minds to that. But if you play with him, he'll take you further than you've ever gone before." I don't know if that meeting ever happened. Smith claims it did, but when starting center Dave Tenwick had a chance to write his own column for the student newspaper, he felt otherwise. "Well, if we did have a meeting like that, I sure don't remember it."

This much I can tell you: on December 6, 1957, a little less than four thousand people turned out for my first varsity college basketball game. Wish I could tell you everything that happened, but I don't remember a thing about that game. The box score says we beat Indiana State, and that I hit on eleven of sixteen shots, and hit six of eight free throws for a total of twenty-eight points. I also dished out fourteen assists. For twenty-eight minutes of playing time, that's not too shabby.

The only other thing I know about that night comes from a column printed years later. In it, a sports editor says that this was the night when Bearcats play-by-play announcer Dick Baker, broadcasting on WSAI-AM radio, first referred to me as the Big O. At first when I made a play, he called me O. "O does it again." In recollection he would say he had been doing it since my freshman season, while watching me play, but that this was the first time he had a chance to share the nickname with listeners.

Days later we played a strong Temple team led by All-American Guy Rodgers. Dozens of writers from Boston, New York, Philadelphia, and Washington covered the game. I had thirty-six points and eighteen rebounds in another win. After the game, Temple coach Harry Litwack called me the greatest sophomore player in the country. Then we were at home for our holiday tournament. My thirty-six points against St. Bonaventure helped us pull away in the second half. A night later, another big game against Xavier led us to the tournament title. Four games into the season, I led the nation in scoring, and our team was ranked fourth nationally. After ten games, my average had leveled off at about thirty points a game. A sportswriter with a hangover and too much spare time gave us the nickname, "the Firehouse Fo' Plus the Big O."

The next game took us to New York City.

Playing in Madison Square Garden is special. New York City is the center of the media world, and a good performance there means untold possibilities and national exposure. In 1958, this was even more true than today. Without cable television, players weren't seen by fans as they are now. Visiting athletes were known only by reputation. When I was in college, few people had actually *seen* Wilt Chamberlain. I mean, everybody knew there was a seven-foot giant who played at the University of Kansas. We all were awed by the idea of Wilt. Maybe someone had even seen a few seconds of footage of him. But most fans didn't know what he looked like. In New York, the media and wire services saw everyone. An appearance in New York meant that you, Wilt, or me would be playing on the biggest imaginable stage, in front of all of the people who would report to the world, tell the nation who you were or were not, what you could or couldn't do.

I didn't know that much about the history of Madison Square Garden. I'd read briefly about it. I knew, vaguely, that college basketball was still recovering from the point-shaving scandals of the early 1950s, and that New York's college basketball scene had been devastated by the problems with CCNY, Long Island University, and NYU. I guess, to generate a spark, the Garden would bring in big-name college teams and players for a two-day, four-game tournament. That was about the extent of what I knew.

If anything got to me, it was riding in a taxi. Coming from the Hotel Paramount, up Eighth Avenue to a pregame workout, I was dumbstruck by the majestic chaos of New York City, and gaped and stared out the window. "Look out," I told the cabby. "Man, you're worrying me with the way you drive." "Look at all those big buildings." "Never saw so many movie theaters in my life." "Man, this is a big town."

On January 9, 1958, under the headline "Cincinnati to Meet Seton Hall Tonight," *The New York Times* ran this story:

> Cincinnati, one of the strongest collegiate basketball teams, will meet Seton Hall in the second game of the double-header at Madison Square Garden. Another team, Xavier of Ohio, will play against Iona in the opener at 7:15.
>
> The Bearcats of Cincinnati have won eight of ten. It wasn't until Connie Dierking was sidelined by a broken bone that Cincinnati lost a game. That was a week ago, and Dierking, though traveling with the squad, will probably not see action.
>
> The star of the Bearcats, Connie (sic) Robertson, will

be making his first appearance in the Garden. The six-foot-five sophomore is averaging thirty points and sixteen rebounds a game.

Whatever marketing plans the Garden execs had, they didn't exactly bring out the fans that night, because our game tipped off in front of a mostly empty building. Connie Dierking, our center—whose name the *Times* juxtaposed with mine—made a surprise start as our other forward. I took my first shot thirty-five seconds into the game, a midrange jumper that missed. A minute and fifteen seconds after that, I used my height and my muscular body to back a defender down, then spun off him and leaped and hit a scooping layup.

There must have been something in the air that day. Not only had the paper juxtaposed my name with Connie Dierking's in print, but Seton Hall's coach kept yelling, "Get Robinson!" His yelling did not help. They were overmatched, and we quickly outran and outscored them. Holding the ball in my right hand, far above my head, releasing and following through on a virtually unblockable shot, I hit jump shot after jump shot. I posted up, ran fast breaks, filled the lane, and finished with one scooping layup after another. By halftime we had blown open the game, and the second half was more of the same. My game wasn't long-range shooting; I think I only took three shots that night from beyond the top of the key. But whether they were layups or running hook shots or those rare deep jumpers, the ball kept going in the basket. Sometimes you find yourself in a game where everything flows, where there's a rhythm to your passes, your shots. I didn't know how many points I had, how many baskets I'd made, how many I'd missed. It's impossible to count your points during a game and keep track of what's happening on the court. I was having a pretty good shooting night, sure, but the whole team was playing so well, running up and down the floor, scoring almost at will, that there really wasn't any reason to think anything of it.

With two minutes and fifty-six seconds left, Coach pulled me, and I sat out the rest of the 118–54 shipwreck. It wasn't until afterwards, when I was cornered in the dressing room, and an eager group of reporters started asking me about my record night, that I asked for a stat sheet and saw the following:

Field goals attempted: 32. Field goals made: 22.
Free throws attempted: 12. Free throws made: 12.

My fifty-six points that game were more than the entire Seton Hall team scored, and set not only a Cincinnati record, but a record for the most points that any single player—college or professional—had scored in the thirty-year history of Madison Square Garden.

I didn't have time to process this news; the questions were coming at me at a machine-gun pace:

"When did you realize you might set a Garden record?"

"I didn't realize it."

"Well, after you learned you had set a record, how did you feel?"

"I felt good."

"Was this your biggest thrill?"

"No, my biggest thrill was in helping Crispus Attucks High School to two Indiana state championships."

They continued shooting their questions, and I answered most of them in the same terse manner, with quiet one- or two-word sentences. It was overwhelming. One writer asked me something, and I mumbled something in return. While three or four others reporters interrupted and fought with each other for the next question, the first one stood there and wrote down my comment and let everybody else swarm. He had dark hair and glasses and stood behind the rest of the mob. Finally, everything was over. I finished with my shower and sat in front of my locker and started drying off. The guy came over and sat down.

"You know," he said, "I want to talk to you. My name's Milt Gross. I'm a writer for the *New York Post*."

I shook his hand.

"You know," he said, "if you're going to be a star, you've got to talk to the press."

I looked at him. "But I don't know them."

Well, Milt got to know me. He befriended me. That first night, he explained the nature of the media and reporters to me, and from that point on, whenever I came to New York, we'd meet. Milt took me out, introduced me to Jackie Robinson and Roy Campanella. For the next seventeen years—the entire course of my basketball life—I knew if I said, "Milt, this is off the record," he wouldn't write it. I knew if I had something that I wanted to get printed, he would get it right. It was an important friendship, one that was mutually beneficial, and also one that would eventually cause problems for me with local reporters in Cincinnati.

When I finally dressed and left the Garden, it was late; the streets were empty and glowing. A light snow was in the air. I was with my room-mate, Chuck Machock. The team bus had long gone, so we walked back to the hotel, talking about the game we'd just played and everything that had happened afterwards.

> *From Jimmy Cannon's column in the* New York Post *on January 10, 1958:* "They knew right away, soon as the kid handled the ball. It was the way he dribbled, crouching, shielding the ball with his body. There was the quickness of his hands, the agility of his body . . . Not many were there either, but as Oscar Robertson's legend increases, the liars will put themselves in the Garden on the big night of Thursday, January 9."
>
> *John Griffin of UPI:* "Not since Hank Luisetti came storming out of the West with his amazing one-hand shots has a basketball player rocked New York in his debut like Oscar Robertson."
>
> *Fred DeLuca of International News Service:* "An historic performance that brought back memories of the great-ness in the arena that was once the mecca of the nation's hoop sport."
>
> *Louis Effrat, covering the game in* The New York Times: "He's merely wonderful."

Word was out, and now the publicity machines moved into full gear. Supposed analysts compared me to Willie Mays, and name coaches—like Joe Lapchick—declared that I could become the greatest player of all time. Playing in Philadelphia's famous Palestra, a bunch of reporters and fans sat anticipating my performance, treating me as if I were a show pony about to do tricks. St. Joseph held me scoreless for the first seven minutes, but I found a rhythm and managed to eke out forty-three points, and we cruised to another blowout, breaking the century mark yet again. A man who worked with my mom used to tell her that when I was playing, whether it was in Manhattan or in Philadelphia, he could hear the radios and the screaming and shouting all over town. Twelve games into my first collegiate season, I was declared the front-running candidate for the Gold Star Award, traditionally given to the player of the year. Our home games sold out for the rest of the season. Our road games, too.

Children used to stand on the sidelines before games, watching me shoot, and usually I made the time to throw some passes or kid around. Teammates joked about me wearing shades to avoid my adoring public. I knew they were kidding, and laughed along with them, but didn't really know what to make of it all. My mom has always claimed that no matter how much I protested, I actually enjoyed the attention, but that I was too humble to ever show that I enjoyed it. I'm not one to disagree with my mother, and certainly not in my autobiography. But I *can* tell you there is nothing exciting about having crowds following you into the men's room to ask for an autograph.

In retrospect I understand things a lot better now. Baseball was still the most popular sport in the nation back then, in no small part because of how well it translated to radio broadcasts, newspaper stories, and box scores, the dominant modes from which people received their sports information at the time. Television was still developing as a medium, and the broadcasting of sporting events developed slowly. (If you can find a tape of it, try to follow the ball during Bobby Thompson's famous home run off Ralph Branca. Hell, try to find the ball.) As the quality of pictures got better, the sports that best translated onto television screens would grow in national popularity.

At the time, however, basketball was a series of blurred images and still photos; it was bulky men in crew cuts lumbering across the lane for hook shots, short athletic men darting around; it was underhand free throws and long-range set shots. Big men played close to the basket. Little men handled the ball. This was how the game was played.

A posed shot in 1959.

From left, Henry, Bailey, and me.

Me at an early age.

My eighth-grade team with Coach Tom Sleet.

The state champion Crispus Attucks Tigers, 1956.

Outmaneuvering
an opponent as a
high school junior.

Oscar Robertson,
Indiana's Mr. Basketball,
up against Kelly Coleman,
Kentucky's Mr. Basketball.

Setting up for a free throw, 1956.

Easing the ball into the basket against
Kansas State in 1958.

A jumper against Indiana State
in the 1959 season opener.

Dancing with Yvonne at home.

The record-setting game in Madison Square Garden.

I don't know if I was the first six-foot-five, two-hundred-pound athlete to handle the ball as much as I did, let alone play the way I did. I do think it's safe to say that my performance at Madison Square Garden was a touchstone moment for the sport of basketball. I think that watching someone with my athletic ability, size, skills, and basketball knowledge gave experts a sense of the future. Along with Wilt Chamberlain, Bill Russell, Elgin Baylor, Jerry West, and a host of other players who would dominate the upcoming decade, I represented a step forward in the game's evolution. To a large degree, I think that's what people were responding to.

Does this mean that from then on my life was coming up roses? Attention goes both ways. The day after our team returned from New York, I was in the Cincy cafeteria, walking through the food line with a friend, Wilmington College's John Bryant. A black woman behind the counter named Priscilla was ladling out meat and potatoes. When I showed her an excellent, slick black-and-white photo from the Seton Hall game, she said, "Oscar, I want that picture, with your signature."

"Sure, I'll be glad to get you a copy."

"No, no, I want *that* picture. Right there."

"Priscilla, I guess you don't understand. This is an original photograph of a great moment in my life, and I intend to keep it. I'll speak to the university sports publicity department. I'm sure we can get you a good copy."

"I understand all too well, Oscar. You're getting pretty high and mighty. Well, in two or three years, you'll be right back here with me, washing dishes."

I surveyed her and measured my thoughts. "Priscilla," I replied, "One day I'll be playing professional basketball, and you'll still be right where you are now."

———

I WAS AN INTENSE COMPETITOR. My face could be calm and smooth. Just as easily it could contort. I talked to refs. I was competitive. "He can't be such a Superman if he complains so much," one referee told a reporter, though he made sure to keep anonymous when he said this. The truth is, most of the time, when I looked mad, I was mad at myself. I knew I should have been doing better. But I was a rough player. I knocked guys around, and got knocked right back. You just had to expect it, up to a certain point.

Of course, that line got crossed.

I broke the color barrier on the University of Cincinnati's basketball team the same year the school entered the Missouri Valley Conference. Our conference schedule called for our team to visit to St. Louis, Houston, and Denton, Texas, all racially charged cities. In St. Louis, for example, racial tensions had caused the Hawks, then the city's NBA franchise, to trade away the draft rights to Bill Russell. In my mind that's about the single worst front-office mistake in NBA history, right up there with picking Sam Bowie ahead of Michael Jordan.

One road trip had us playing a game in Houston first, then up to Denton, Texas, for a game against North Texas. In Houston, we stayed at the Shamrock Hilton Hotel, a plush, downtown hotel. At around midnight the hotel manager called Coach Smith's room. Said they had to get that black kid down from the end of the hall and out of the hotel.

"I called Harry Faulk, the athletic director at Houston, and asked him what the hell was going on," Smith recalled for an interviewer. "He told me they were expecting Oscar at Southern University for the night. The thought crossed my mind to pull the whole team out of the hotel and forfeit tomorrow's game and get on the next plane back to Cincinnati."

I was in my room. I'd been lying down on the bed for a little while, when a knock on the door interrupted. Coach Smith came in and said that I couldn't stay here. Well, I thought the whole team was moving. "What do you mean?" I asked. "Where are we going?"

Coach explained that we weren't going anywhere. I had to go over to Texas Southern, a local blacks-only college. "They don't want blacks staying here," he said.

I didn't know what to say or do. But I went. The Texas Southern basketball coach got out of his bed in the dead of night, helped me out, and found me a spare dorm room. Decades later, at a funeral for Wilma

Rudolph, that man who'd coached TSU told me who he was. I was glad to meet him again, and I told him that I appreciated what he did for me that night.

In that dorm room, I laid down on a little bunk bed.

As much as it bothered me that the hotel wouldn't let me stay there, I was just as bothered at being the only person who had to move. All this talk about being a team and winning and losing together, staying together and doing things together—as a team. What just happened? I asked myself. What the hell's going on here?

I had forgotten momentarily that this was America.

The next day, nobody said anything to me, not anyone from the school, not a teammate. I didn't say a word to them either. We flew from Houston to Dallas, then took a silent, tension-heavy bus ride into Denton and the arena, where I discovered a black cat loose in the locker room, apparently some kind of small-minded comment on me playing there.

The shock of that discovery wore off, and I composed myself, figuring that they put the cat there to rattle me. I wouldn't give them the satisfaction, wouldn't let myself be rattled. I dressed, then went onto the court for warmups. The place exploded. It was a packed house, and maybe they did not know about what had happened the previous night, but if they had, they probably would have been happy about it, at least from the way they screamed, booing, questioning my ancestry, yelling every name in the book. Programs flew from the stands. Hot dog and cinnamon buns. All of it raining down. All of it directed at me. Even in the smallest Indiana high school I'd never seen anything like it.

I didn't take any warmup shots or get loose, but just stood in the middle of the court, my arms crossed. I didn't know if I was going to play, did not know what to do, but the longer I stood there, the angrier I became. It's probably good that none of my teammates came up to me or said anything. I was so disappointed that if someone had put a hand on my shoulder, I don't know what would have happened.

Something inside me said, *Play the game.* So I did. I scored only thirteen points, my low for the season, and some papers would make it out as if this kid named Gary Phillips had a lot to do with stopping me. The truth is, under the circumstances, it was one of my best performances in college. I hadn't gotten any sleep the night before, hadn't warmed up, and was mad as hell, really not in the right state of mind to play the way I usually did. We still pounded them, 70–53. "Beat them and made them like it," as Coach Smith put it.

Afterwards, a newspaperman asked how it felt to be the star, yet be forced to live away from his teammates. I answered, "How would you feel if you were me?"

Then I waited until we were back in Cincinnati and went to see Coach Smith. I told him that I did not think he had anything to do with what happened. If I thought he had anything to do with what happened in that hotel that night, I would have left school and never come back. But, I also said, he'd checked me into that room. The university and the athletic department and, yes, the coaching staff, all of them knew the travel plans; they were responsible for making and okaying them. I said that I did not ever want to go anywhere again with the team and yet be kept separate from them. I did not want to attend any civic functions or any public team functions. I didn't blame any players on my team for what happened, but if I couldn't stay with them, I wanted nothing to do with team functions that promoted this school, and I didn't want any questions about it. If anything like this happened again, I told him, I would leave UC.

From that day forward, I grew up fast.

ON THE LAST NIGHT IN APRIL, I scored twenty-four of our last twenty-six points, and fed Larry Willey on a floor-length pass for the other basket to lead Cincinnati back from a nine-point deficit in the final ten minutes of regulation play. In the last ninety seconds of the game, I made six consecutive free throws, helping us to clinch the 86–82 victory over Wichita, securing the Missouri Valley Conference championship in our first year in the league and earning the school its first berth in the National Collegiate Athletic Association (NCAA) Championships. It was a big feat. You could be the second-best team in the nation, but if you didn't win your conference's title, you weren't going to the NCAAs.

When we returned from Kansas, more than three thousand fans were waiting at the airport.

We were 24–2, ranked in the Top Ten, and heading into the post-season. It was a two-hour trip to Louisville, Kentucky, for the Midwest Regional. Our fans drove down in a caravan, and we easily won the opening game. This meant a day of rest before we played top-seeded Kansas State for a berth in the final four. The game took place on the same day as the Indiana state high school basketball championship. Just before the opening tip-off, I walked over to press row and spotted a reporter I knew named Bill Staubitz. Bill was from Indiana and was a big basketball fan. I knew he'd listened to the high school finals on his car radio, so I asked how Attucks was doing. Bill told me they won.

A sold-out crowd booed me on three particular plays when, as Kansas State broke ahead for a fast break, I stood with my hands on my hips or jogged up court. Each time I ended up with the defensive rebound after a missed shot, one time driving back down the length of the court, where I scored on a driving layup.

Bob Boozer led a Kansas State team that was much larger in the front-court than we were. It was a physical, grueling game, played to their strengths. With less than a minute left, we were trailing by two, and I was at the foul line. I hit the first shot, then began my normal ritual on the second, breathing deeply and composing myself. The rules say that from the moment the referee hands you the ball, you have ten seconds to shoot, but that you can hand him back the ball, at which point the count will start over.

A teammate yelled: "He's counting, Oscar. Shoot it."

Well, I hurried the shot, missed, and Kansas got the rebound. We ended up going into overtime, where I fouled out in the first minute or so, the first time in my college career that I was disqualified from a basketball game. That was the end of our season. Looking back on that game still vexes me a little. It wasn't that the referee was wrong. It was the rule. I could have just tossed the ball to him, stopped the count, and stepped off the line. A bunch of us from the team later reviewed the game on a movie screen a dozen times. The ref was letting free-throw shooters, myself in-cluded, take long counts, sixteen to eighteen seconds' worth, through the whole game. Inconsistency is one of the things that I've always hated about referees. Throughout my entire career, it always got to me. At the same time, the fact of the matter is that the ball was in my hands. And nobody missed that free throw but me.

Bob Boozer and I would be teammates on two different NBA teams, and in the years to come, he would kid me endlessly about that free throw. What could I do but laugh? One of the things that sports does is teach you that loss *is* part of life. It doesn't teach you how to deal with loss, how to be graceful in defeat, how to accept the idea that sometimes you will lose, or how to look at your mistakes and learn from them and improve. That's up to each person. Some things are easy to get over. If you do your best and lose, you can accept that. Mental mistakes and moments where you weren't given a fair chance, the chance you deserved, those are harder to swallow. Nothing is more irritating than the mistakes you make on those matters within your control.

Afterwards, George Smith said to me, "Forget about it, it's over. Over for me and for you. You can't win them all." At that time, when you reached the final eight, the NCAA tournament had consolation games, where the losing teams played one another. We stayed in Louisville for a day, sulking, and then took the court against Arkansas.

My fifty-six points in that game equaled my Madison Square Garden performance and set a then-NCAA tournament record. It didn't really ease the sting of the original loss.

Our team ended the season with a school-best 25–3 record. My season total of 984 was the most points by a college sophomore in basket-ball history, as was my 35.1 points per game scoring average. I was only the third sophomore to be voted a first-team All-American, making the team with Wilt Chamberlain, Elgin Baylor, Guy Rodgers, and Don Hennon. With five more votes than Wilt, I was also named the college player of the year, the first sophomore to win the award.

During the next months, I attended sixty-four sports award banquets and ate more rubber chicken than any one person should ever be exposed to. This wasn't easy for me. Award events are usually a mixture of the uneventful and the boring. And getting up in front of a group of people that I didn't know anything about, and talking about this and that, wasn't something I was comfortable with. In the end, I think the whole process was good for me. I did a lot of hand-shaking and, slowly, my social skills began to grow.

Sometime that spring, the Cincinnati Royals selected me under the NBA's territorial rule, but I didn't pay attention. I still had two years of college left. Besides, other things were happening.

Austin Tillotson's wife Gladys taught elementary school in Cincinnati. One day I was at Austin's house, and he told me about a lady his wife taught with, a woman he'd met a few times and thought quite highly of. He felt I should meet her, maybe get to know her. I got her number and gave her a call.

Yvonne Crittenden was her name. And she doesn't remember things that way. According to her, I saw her at a fraternity dance as I was passing through the building on my way in from practice. I asked my friend John Bryant for her phone number.

Either way, we ended up on a double date with John and his girlfriend. We went to see Carmen McRae at some smoky little nightclub.

Yvonne was petite and reserved. I thought she was lovely, a true lady. But I was so shy that I really did not have much to say to her. If she didn't talk about sports, there wasn't going to be much of a conversation. I spent most of the night talking to John.

But during the intermission, Yvonne and I did talk a little basketball.

CHAPTER SIX

"What They Eat Don't Make Me Fat"
1958–1959

I N 1 9 5 9 , a fourteen-year-old Negro boy was appointed as a page in the House of the Representatives, marking the first time since Reconstruction that a black man, woman, or child did any work besides sweeping or cleaning in that building. Jesse Jackson was a freshman at the University of Illinois, and like every other guy in the colored dormitory, he followed basketball. One day his dorm erupted in an argument over whether I could be a player in the National Basketball Association. One of my old Attucks teammates, Edgar Searcy, also lived in the dorm, and he insisted I would make it. He passed around a magazine photo taken my junior year during Cincinnati's tournament rematch against Kansas State. "It showed Oscar coming down with a rebound," Jesse told an interviewer. "Both of his legs were spread-eagled, and both of them were higher than the other players' heads. With that one photograph, Edgar finally convinced us. I had no doubt that Oscar would be successful."

I guess he wasn't the only one, because my junior year was barely underway when Abe Saperstein came courting. The owner of the Harlem Globetrotters, Abe was in a quandary. When Wilt Chamberlain had left college after his junior season and turned pro, a rule prevented college players from playing in the NBA until their class graduated. So for the then-astronomical sum of sixty-five thousand dollars, Wilt had spent that 1958–59 school year as part of the Globetrotters' famed magic circle. But now Wilt's class was moving toward graduation. Soon "the Stilt" was going to be playing for the NBA's Philadelphia Warriors. Abe needed a new meal ticket, and I guess he thought I could be it.

Willie Gardner played on the Globetrotters. Abe knew that Willie had grown up with my brother Bailey, playing on the same Crispus Attucks team together. He also knew that Willie had introduced me to several Trotters, including Marques Haynes and Goose Tatum, and that these two had watched me play since high school. Abe called Willie and told him to bring me up to Indianapolis, where Abe had offices for the Globetrotters and also the Indianapolis Clowns, a barnstorming Negro baseball team.

I knew Abe had Willie on the carpet, and he must have been pushing on him pretty hard. That was the only reason I agreed—because of Willie. Once I got to his office, Abe made a pitch about playing with the Globetrotters and painted me a pretty picture of all the opportunities I could have, including the chance to travel around the world and visit every continent while playing basketball. Then he offered me seventeen thousand dollars.

I might have had a great time playing for the Globetrotters. I *did* know and like the guys on that team, and it would have been fun to travel the world with them. It might have been a challenge too. It's no secret that I played textbook basketball, fundamentally sound, without a lot of unnecessary flash. In his book *Elevating the Game: Black Men and Basketball*, Nelson George wrote that the musical equivalent of my game was Nat "King" Cole, the smooth, understated, yet swinging vocalist, a man who blended the crooning big-band singing tradition with the slick blues he played as a pianist. Meanwhile, the Globetrotters were all flash and fun and gimmicks, the basketball equivalent of Tommy Dorsey's drummer, Gene Krupa. I could have adjusted, of course. I had the skills to do any and every possible thing with a basketball, and it would not have been hard to learn how to play the Globetrotters' way. It's actually a lark to imagine myself in the middle of a magic circle, spinning the ball on my hand and bouncing it through my legs, off my knee. Wilt always said his time with the Globetrotters broadened his game. Maybe it could have done the same for me.

But not for seventeen thousand dollars.

"Abe," I said, "you've got to listen. First of all, no. Second: I made the dean's list a couple of times. I'm successful playing basketball. Why would I want to go to the Trotters to make seventeen thousand dollars?"

He said, "What if you get hurt playing college ball?"

"I can get hurt here with the Trotters," I replied.

Willie took me back to Cincinnati, and that was the last time I ever spoke to Abe Saperstein about that.

With all the publicity I'd received during my sophomore year, there was no doubt I was going to be a marked man; other teams were definitely going to try to key on me, so of course I had to stay sharp. During the summer, I'd honed and evolved my practice routine, throwing some strange new drills in along with all of my basics, going so far as to seek out the right man to guard me, one-on-one. I experimented against the highest leaper and pole-vaulter on campus, against guards, burly forwards. So much of my game repertoire was impromptu—stuff I made up once I got into a situation where the defense dictated the move—that I felt I had to be prepared for any situation, especially if teams were going to be keying on me and throwing junk defenses my way. I figured it was like being a guy out on a diving platform, where after you've done a dive so many hundreds of times, any move becomes second nature. Or a boxer who has been in a ring so long that his reflexes become accustomed to feints and punches.

Connie Dierking had graduated and moved on to the NBA. But with me, a very talented point guard named Ralph Davis running the show, and Mike Mendenhall at guard, expectations were so high that capacity at the Armory Fieldhouse was expanded to eight thousand and all tickets were sold out well before the 1958–1959 season began. Sophomore John Bryant, the basketball program's second black player, gave us some depth, along with Mike Mendenhall.

Although we were a preseason top twenty team, and deservedly so, I think that in the long haul, the fact that Cincinnati was a private school hurt our national championship hopes. As a private school, the university accepted only top students, and I don't think the basketball program could recruit the kind of athletes that we really needed to go ahead and win. (Indeed, it wouldn't be until after I'd graduated that the school became a completely public institution, and this was rectified.) Moreover, Coach Smith was a stickler on moral matters—he used to try to keep us away from reporters he felt drank too much. Before I came to school, one player on the team was married and had a kid every year that he was in college. George kicked that player off the team for having so many children, and then he instituted a rule that if you were married, you were off the team. My junior year, a talented player named Spud Hornsby was kicked off the team for this very reason, basically killing any chances we had at a national championship.

The fact is, we were still one of the best teams in the nation. Ralph Davis and I got along really well, we talked a lot and spent a lot of our time together on the road. But all the guys were supportive during what was to be a contentious and difficult season. I think they knew how hard it was for me. One problem after another seemed to erupt that year. It was a season of brush fires and storm clouds and controversies. I didn't have much of a social life—basically all I did was play ball, practice, and go to class. When class gave way to the work-study program, I worked. I was a member of the team; at the same time, I was not allowed to join an honorary sports fraternity for varsity letter winners. I was a star, yes, but a black star; it set me apart, whether I wanted that or not.

Everyone called me "Oz," short for Oscar. It's an obvious and simple nickname, one that is associated with more than the word *wizard*—which I guess is what people considered me with a basketball. To me it meant the Land of Oz, a separate, alien world where I spent the 1959 college basketball season—isolated, in a combination of hothouse and fishbowl. Due to a mixture of fame and shyness, I was virtually unable to go outside, and I didn't spend too much time hanging out with my teammates. Instead, most of my friends were older—the Tillotsons, the Browns, the Pauls, Art Hull, people with the experience and maturity to advise me. I remember that Yvonne would come to my games and I would go over to her house sometimes, but if we went to a restaurant for dinner or to a movie or just walked around campus, I had to be able to spot con men. Once in a while I might have a beer with the guys over some pizza, talking about school or basketball.

One time, friends from Attucks came up to see me play. Afterwards, we went to a local restaurant named Frisch's. My buddies were in a good mood and started goofing around, grabbing handfuls of the complimentary candies out of the bowl on the front counter. I turned to John Bryant. "We can't be too close to goofy stuff like this. Sooner or later, for some little incident, we are going to get nailed for just being around when something happens." Not long after that, a teammate and a bunch of people barged into my room, drunk. They woke me out of a sound sleep. I made myself a cup of coffee and waited until they left. The next day I found the guy and took him aside and told him, "Don't you *ever* come around to my room to make your scene. I don't know who may have seen you come in. I don't know the stories that might circulate, where they might go. Pick someone else's door to bang on, okay?"

I had an expression back then. *What they eat don't make me fat.*

THE SEASON WAS ABOUT A MONTH OLD when our team flew to North Carolina for the Dixie Classic, a three-game holiday tournament. When I got off the plane at the Raleigh-Durham Airport, the first thing I saw was a pair of water fountains, one marked "Colored," the other, "White." We went to the campus for a practice, and then the bus drove through downtown, past the hotels where the other teams were staying. Coach explained that no hotels downtown would accept black people as guests. Our team was going to be staying in an unoccupied fraternity house at North Carolina State.

I still have mixed feelings about that. In the days after that earlier trip to Houston and Denton, I'd sought out Coach Smith and made it perfectly clear that I did not want to be kept separate from the rest of the team. So to some degree I appreciated the gesture and unity. But until my dying day, I will believe that all my school would have had to do was tell North Carolina State and the tournament planners, *If Oscar Robertson and John Bryant can't stay at the hotel in downtown Raleigh, we're not going to play.* If they had shown some backbone and said that, I expect that everything else would have taken care of itself. But they did not. Instead, a conscious choice was made in the other direction. We backed down and capitulated. I've heard the minutes from the University of Cincinnati's board meetings when this trip was discussed. It is undeniable. The trustees knew about the racial climate in North Carolina. Why else would they have had to vote that it was okay to go down there, unless there was a tacit knowledge that black players would have to stay separately from the team? They made this decision, and the athletic department and Coach Smith knew all about it. They were on the trip with us, and they stayed downtown, in the hotel. (To the credit of my teammates, we all stayed together in a fraternity dorm that was empty for winter break, where we were joined by all four of the black players from Michigan State University.)

Before our opening game, I received a letter from the Grand Wizard of the Ku Klux Klan, reading "Don't Ever Come to the South." It's just amazing what some people do, and how they can continue with their lives afterwards as if nothing happened.

When I went out on the court, the arena was in a racist frenzy. Countless times during our opening game against Wake Forest, shouts of "nigger," "porter," and "redcap" reached the court. Wake Forest's forward, Dave Budd—who would go on to play for the Knicks—made things worse, getting in my face and guarding me tight all night. Budd meant no malice. He was playing the game as hard as he could, the best way he could, but his antics only seemed to make the crowd crazier, and the crowd seemed to rile him up even more. When he'd guard me, he'd grab at my jersey, elbow me, and take more shots at me. It's part of the game, and I understood that. But I also knew that an official's job was to keep control.

The main referee working the game that night was a guy named Jim Enright. Enright was reputed to be the best official in the Big Ten conference and was also a sports editor of a major Chicago daily newspaper. He had a great reputation throughout the basketball world. But that night Jim Enright did a terrible job. A player kept putting his hand out in front of my face when I had the ball, almost hitting me around the face with his hand. Of course, face guarding is illegal. I dealt with the face guarding by smashing the ball against Budd's fingertips, which had to hurt like hell.

Midway through the first half, there was a loose ball. Budd hit the floor, diving for the ball, and so did I. Our legs and bodies tangled up, and we rolled around and started wrestling for control of the ball. Other players thought we were fighting and gathered around. The crowd went insane, just like in Texas. People were screaming every curse word in the book. Coins and hot dogs flew out of the stands and onto the court. When I got up, there was a circle of players around me, and Budd was standing, too, right in my chest, huffing and puffing. I wasn't a big ruffian when I came up in the ghetto, but I was going to take care of myself. I grabbed the ball. I don't think I was speaking to Budd so much as to everyone in the arena when I said, "Man, I ain't going nowhere."

I don't know how many points I scored that night, but I contributed enough to help us win by twenty. Afterwards, Coach Smith stormed into the officials' dressing room and cussed them something fierce. Then he went into our dressing room and hugged me and started crying. It was a big moment. Even if I didn't believe that the man understood me, I also knew his heart was in the right place. A cynical friend of mine used to tease me that George's tears and hugs that night kept me at Cincinnati for the year and a half until graduation. He might be right.

Meanwhile, my brother Henry had driven down to the tournament with some friends. He was in another part of the locker room, remonstrating with a few members of the Cincinnati athletic department. Any remarks about how I'd been treated on the court fell on deaf ears. My brother was bluntly told he had no business being at the game. He should have stayed home in Indianapolis.

When I got back to the dormitory at the end of the night, I compared notes with Johnny Green and some of the other guys from Michigan State. Johnny said he'd gotten the hell beaten out of him too, and that the refs hadn't done a thing.

The rest of the tournament was filled with tension and punctuated with verbal outbursts. Afterwards, when reporters asked me about one game, I just had to bite my tongue. "They won and we didn't," was all I said.

It was New Year's Eve. Even though we'd lost two of three in the tournament, we wanted to do something to bring in the new year. So the black players from our team and from Michigan State's squad had an impromptu party in the dormitory. I remember that we got some pizzas and some beer and hung out in the lounge until three or four in the morning, talking about the way the world was and why this shit happened to us.

BY THE TIME WE GOT BACK to campus, the school was awash in gossip. My co-op job at the Gas and Electric Company was rumored to be nothing more strenuous than going to the factory, turning on a calculator at the start of the day, and turning it off when I left for home. When Walter Paul brought my mother to a home game in his private car, of course word spread that Mom had a private limousine and chauffeur taking her up from Indianapolis for home games. I heard about these second- and third-hand from friends and from other, less reliable sources. It wasn't long before I heard from the NCAA as well.

They sent a letter to the athletic department saying that Cincinnati could no longer use its co-operative employment course in connection with certain grants-in-aid. My name wasn't mentioned, but now students would have to pay their own room and board during the weeks they worked for Cincinnati Gas and Electric, Procter & Gamble, or the Hudepohl Brewery—all offices that in one way or another were connected with

Walter Paul. That was fine with me though, because soon enough I got hired as a trainee by the Thomas E. Wood Insurance Company. It probably wasn't a coincidence that Wood was the major stockholder of the Cincinnati Royals. Soon enough the NCAA called again. Now I wasn't allowed to participate in the co-op program anymore. Never mind that other players on the team could keep their jobs. I couldn't work, and the case was closed.

Walter Paul called me up one day, and we met in his office. He knew the co-op program had been one of the reasons I'd signed with Cincinnati. Over lunch, Walter and I discussed the school and getting ready for the NBA. I told him I wanted to stay in school. Walter said fine. I told him I would stick it out and stay in business administration and graduate in four years. "Nobody's going to say I took the easy way out." I don't know how long we sat in his office talking that day, but eventually we came to an agreement. That was one of the things I always appreciated about the man. Even when we had different points of view, we never had a disagreement. We'd just talk through a situation and come to some understanding before we left the room.

Before our team hit the road for a trip back down to Denton, Texas, I reminded Walter—and anyone else who would listen—that if they kept the black players apart from the team, I wasn't coming back to school. I even pulled John Bryant aside and let him know to take some money with him on the trip, because if there was a repeat of the shit that happened last year, we'd be paying our own way home. On the plane ride, I had a vague sense that something might be wrong with the guys. I didn't know if it was because of the incident in North Carolina, if the guys were wondering about the NCAA stuff, whether they were worried about taking another trip back down to Texas, or if for some reason they thought I was mad at them. But something seemed a little off.

In any case, the entire team stayed at a university dormitory, and we won—commandingly.

From Denton we traveled to St. Louis. Our first night in town, John Bryant and I entered a restaurant together, and every eye in the place jerked toward us, and less than a minute later, the place was empty.

At the same time, there are memories that more than make up for all the hate and problems: the lady in some other restaurant who came over to my table and said she was from Nashville, that everyone in that city knew I'd been born among them, and that the whole city was proud of me. And the scene in Denton, after a brutal game: People in the stands directly behind the bench had just spent two hours harassing me, calling me every name I'd ever heard, plus fifteen or twenty new ones that just about had me peeking out from the huddle, asking, *Just where do you get this?* The game was over, and then a twelve-year-old boy asked me for my autograph. I was in no mood and said no. John Bryant told the kid to hold on a few minutes. I cooled down, and Bryant brought me back out and, sure enough, I gave in and signed the kid's program. He looked up at me. "We sure would be obliged if you would join us for a church supper at the Denton Methodist Church. We know you'd be welcome."

Things like that made the whole night worthwhile. That, the forty or so points I scored, and the win we walked away with.

In the January 19, 1959, issue on page 54, *Newsweek* ran this story under the headline "How to Stop 'Big O'":

When Oscar Robertson, the "Big O" of the University of Cincinnati, grabs a ball near mid-court and starts driving toward the basket, a sudden shimmering attention grips basketball buffs. Here, the fans know, is sheer artistry. Tall and quick, Robertson squirms, dribbles, fakes, pivots, and finally, with infinite grace, he shoots. More often than any other college player in the country, when Oscar Robertson shoots, he scores.

As the current season entered its second month last week, Robertson was demonstrating that his sensational sophomore year (984 points, the most ever scored by a soph), was no fluke. In his first ten games, he had scored 322 points, an average of 32.2 a game. But Robertson, six feet five and 199 pounds of pure athlete, is much more than a scorer. He also leads Cincinnati (which has lost only to North Carolina and N.C. State in ten games) in rebounds and assists. "He does everything," says Joe Lapchick, the veteran coach of St. John's. "How can you stop a guy like that?"

How indeed, do you stop Oscar Robertson? No one has a guaranteed system, but last week a *Newsweek* poll of college coaches and players, whose teams have faced Cincinnati this season, produced these suggestions:

Frank McGuire, coach North Carolina: "The only way to stop Oscar is to keep him from getting the ball. We put a tall man in front of him and a tall man behind him." (Against McGuire's double-teaming, Robertson scored 29 points.)

Dan Englehardt, six-foot guard, North Carolina State: "I played between Oscar and the ball. I watched his eyes and kept my hands up, but it didn't seem to bother him. He hit long jump shots with my hand in his face." (Against Englehardt's harassing, Robertson scored 29 points.)

Gary Phillips, forward, Houston: "I played man-to-man and watched Oscar's midsection. He can fake his head or his shoulders all he wants, but wherever that belt buckle goes, he's got to go." (Against Phillips's man-to-man, Robertson scored 13 points, his lowest total of the year.) [*That was during the awful game in Texas. I think Phillips had less to do with my point total than racial harassment did.*]

The only player polled who wasn't overly impressed by Robertson was Tom Sanders, a six-foot-six center at NYU. "He's not so tough. His fakes aren't so good, and he's not so fast." (Against Sanders, Robertson scored 45 points, his highest total of the year.)

Perhaps the surest method was offered by Lou Rossini, the NYU coach. "Put your four best men on Oscar. Then tell your fifth man to cover his teammates. That might stop him."

We weren't too long into the new year when I got called to the coach's office again. A guy named Jeremiah Tachs, from *Sports Illustrated*, had come to see me. Coach Smith told me he wanted me to talk with this guy. I said I really didn't want to. Coach said, "*Sports Illustrated* is the most influential sports magazine in the country. You've got to talk to them." So I said okay. Jeremiah came to my dorm room, and I sat down with him. First we talked about Bill Russell and how people in Boston were treating him, even though he was a great player for the Celtics. We talked about how Bill's kids had problems going to school in Boston and went over the story about Bill driving back after one season through Mississippi to Louisiana, where he's from, and how he couldn't stop and eat, and was harassed, and what a shame that was.

I'd say we talked about Bill for a good half-hour or so. The reporter seemed to be a decent guy, so I started to loosen up a bit. Then he asked about the University of Cincinnati.

I said that sometimes school is great. And then sometimes it's not so great.

He asked if I was thinking about leaving school early to go to the Globetrotters.

The question stopped me cold. I had no idea that people even knew about my meeting with Saperstein, let alone how much they knew. I'd turned down the Globetrotters' offer, but the NCAA was watching my every move. I told the reporter that I wasn't going to play for the Globetrotters. I told him that I'd met with the Globetrotters. He nodded and asked me about that some, and we talked for a while, back and forth. I guess our whole conversation lasted a bit more than an hour, and then we shook hands and, after making arrangements with their photographer, parted.

I didn't read *Sports Illustrated* back then. I didn't see the article when it came out, knew nothing about it, really. I found out about the article the way I found out about most bad news back then: Coach called me.

"What the hell's going on?" he said.

"What are you talking about?"

"We've got this article."

"What article?"

"Come over to the office."

Coach Smith was waiting, along with Tom Eicher, our PR man, and the university's athletic director. The room was silent and tense as they sat me down and pushed the magazine at me. It was opened to the article. Two pages, with a separate full-page spread. "What Price Glory For Oscar?" About a third of the way in, I read:

> In the wake of these achievements, an unprecedented tidal wave of publicity has engulfed him: an endless stream of press, radio, and television interviewers; magazine and news-reel cameramen; bids for personal appearances and award presentations; to say nothing of the pressing crowds who simply want to meet him, shake his hand and get his auto-graph. He has been serialized, eulogized, taped, televised, photographed, biographed and recorded. Not a day goes by without at least one interviewer trying to catch him in his one free hour between classes and team practice, or meeting him at an airport en route to a game, or phoning to request such a session. And the remarkable thing is that, in all the reams of copy, so little of Oscar Robertson has emerged other than his ability as an athlete.

If you have to know, reading that part gave me a perverse sense of pride. I almost smiled. But Coach wasn't smiling, and I knew this was se-rious and kept reading.

There were paragraphs about my quiet nature and background about where I was raised. And then:

> In those two items lie the keys to Robertson's personality and his future actions. He is highly sensitive to the problems he faces as a Negro, and he is wholly dedicated to becoming a professional athlete and making a lot of money at it. As noted, these facts have largely been unexplored, likely be-cause they lead relentlessly to the conclusion that Robertson

is not happy at Cincinnati and wonders whether he soon will
have any reason for staying there . . .

I was getting pissed off at *Sports Illustrated* and their conclusions. I
kept staring. The words did not change, but sat on the page:

> . . . A guest reporter on campus, well treated by Basketball
> Coach George Smith and Public Relations Man Tom Eicher,
> both hospitable men and devoted to their athletes, is reluc-
> tant to come away with a story which will cause distress
> to such hosts—indeed, to all of Robertson-worshipping
> Cincinnati. But the facts are inescapable.
>
> In his Coke-bottle-cluttered dormitory room the
> other day, Robertson tried to explain this. As he spoke—
> haltingly, one careful word at a time—he tossed, bounced,
> and fingered the basketball he always keeps in the room. It
> wasn't, he said, the mere fact that on certain trips with the
> team he was obliged to take segregated quarters, or that
> "Hell, there's a café and a movie house just a few steps off
> campus where I'm not welcome," or the abuse he takes from
> spectators on certain road games. It was that and more,
> which he summed up as, "There's no real social life for me
> here . . ."
>
> Robertson does not believe that he'd be better off else-
> where, and he does not care to fix the blame. He is the
> shining star of a team of basketball players, among whom he
> cannot forget he is not an equal, though he will not be quoted
> in the words with which he expresses his true feelings.
>
> Would he be happier playing with the all-Negro
> Globetrotters? The answer is obvious. "Sure, I'd like to play
> with them. When they come to town I go down and sit on
> the bench, and when I come back afterwards people say,
> 'Hey, we hear you've signed to play with the Trotters.' Well,
> it's not true. But they're a swell bunch, they get to travel all

over the world, they put on a good show, have a good time together . . . and make money. Sure they don't play real basketball. They're putting on a show and they know it—man, you can't be serious *all* the time—and they're enjoying themselves."

Watching Robertson's animated face as he says this, it is difficult to doubt that he will one day choose to do the same as Wilt Chamberlain did last year—leave school for a year of fun and companionship (even more than for Globetrotter cash) before joining the pro basketball league.

The likelihood is increased when it becomes clear that he has lost interest completely in his studies. "Statistics, theories of economics," he says, with a wave at the books on his desk. "I can't work at that stuff. It bores me." He was, it should be noted, an excellent student in high school, a fair student last year and a poor student this year. The decline is the direct result of his growing and now firm conviction that his future spells out basketball and nothing else.

Finally, it is abundantly clear, though he will not be quoted on this, either, that he has learned everything he can as a college player and has already achieved more fame than he could have hoped for in order to enhance his value as a professional. This last, he will admit, was the real reason why he chose Cincinnati over the 75-odd schools that bid for him. Though many other reasons have been offered, Robertson says, "I did want a college close to home. But I also wanted to play with a team that played in New York and Philadelphia and some of those other big places in the East. That's where you get the prestige."

The eyes were on me. I began, dimly, to understand, to see the thread connecting the tension I had felt after those problems in North Carolina and the rumors on campus when we'd returned. I'd thought that nobody knew about my meeting with Abe Saperstein. But everybody did. Some on campus thought I was going to leave the school early to play for the Globetrotters. I sat in the office and three pairs of eyes were bearing down on me, and I understood that each person in the room believed I was leaving as well. Seeing my feelings about race on paper, in black and white, reading about my problems with the campus, it made them sure that I was unhappy. It confirmed all their fears. They read about me jumping to the Globetrotters and were ready to believe I was going to jump, that every worry they had about me was true. I clenched my jaw and kept reading, pausing over the final two paragraphs.

> There is, Robertson apparently feels, no room further up for him in his present situation. There is only a way out.
> If he takes it, much of the glory that is Cincinnati's today will turn to ashes. But it is ashes in Oscar Robertson's mouth already.

I am now mature and levelheaded enough to be able to separate my words in this piece from the author's intent. Looking over the article right now, I can clearly see where I am paraphrased on the page, saying I do not want to leave school, and do not care to blame anyone on the campus for the racial situations that have arisen. I also see a place in that same paragraph where I am not quoted, but the author has decided my true feelings, and speaks for me without compunction or responsibility. But my words never prove his ideas. Rather, he used my "animated face" to decide that I was going to leave college for the Globetrotters. This, even as I was telling him I had not talked to the Globetrotters, was not going to play for them. I see where he used phrases like "apparently feels" to couch more of his conclusions, putting them in sentences that all but shout "fact," as if they were my actual words and thoughts.

I looked straight at Coach Smith. "This is not true," I said. "I didn't tell this guy any of these things."

"You've got to apologize," Coach told me.

"Apologize?"

"You've got to answer to the public, tell them you are sorry for saying the university is racist. Say you're not going to the Trotters."

"Wait a minute," I said, "Coach, I never said this stuff to begin with. We talked about Bill Russell's situation and about Abe Saperstein. I told that man I didn't want to go play for the Globetrotters. I'm telling you what's in this article is not true. Why should I have to go and tell the press that I'm sorry for what I did not say?"

"No," Coach said. "You've got to go tell the press—"

"This guy writes this garbage because he wants to cut me up, and I tell you that I didn't say these things, and now I've got to go explain to the press that I didn't say them? I don't want to do that. I'm not going to do it. I'll tell you what happened and I'll tell the team, but I'm not going to apologize for things I didn't say."

Something you've got to understand about athletes and the media. You don't see all the good things a newspaper writes about you. You don't see every complimentary feature, especially if you get the kind of attention I did. If you are checking your clippings all the time, there's no way to keep your head on straight. People are coming to ask you questions constantly, and that's what you deal with, the person and his or her questions; rarely do you see what they write about you. About the only time you truly know what's being written about you is when something bad comes into print or gets put on the air. Then coaches and sports information people are ringing you like crazy, asking you what's going on and, more importantly, making plans for damage control.

That's what happened here. After the *Sports Illustrated* piece, every local sportswriter and columnist was salivating, knocking on the door for a response. A lot of them were used to my short after-game comments and didn't seem to hold them against me, because they sensed I was naturally quiet and sincere. At the same time, maybe they were a little irritated because I seemed to open up more for reporters from New York newspapers and national magazines. It didn't matter that I talked to Milt Gross of the *New York Post* because I trusted him. It didn't matter that I'd been forced into talking to *Sports Illustrated,* and then was misquoted and used. These local guys had never taken the time to know me. And Coach Smith kept me away from most of them. One columnist had even refused to write anything when I'd told him about finding a black cat in my locker, and half of them showed the same provincial, small-minded racist attitudes that made my life so difficult in Cincinnati, so it was impossible to trust them.

But none of this mattered to them. All they knew was that the quiet black kid talked to national papers and not to them. I'd gone and caused big news, come out in one of the largest forums there was at that time for sports, slammed the school, and claimed I was leaving early. Those guys were in a frenzy to get the word from me themselves on what my plans were.

But I said nothing to them. Did not address the article in the slightest.

If I had spent my NBA career with the Celtics or the Lakers or in any city but Cincinnati, none of this would have mattered. I would have had a chance to establish new relationships with the sports reporters in that city, would have moved on without a beat. But the Cincinnati Royals already held my professional rights, so I ended up spending ten years—the majority of my career—playing pro ball in Cincinnati, dealing with the same reporters and editors. *The Cincinnati Enquirer*, the largest paper in town, wrote yards of column inches about the article.

Let them write what they want to write about me, was always my attitude. *But what happened in the game? Tell me what happened in the game.*

Over time, this became my strategy/philosophy. In the end reporters could write what they wanted. I still played. They couldn't change what I did, no matter how they described it.

―――――――――

IF THE UNIVERSITY administration did not understand my needs or rights, I think that the guys on my team, more than anyone, saw what I went through. I believe they knew even more about some of the things I went through than I did, because they got to witness them firsthand. Nobody was ever jealous of the national attention I received, in part I think because they also saw the downside, the weight of the glare, all the obstacles that were put in my way. And while the guys and I did not hang out all that much, I think that in some ways all the tensions and controversies that swirled around me made us a closer team when we hit the floor.

On the whole, the basketball court was the one place where the craziness didn't reach us, almost as if we were safe out there, untouchable. Playing great ball, we took the conference for the second straight year and went into the NCAA tournament with a winning streak of sixteen games, where once again, playing to get to the final four, we met our old foil, Kansas State.

During our pregame meeting, I told John Bryant, "If the rest of you guys play a little bit, we'll win this game." He looked at me, speechless, maybe a little hurt. But he knew I was serious. I went out there and once again fought and clawed against Bob Boozer, lighting him up for twenty-four points and seventeen rebounds. The game was tight throughout, but with three and a half minutes left I hit a jumper to put us up by five, giving us firm control. It wasn't going to come down to free throws this time.

I remember being at the free-throw line and, during those final seconds, the sense of relief and joy. I remember the clock counting down, fans mobbing the court, and me and my teammates hugging one another and celebrating. And I'll never forget that my teammates raised me on their shoulders that afternoon. The whole crowd was standing and clapping, and it was really one of the best feelings I've had in basketball. We were going to the final four.

Next up for us was the University of California. But Pete Newell, their Hall of Fame coach, decided that I wasn't going to beat them. If I was playing outside, he made sure to double-team me on the perimeter. If I was posting up, he had a guy fronting me and zone help sagging in, so there would be three or four men around me. This left other guys on our team open, but Newell decided that he would rather have those guys taking open shots than me. Newell also made sure to hold the ball on offense, reducing the number of possessions in the game. This meant we had fewer trips down the court, fewer shots, and more pressure each time I had to decide whether to pass or shoot.

Playing in front of the largest crowd of the tournament, California's star center, Darrall Imhoff, tore us up, putting up twenty-two points and getting sixteen rebounds. As for me, I had a decent game, scoring nineteen points and grabbing nineteen rebounds. But I didn't hog the ball. Since grade school, I'd been taught to pass when guys were open. I passed. We ended up losing by six, and California went on to win the national championship, beating tournament MVP Jerry West and West Virginia in the title game.

We finished the season ranked in the top five, with a 26–4 record and two straight conference titles. I led the nation in scoring for the second straight year, and my two-year scoring total was the most points anyone had scored during two years in college basketball history. We averaged almost 7,800 fans in our 8,000-seat home arena, played high-profile games all across the country, and now had recruits *wanting* to come to play for Cincinnati. By all accounts it was a successful season. The program was turned around.

Not long after we got back to campus, I was hanging out in the dorm one night, talking with John and two or three of the other black athletes, football players I think. Someone came and said that the rest of the basketball team was over at the student bar, drinking and hanging out. We talked about it a little and got one another worked up, because we weren't welcomed in there. So finally I said, "Come with me." I walked ahead of them, and we went to the bar. The bouncers and staff looked at me but didn't do anything. And sure enough, the rest of the guys were inside, drinking and hanging out. So we joined them. Nothing happened. We stayed for the night and talked. I doubt that if I hadn't been leading our group that would have happened. But it was another small victory. And I never stepped inside that place again.

The following spring, my mother became ill. She had been feeling weak for a little while, and over the course of a week, pain increased through her stomach. The doctor said it was her kidney, some sort of infection, and it was serious. Mom was hospitalized, and surgery was scheduled.

The surgery was successful, but while Mom was in the hospital, we learned that the bill was going to be huge. On top of this, Mom had recently been taken on some house repairs by a crooked contractor.

I visited her in the hospital room. I could see she was in all kinds of pain, but that she was trying to hide it. I finally couldn't take any more and left. A nurse came in the room and asked my mother if that fine-looking man was her son. Mom said I was and admitted that she had just won the battle of her life, hiding the extent of her pain.

"I don't think you pulled it off," the nurse said. "When I passed him, tears were rolling down his cheeks."

Seeing my mother in that kind of pain was hard enough. That she had to go into debt to pay for her surgery made me furious. That we didn't have anything and meanwhile people were making money off my talent and still treating me like their property incensed me.

To this day I cannot swallow the fact that the day after my mother got out of the hospital, she couldn't rest and recover at home, she had to go back to work.

At the same time, what could I do? I couldn't join the NBA for another year. Jumping to the Globetrotters for dirt wages definitely wasn't an option. Especially not after all the speculation. I'd look like a hypocrite. Like a fool.

"Mother," I said, "Someday, if I am able, I will do all I can for you."

CHAPTER SEVEN

Gold
1959–1960

IN LIFE, IF YOU ARE PATIENT enough to let time run its course, solutions sometimes make themselves apparent. For me, the one obvious solution to any problem was basketball—all the time. The game itself was therapeutic, released my aggression. When the Cincinnati Royals' season ended, Jack Twyman, Jack Fitzpatrick, and Connie Dierking would come down to the school for pickup games, or meet me and some other guys at some other local gym. The places weren't air-conditioned, so they were your typical, humid sweatboxes, but we'd run up and down all afternoon, playing some great basketball, competing and having fun. Afterwards I'd shower, and Yvonne and I might go out to a movie or stay at her house and listen to records. My future was taking shape in all kinds of ways. I saw my profession clearly and was in love with the woman I wanted to spend my life with.

That summer I was invited to participate in the Pan-American Games in Chicago. The Pan-Ams were one of the premiere venues for international competition at the time. Every four years, nations from throughout the Americas (North America, South America, Latin America) came together for two weeks of competition and friendship. The basketball team practiced in Chicago. Probably my biggest thrill of the competition was getting to play with and know Jerry West. There'd been a lot written about the two of us, and the media tried to set up some kind of rivalry because I was black and he was white, especially when both of our teams made it to the final four that year. In Chicago, we had time to talk and practice together. Both of us are country boys—I was from Tennessee; he was from Cabin Creek, West Virginia, and it didn't take long for us to hit it off. Like everyone else, I called Jerry "Zeke," in honor of his nickname, "Zeke from Cabin Creek." He took to calling me "Doughnut," because doughnuts looked like big O's.

DePaul's Ray Meyer coached our squad. One night he called George Smith and told him to come up to Chicago, check out the situation. "I don't like what the grapevine is saying about Oscar not finishing his senior year."

Of course George took the first plane up. I was silent for a while, not sure what to say, half-angry at him because I'd told him I wasn't going to play for Abe, half-amused at the way he was chasing after me, but also a little annoyed at him for that too.

"I'm not going anywhere," I said. "I gave you my word. That's that."

George took the next flight home. But it wasn't until classes opened in September that he and other college authorities were certain that I'd be back. Meanwhile, all eleven of the school's home games had sold out, and close to a thousand people were already on a waiting list for season tickets. Now magazines were calling me Basketball's Moody Marvel and reprinting claims that I had lost interest in my business administration courses. In fact, I made the dean's list that semester. Maybe part of the reason I studied harder was to show up anyone who wrote that I wasn't studying. And while there were professors who refused to give me a break, I also had wonderful teachers, like Dr. Sheehan in marketing. He used to make the class get up and give an impromptu speech for maybe three minutes. Obviously this was the last thing I wanted to do, but I did it like everyone else, and it was great. I learned about constructing an opening, a body, and a closing summation. That class was one of the little things that eventually helped me overcome my shyness.

Of course I wasn't a scared eighteen-year-old anymore. Dave Tenwick, one of my teammates, liked to say that my dorm room that year was like Grand Central Station, jammed with friends constantly coming and going and watching basketball games on the television. Coke bottles and basketballs were all over the place, and the atmosphere was relaxed. If I wasn't completely happy with the system I was in, at least I'd grown comfortable enough to exist in it. And while I missed Yvonne, at least I had friends around and dropping in.

Our team went into the season ranked as everyone's favorite to win the national championship, which marked the only remaining goal I really had, my one piece of unfinished athletic business at that time. I wanted to graduate, and I wanted to win the national championship. At this point, everyone in the nation seemed to agree I was the best collegiate player. Indeed, for the first time, it seemed even the most hostile fans acknowledged my abilities. When we played in Houston, people who had been throwing things during my junior season rose and gave me a standing ovation that lasted several minutes.

I understood the game at a deeper level than other collegiate players, and I started pacing myself, not out of disrespect or haughtiness, but strategically. I tested my opponents' abilities early and gauged officials to see what they'd let me get away with, then used the second half to exploit whatever openings I'd observed.

We opened the season on fire, drubbing a solid St. Joseph's ball team by forty-four points. (I scored forty-eight points on eighteen of twenty-six shots, fourteen rebounds, and six assists.) Soon after, an early-season showdown pitted us against the fifth-ranked Bradley Braves. I scored eighteen in the first half, but we couldn't shake free, and led just 38–35 at the break. With the score at 44–43, I scored nine straight and had twenty-four points, thirteen rebounds, and eight assists in the second half alone. We won going away, and I matched my season average of forty-two points. I remember coming back to the locker room after the game and discovering that an envelope stuffed with money had been left in my locker. I figured someone had put it there to trap me, and I didn't want to jeopardize my future. I left it right where I found it.

Next on the schedule was a trip back to New York for the Holiday Festival at the Garden. In our opening game, I had forty-seven points. The next night we were matched up against St. Joseph's again.

A twenty-five-year-old prodigy named Jack Ramsay coached the Hawks. Two decades later, he would coach the Portland Trail Blazers to an NBA title. Ramsay had a reputation as a whiz. Determined not to let me torch his squad again, he drew upon Pete Newell's blueprint and came up with a junk defense. It looked like a box-and-one, where four men played a zone, while one man stuck with and shadowed me wherever I went. But in reality, it was constantly changing. Three men played a zone in the form of a triangle, with two men guarding the baseline, and one clogged up the lane. The other two defenders played man-to-man. If I was outside with the ball, Ramsay had his team play a normal box-and-one, with Frank Majewski guarding me and the other men playing zone in the form of the box. But when I went inside, two men surrounded me; Majewski fronted me, while Vince Kempton pushed on me from behind. The other three men employed a triangle-shaped zone, with each guy continually ready to rush in and help defend me.

I still found openings. Midway through the first half, I took a pass. While Majewski and Bobby Clarke surrounded me, I spun and jumped and made the shot. Once I grabbed a St. Joseph's pass from underneath their basket in one fluid motion, flicking the ball out of the air and shooting it, scoring before anyone had a chance to surround me.

I totaled seventeen rebounds and five assists. I also made key steals, guarded the middle against cutting Hawks players, and boxed out. I deflected dribbles, started the fast break with defensive rebounds, and jammed their outlet passes to clog up their fast breaks. I set screens, fought through picks, and dove for loose balls. In other words, I played my usual game. My twenty-five points were a personal low over our first ten games and the fourth lowest total of my career to that point. But with all that attention lavished on me, Bob Wiesenhahn, an unheralded six-four junior, went unguarded. He ended up with a career high of twenty-eight, and we took the win.

But afterwards, our locker room was like a morgue. Nobody had expected a team that we'd beaten so badly to play us this tough. Reporters asked how many men guarded me. "I don't know," I answered. "All I saw were hands, and I just wanted to get rid of the ball."

The next night we played Iowa for the Holiday Festival Championship. It was December 30, 1959. Less than two hours before the game, I was lying quietly on my bed in the Manhattan Hotel, completely absorbed in a television show. At 8:00 P.M., Bob Sweeten, the student manager, came into my room. "Come on, Oscar. We've got to go down now."

Iowa came out and pasted us, speeding to a 24–13 lead in the first nine minutes behind their backcourt of Ron Zagar and Mike Heitman, with six-seven sophomore Don Nelson working on defense and making his usual hustle plays. Seventeen thousand five hundred basketball-crazed New Yorkers were buzzing at the thought of an upset. George called time-out. In the huddle he told them, "Give the ball to Oscar and get the hell out of the way."

Up to that point I had three points, had missed several free throws and shots, and been called for traveling twice. After the time-out, immediately I drove and scored and got fouled for a three-point play. I stole a rebound and converted the layup. I hit a jumper from the side. Another jumper from out front. A drive. A couple of fouls. Fifteen straight points. When the half was over, we led 54–42, and I'd accounted for thirty-three points.

I ended up with fifty points, thirteen rebounds, and four assists, as we cruised to the tournament title, 96–83. After the game, I explained the comeback in my usual matter. "We were behind. I had to start sometime."

Someone asked if this was my best performance. "It was all right," I said, "but I missed a few easy ones."

"Do you have any weaknesses?" another reporter asked.

"Sure. Lots of them."

"Name one."

I grinned. "This is one. Talking to reporters."

Navy coach Ben Carnevale was in the stands watching. "Would you trade a battleship for him?" he was asked. "I'd give the Polaris missile for Oscar."

After thirteen straight wins, we lost at Bradley by a point, then began another winning streak. On February 1, 1960, five minutes into our win over Drake at the Armory Fieldhouse, I drove for two quick layups and broke Frank Selvy's all-time collegiate scoring record. The game was stopped for the announcement, and at halftime, George Smith and I walked out on the court. George handed me the basketball I used to score the points and spoke into the microphone. "It could not be presented to a more deserving student-athlete and great star." People think that if you are quiet and stoic, you don't care, don't feel. But as the crowd stood and clapped, I was overcome, suddenly uncomfortable with all the attention. Meanwhile, there was another half to play. I wiped my face on the sleeve of my warmup jacket, took the ball, shook George's hand, and promptly walked off the floor.

A week later, I entered our game against North Texas State leading the nation in scoring with an average of thirty-three points a game. North Texas's Jim Mudd was fifth, averaging almost twenty-eight a clip. I hit my first nine shots before missing, nailed a fifty-foot shot at halftime, and with a little more than three minutes left was pulled from the rout, having scored fifty-seven points. A team official saw that I was one shy of the conference record, so George put me in. I ended up with sixty-two points on twenty-three of twenty-nine shooting, made sixteen of nineteen from the free-throw line, and had nineteen rebounds. We destroyed North Texas 123–74. George told reporters that he put me back in the game because, "I felt we owed him that chance." When the press came to me, I was even more succinct. "Had fun tonight," I said, and that was the end of the interview.

THE ONLY LULL in my scoring clip came against Duquesne, in Pittsburgh. Before leaving for the trip, I gave Yvonne the little ring I'd bought for her and asked for her hand in marriage. She said yes, and my head was still in the clouds at tip-off.

We took our conference title yet again and rolled through the NCAA tournament and were a game away from our second consecutive final four appearance. On March 12, we played highly seeded Kansas on a supposedly neutral court, located in Manhattan, Kansas. The crowd was insane, and the game was tight; with eight and a half minutes left, we trailed 63–61. I scored on a twisting layup, then hit a long jumper to give us a lead that we wouldn't relinquish. I scored twelve of our last twenty-one points and ended the night with forty-three points, fourteen rebounds, and three assists, as we stretched our lead and won, 82–71.

Once again we were in the final four. And once again we were matched up against Pete Newell and the University of California. We'd won fourteen straight and were 27–1. California was 26–1 and the best team in the West. This was the game we'd wanted all year. Now we had it.

The game was played in the old Cow Palace auditorium in San Francisco. "Our whole game plan predicated on being able to reduce the damage Oscar was going to do to us," Newell later said. "You have to play him with one man on him and the other four guys really helping." It wasn't a new plan. It was the same one California had beaten us with last year, the same plan Jack Ramsay and St. Joseph's and a bunch of other teams had tried. But we'd beaten St. Joseph's this year. And with Paul Hogue and Bob Wiesenhahn and Carl Bouldin in our lineup, we had the players, I felt, to be able to deal with Cal.

Darrall Imhoff was still controlling the paint for them, and we had no answer for his running, sweeping hooks, but we hung tough. California ran a deliberate, half-court offense that slowed the game down, and when we had the ball, two and three guys were constantly running at me. I did what I could, driving, dishing, trying to hit open men. Midway through the first half, John Bryant grabbed me. "I'd rather see you taking a fifteen-foot jump shot than see someone else take a two- or three-foot shot." I told him, "Look, if someone's open, you give them the basketball. It's just the way the game is played."

This isn't to say I wasn't aggressive. If you watch the tape, you can see me bring the ball up court, drive past one defender, head down the left side of the court, and hit a running jump shot with three defenders collapsing around me. You can see me drawing two men on one drive after another and dribbling away from all the defenders to take arcing, fadeaway jumpers from the baseline.

The truth is, we didn't have the personnel to win that game. Everyone thinks we did. Everyone thinks that because I was on the team, we had a great bench and a talented squad. We did have a talented squad— in three years we had gone from an average team to one of the best programs in the nation, so we had talent. But we were always a small team. I played forward, and I was six five. Wiesenhahn was six four. We just weren't big enough to deal with Imhoff and the other California trees. Maybe if I had moved to the backcourt and played point guard, I could have done some things to change the game, penetrated more and pounded their guards. But we hadn't played that way all year, and George Smith wasn't the kind of guy who would experiment with something like that in such a big game. Besides that, I was kind of acting as the point guard anyway. When California double- and triple-teamed me, our guys got passes and had opportunities. We didn't score when we should have, and that can't happen in big games.

Winning basketball often comes down to simple things. You've got to have good players, play good defense, and get defensive rebounds. You've also got to make sure your stars don't get into foul trouble, and you need to make the most of your opportunities and open shots. We didn't make the most of our opportunities, but at the same time we didn't really have the manpower to be able to take those chances and do something with them.

Sometimes you get beat and that doesn't mean you played badly. Sometimes the other team just plays better. If California's shots hadn't been falling, or if Imhoff had been off that day, then maybe we would have won. Sometimes the shots fall, and you're meant to win. And if you're not meant to win, you're not going to win, no matter what you do.

Imhoff totaled twenty-five points and eleven rebounds, and California took the game 77–69, ending my dream of a national championship. I finished with eighteen points and ten rebounds.

A week later I was named the college player of the year for the third straight season, the only player to be so honored at that time. In the three years I played on Cincinnati's varsity team, the Bearcats had a combined record of 79–9. I scored fifty or more points five times in my collegiate career and accumulated at least forty in twenty-three games: twenty-seven percent of the varsity contests I'd played. After my senior season, my jersey and number, twelve, were raised into the rafters, retired, never to be worn again. More importantly, now players *wanted* to come to Cincinnati. Paul Hogue, our sophomore center from Knoxville, Tennessee, said that part of the reason he came to Cincinnati was to play with me. Tom Thacker, George Wilson, and others felt the same way.

I'd come to Cincinnati as the only black player on the basketball team; the year after I left, they had three black players in the starting lineup; the year after that, four. And while some people may have second-guessed me for constantly passing the ball against California, I think that the experience Paul Hogue, Bob Wiesenhahn, and Carl Bouldin gained from that game helped them during the following two seasons when they were led by a new coach. Cincinnati finally did win national championships, without me on the floor, and won them back-to-back.

I graduated in June 1960, along with the rest of my class. Although I made the dean's list a few times, I didn't quite get to graduate with honors. Even though I'd had some difficult times at the University of Cincinnati, I also received a good education. My conduct in the classroom and performance on the basketball court helped to wear down some of the resistance to black students. While a student at the University of Cincinnati, I met people who would remain friends and advisors throughout my adult life.

Perhaps my experiences would have been different if I had been a white athlete. Maybe people would have treated me better or there would have been fewer controversies. But when I was just a freshman, sitting in Austin Tillotson's house while he told me that black people did not come to the University of Cincinnati for a reason, I decided that I was glad they chose me, because I could handle that responsibility. And I know that whatever problems I had during my four years there, I did handle myself well. I left things in much better shape than they were in when I arrived. And I met my wife there.

———

YVONNE WAS BORN in Montgomery, Alabama, the eldest of four children. Much in the same way that my family had come to Indianapolis, the Crittenden family had moved to Covington, Kentucky, during World War II's great migration. Ultimately, Yvonne's father established a tailoring and dry cleaning business. She's told me they weren't a rich family, but solidly middle class, and that she never had to experience the kind of poverty in which I was raised. Her father insisted that all of his children go to college, and Yvonne graduated from the University of Cincinnati in 1956, months before I arrived on campus.

Yvonne is intelligent and gorgeous as well as being a talented artist and art collector, a pianist, and a voracious reader. In the two years we'd been dating, she'd become the person I went to with problems and bounced possible solutions off, who I laughed with and vented to and never got tired of talking with. She was the person I truly loved. Our wedding was scheduled for June, right after my graduation.

Before graduation, I went out to Denver to try out for the Olympic team. The tryouts were different then. Invited players were put on teams. These teams played every night for five nights. The players from the tournament's champion team got to place their starting five on the Olympic team, while the coaching committee chose the rest of the players from the other teams. I was on a team with Jerry West, Terry Dischinger, Adrian Smith, with Walt Bellamy as the fifth man. Ohio State's starting five was there, along with some small-college teams, a university team, and a bunch of Amateur Athletic Union (AAU) teams. The AAU was a league of adults who were out of college but played competitive basketball, sometimes touring. People called them amateurs because the players held down jobs, working at Phillips, or some other oil company, or Goodyear tire, for example. But they were really pros; they got paid to play basketball, and the jobs were their front.

It was a strange process. If my memory serves correctly, teams switched players during the tournament. After one AAU team advanced, they'd claim some of the better players from a losing team and use them to reconfigure their starting lineup. But with me and Jerry West at guard and Bellamy in the middle, we were strong enough to prevail. We ended up winning the tournament and making the team. Now Pete Newell wouldn't be tormenting me anymore. Instead of figuring out ways for the University of California to shut me down, Pete would be coaching me and coming up with ways to get me the ball.

Pete told me he stayed up all night with members of the committee, picking the team. A lot of the AAU guys ended up making it because the AAU was powerful in those days, and they used to control who went to the Olympics. So Les Lane, Burdie Haldorson, and Allen Kelley, all of them forgettable players from the AAU ranks, made the team. But John "Hondo" Havlicek didn't make it. Lenny Wilkens didn't make it. Tom Sanders didn't make it.

Still, with or without the AAU guys down at the end of the bench, we were one of the most talented amateur teams ever assembled. Three players from that team—me, Jerry West, and Ohio State's great sophomore Jerry Lucas—ended up in the Basketball Hall of Fame, and Bob Boozer, Walt Bellamy, Terry Dischinger, Darrall Imhoff, Adrian Smith, and Jay Arnette also starred in the NBA. I think the only amateur team ever that could have given us a game would have been Bobby Knight's 1984 Olympic Dream Team, with Michael Jordan, Patrick Ewing, Chris Mullin, and Alvin Robertson. I don't know who would have won, but such a game would have been something to watch, especially with Pete Newell coaching against Knight.

When I returned from the tryouts, I had missed two weeks of a class in sales cost and analysis. The professor wanted to fail me. He even told me, "You can't pass this class." Of course, this would have meant postponing my graduation and would have caused all kinds of problems—I had a wedding coming up and had to get ready for the Olympics, and this was the last thing I needed. I went to see the president of the university about it. I'll always be grateful to Dr. Langsam; he made a deal with the professor.

Since the final exam comprised the majority of my grade, I would receive whatever grade I got on the final. I scored a B-plus. The professor still gave me a D for the course.

Yvonne and I were married on a perfect June day. Thank goodness for Gladys Tillotson. Out of the goodness of her heart, Austin's wife, a teacher at the same school with Yvonne, ended up helping with most of the details and arrangements for the wedding, and she did a beautiful job. The ceremony took place at the Carmel Presbyterian Church in front of our parents, families, and friends. I was decked out in a morning coat with long tails and the whole nine yards. Yvonne was as lovely as I've ever seen her, and even now I can close my eyes and visualize the flowers and her veil.

That summer, Yvonne and I stayed in New York for a while as she finished her master's program. After a few weeks, I left to stay with the Olympic team, an hour away from the city, up at West Point. Meanwhile, Yvonne went back to Cincinnati. The Olympics were to be held in Rome, Italy, and we made a plan to meet there for our honeymoon. So Yvonne went to Rome alone, and our team went on a tour.

We played exhibition games against AAU teams in New York and Cincinnati, but in Cleveland the floor was so bad because of condensation that we had to cancel the game. Then we left for Zurich and played a game there. We spent a couple of days practicing in Lugano, Switzerland, and took the train over the Alps into Rome. I wish I could say that I got a lot of sightseeing done, but Coach Newell had us in battle mode, isolated and getting ready for the task ahead.

The 1960 Olympics were the first Summer Games to be televised in the United States. CBS paid $394,000 for the broadcast rights to what became a two-week coming-out party for some of the biggest stars of the new decade. Coach Newell did not want us to be tired or carousing in the Olympic Village, so our team arrived in Rome one or two nights before we were going to play. He didn't let us walk in the opening ceremonies for the same reason. Never mind that most of us were twenty-one-year-old basketball players, superbly conditioned and in the best shape of our lives. Walking around a track might tire us out.

Yvonne arrived in Rome before us. And while Coach Newell knew that we were recently married, it goes without saying that he didn't want anything to break my focus. She couldn't stay at the Olympic Village and instead stayed at a hotel in town. As for me, I roomed with Terry Dischinger, Purdue's six-foot-seven forward, who spent an inordinate amount of time sleeping.

The biggest star to come out of the Games that summer was Cassius Clay. He hadn't yet changed his name to Muhammad Ali when the Olympics started. He wasn't a favorite in the light-heavyweight division. Nobody knew who he was. But already he was saying he was the greatest. At first he wasn't boisterous about it. He was just a boxer, and he wasn't very well educated, and he thought this was a strategy to promote Cassius Clay. So he said he was going to win. "I'm going to win the gold medal." Even then he was really something, just great. And the more he went around talking, the more people he had following him around. He loved it. Then he went out and proved it, pummeling his Polish opponent for the gold medal. That was how the nation first discovered him. And Cassius was so proud that he didn't take that medal off for two days afterwards. Who would have guessed that just a few months later, he'd be so infuriated by the way blacks were treated in his hometown that he'd throw that medal into the Ohio River?

I was amazed at the way he could talk and make predictions like that. I'd been a boxing fan since my childhood, when my brothers and I used to listen to Friday night fights on the radio. So one day, we were in the Olympic Village together, and I asked him about the secrets to being a great fighter.

"Angry boxers don't win," he said.

"What do you mean? You're getting hit. Don't you get mad?"

"It doesn't matter," he answered. "You have to remain calm. When you get upset, that's when you get beat."

That made an impression on me. I took that into my game and always tried to remember it on the court.

Another person I met at the games was Wilma Rudolph. After Ray Norton lost in both the one hundred meters and the two hundred meters, Wilma became the heart of the team when she won gold medals in the one hundred and two hundred meters and anchored the winning four-hundred-meter relay team. She was a tremendous, graceful runner, and just as graceful and lovely as a person.

I'd known of Wilma before the Games. One of twenty-two children, she hadn't been able to walk without braces until she was nine, but once they came off she started to run. She'd become a star at Tennessee State University in Nashville. I'd heard and read about Wilma whenever I used to go back and forth to visit my grandparents in Tennessee.

When we met at the Olympics, we immediately understood each other. We were from the South and the country, and we talked about Tennessee and Nashville and the life there. We were dear friends from that point on and would remain so for the rest of her life.

It's quite something when you think about it. Cassius was from Louisville, Wilma from Nashville, and I was from tiny Bellsburg. That's three of the Olympic Games' major stars growing up 150 miles from one another.

Jerry West and I were named the co-captains of the basketball team. He talked even less than I did, although by now I had started to come out of my shell, especially on the court. There are people who you admire, players you respect, and Jerry was one of them. Pete Newell always has been one of my favorite coaches, and the Olympics were one of the few times in my life I played for someone I considered a great person. I'd always respected him for the defenses he came up with to try to stop me. And when I was on his team, I appreciated the way that he trusted my knowledge of the game.

Basketball has since become an international game, but in the early 1960s, it's safe to say that no country played the game at anything close to the level that America did. We played five games to get to the title game and won easily every time. In the semifinals, we were matched against the Soviet Union. The Cold War was underway, and our two nations were mortal enemies, so the hype for the game was unbelievable. In the columns of untold reporters, it was depicted as more than a contest between teams: more a battle between ways of lives.

Naturally, the international officials were in over their heads. Afraid that real war was going to break out on the floor, they called all kinds of fouls: even the slightest contact drew a whistle. We still were in control and led by eighteen at halftime. But foul trouble hurt us in the second half, and Russia drew to within ten.

Coach Newell called time-out. In the huddle he told us to press, pick them up full court, and get right into them.

Well, we went out there again and just destroyed them. Their guards simply couldn't handle our quickness, and we jumped and trapped them and caused one turnover after another, outscoring them 25–1 in what I am proud to call one of the greatest displays of pressure defense of all time.

The final score was 81–57. Two days later we destroyed Brazil in the gold medal game. Jerry West and I stood on the top rung of that podium representing our team and our nation. Jerry was so nervous that he felt his pants shaking. I remember standing there and looking out into the crowd, searching for my wife. During the game I hadn't thought about anything but winning, and afterwards I was happy because we did. But when the first notes of the "Star-Spangled Banner" played over the loudspeaker, I really felt it. I remember wishing that some of the guys I'd played ball with in high school could have been up there, all the people that pushed me, who I played against, who helped me get to this point. I remember thinking about all the sacrifices I'd made and all the hell I'd been through. And now I was on the podium, representing my country, accepting an Olympic gold medal. It was overwhelming.

CHAPTER EIGHT

Rookie Stardom
1960–1961

PROFESSIONAL BASKETBALL leagues date back to 1898, just seven years after James Naismith, a Canadian, invented the modern basketball in 1891 and nailed up that peach basket in the gymnasium of the Springfield YMCA. As I understand it, basketball was almost barbaric back then. Steel cages were erected around the court, and players armed themselves with knee, elbow, and shin pads, which they used as both padding and weapons. Often, games were played in conjunction with concerts or dances. At halftime, fans would get drinks at a bar and socialize; afterwards, bands would play, and there'd be dancing. There were untold small-time professional leagues and touring teams, including the American Basketball League, the Metropolitan League, the Philadelphia League, Tri-County League, and the Eastern League. A barnstorming team called the Original Celtics featured Joe Lapchick and was thought by many to be the best team of the time. Most of this activity took place up and down the Eastern seaboard.

During the late 1920s, the American Basketball League (ABL) emerged as the strongest of these early leagues. Along with the Midwestern Basketball League (founded later, in 1937), the ABL provided part of the foundation for what would eventually become the National Basketball League (NBL). The NBL had franchises in New York, Boston, Chicago, and Indiana. Initially, it was a regional, almost provincial league. Three of its eight teams—Buffalo, Rochester, and New York City—were within New York State. Other teams based in relatively small and obscure towns (Oshkosh, Dayton, Fort Wayne) came and went. In those days, the National Basketball League's status was national in name only.

The NBL and a few smaller leagues eventually consolidated in 1949 to become the league we all know today as the National Basketball Association (NBA). At the end of World War II, however, the NBA was a fledgling and struggling organization. CBS's broadcast of a double-overtime game between the Boston Celtics and the St. Louis Hawks for the 1956–57 NBA finals was the first nationally televised basketball game. For the following season, NBC paid five hundred thousand dollars to televise Saturday games into the twelve million homes with television sets. But their broadcasts generated so little interest that Nielsen reported the ratings as IFR (Insufficient for Reporting)—the numbers were too small to be measured.

Things began to change in 1960 when the Lakers moved their franchise from Minneapolis to Los Angeles. For the first time, the league had a truly coast-to-coast, national presence. Just as importantly, 1959 to 1960 marked Wilt Chamberlain's debut with the Philadelphia Warriors. I've always thought that his gargantuan appeal had a lot to do with that season's attendance figures jumping twenty-three percent.

The Rochester Royals had taken the NBA crown in 1951. A pair of brothers, Jack and Les Harrison, owned the team but were losing money in Rochester. The town was too small to support a professional basketball franchise. Three cities were on their short list for relocation—Cincinnati, Cleveland, and Kansas City. A Cincinnati group was lobbying the NBA for an expansion franchise. They had $125,000 pledged toward the NBA's start-up entry fee of $200,000. At a February 1957 meeting, Maurice Podoloff, then the commissioner of the league, scheduled a test game, held at the Cincinnati Gardens, between Rochester and the Fort Wayne Pistons. The game almost sold out, and the Harrisons agreed to play thirty-one home games in Cincinnati. On April 3, 1957, the terms of the deal went public, and the Cincinnati Royals were born.

I was a sophomore in college during the Royals' first season in Cincinnati. And it was toward the end of their opening campaign that an accident took place that, I believe, hung over the franchise, perhaps ultimately influencing its fate.

Maurice Stokes was a moose of a man, the first star that the franchise had. At six feet seven and 250 pounds, he was stronger and a better shooter than Elgin Baylor, who led Seattle to the 1958 NCAA championship game and had joined the NBA following his junior season. Along with Jack Twyman, Stokes was the heart of the Royals during the late 1950s. He was a physical player, but also a smart, gentle man of humble beginnings—his father had worked for thirty years in Pittsburgh steel mills, and his mother was a domestic. The Royals, led by Stokes and Twyman, along with Georgie King and a decent supporting cast, came to Cincinnati touted as the team to beat in the Western Division.

In the final game of the regular season, while jumping for a rebound, Maurice's legs were unintentionally cut out from under him. He crashed to the floor and landed on his head. After receiving some medical attention, Maurice left the court under his own power. Five minutes later he went back in and finished the game. The team then showered, went straight from the arena to the train station, and traveled all night to Detroit (the former Fort Wayne franchise had recently relocated to the Motor City). They were preparing to begin a best-of-three playoff series against the Pistons the next afternoon.

A half-hour before tip-off, Maurice and teammate Jim Paxson became nauseated and vomited. Everyone figured it was a virus, perhaps food poisoning. Maurice was lethargic in warmups, but he played the game, and the team took a bus to the airport at Ypsilanti, Michigan, to catch a flight back to Cincinnati. Mo had a sandwich and a beer and bowl of soup. Ten minutes into the flight, he became violently ill and lost consciousness in a cold sweat.

By this time the plane was forty-five minutes from Detroit, and an hour and a half from Cincinnati. Pilots and team personnel convened and decided to proceed to Cincinnati. The plane eventually landed, and Maurice was rushed to a Covington hospital. Doctors would later say that only the efforts of the stewardess had kept Maurice alive.

Meanwhile the Royals played game two without him and lost, ending their season. The team then scattered back to their hometowns: everyone except Jack Twyman, who lived in Cincinnati, and Maurice Stokes, who was in the hospital, paralyzed.

When Maurice regained consciousness, his body no longer worked. As doctors were taking tests, one of the technicians made a joke. Maurice laughed, and the technicians realized that laughter was a reflexive action, like breathing. Except for reflex actions such as this—the flutter of his eyelids, or spontaneous laughter—it was impossible for him to do anything. At the same time, his mind was clear as a bell. Maurice understood everything that people said, but his injury affected the part of the brain that controls the voluntary action of the rest of the muscles in his body, so he had no muscle control whatsoever.

Maurice was diagnosed with post-traumatic encephalopathy, meaning a blow to the head was the cause of his paralysis, as opposed to a virus or encephalitis. Some of the players believed that the decision to fly ahead to Cincinnati and the resulting additional forty-five minutes of the flight contributed to the severity of Maurice's illness, but who can say for sure? He had about fifteen thousand dollars in the bank and could not relocate if he wanted access to workmen's compensation as a means of paying for part of his medical bills. Rehab would cost about a hundred thousand dollars a year, and there was no real chance at recovery. In those days, there was no medical insurance and no pension. Maurice had no way to pay his medical bills and no prospect of ever walking again, much less playing. He was twenty-four years old.

Attendance that first year in Cincinnati marked a noticeable improvement from the largely absent crowds in Rochester. But it wasn't enough, and Maurice's accident seemed to spread a cloud over the franchise's immediate future. Tom Wood ran the Cincinnati Gardens that first season; he later became executive vice president and ran the entire team. According to him, the Royals took in $96,000 at the gate that first season. Player and front-office salaries alone were $110,000—miniscule in comparison to the rest of the league, but still enough to put the Royals in the red for the season. The team also had to pay expenses for travel, equipment, rent on the arena, and so on. There were no television rights, no money for playing away from home, no other income whatsoever. The Harrison brothers threw in the towel and sold the team to a group of local investors headed by Tom Wood and a Cincinnati attorney. A rider in the contract stipulated that the price, $200,000, would rise to $225,000 if Maurice Stokes ever played again.

After Maurice's accident, Clyde Lovellette, a highly priced addition the Harrison brothers had made before selling the team, didn't want to play on Cincinnati and forced a trade to St. Louis, where he'd go on to become an all-star. Another starter gave up basketball to play baseball in the St. Louis Cardinals minor league system. Indeed, only the generosity of Ben Kerner of the St. Louis Hawks kept the Royals franchise from folding. The Hawks had just won the Western Division; Kerner believed Cincinnati would eventually make a great natural rival for his team. Kerner literally gave Cincinnati five players, no charge. In addition, he traded Wayne Embry to the Royals, giving Cincinnati a barrel-chested, dependable center for Twyman to team with.

Despite operating on a shoestring budget, the Royals were still hemorrhaging money, saddled with bad luck and failures. While the University of Cincinnati went to two consecutive final fours and consistently sold out the Armory Fieldhouse, the Royals continued to struggle at the box office, averaging around fifteen hundred fans a game. The same Jack Twyman who'd worked out with me when I was being recruited by the Bearcats was the team's highest paid player. An excellent standstill shooter from the outside and a prodigious post scorer, Jack was paid the unspectacular annual sum of twenty thousand dollars.

At that time the league had two kinds of drafts. Since there was no free agency then, these drafts were the only ways for teams to add players. The main draft was for players whose collegiate eligibility had expired, but there was also a supplemental draft known as the territorial draft. In this draft, a team could claim the rights to any underclassman playing within that region. It had been designed to keep players geographically close to whatever fan base may have followed them in college. The Royals had selected me in a territorial draft at the end of my sophomore year, which meant they controlled league rights to me. While this allowed the Royals to claim me, there was a tactical downside—if each team kept the best players from its region, no other team had a chance for choice national talent.

If you were at the top of the league, the mechanisms were set up so you tended to add more ammunition to your talented squad and remain at the top. If you were in the middle of the pack, you also tended to stay there. In 1958, relying on Jack Twyman's jump shot and little else, the Cincinnati Royals won a league-low nineteen games and finished in last place in their division. In 1959, they again finished last, more than seventy-five thousand dollars in the red. When Cincinnati used the first pick of the 1959 draft lottery to select my old rival, Bob Boozer, he turned around and signed a contract with the Peoria Caterpillars, a basketball team that was part of the rival AAU league. The only reason the Royals did not fold or relocate was because they owned my rights and were relying on my arrival to reverse their bad luck, mismanagement, and errors. But until I graduated, the team was on its own.

Hank Aaron has talked about getting terrible service in empty restaurants in Cincinnati, purely because of the color of his skin. And if you mention the city's name to other black major leaguers of the time, you're more than likely to hear story after story about the vulgarities that rained down from the white stands in Crosley Field. By now I wasn't an awestruck kid, happy to see black faces at a baseball game. I understood the city's racial biases well. But the Royals held my rights. I was their savior. No way they would trade me.

Professional sports at this time had a monopoly on player rights. If a team drafted you, they held your rights for good. When your contract ran out, you weren't free to sign with another team, but could only sign with the team you played for. Being traded or cut from the team was the only way your rights changed. If you didn't like a team's offer, too bad. Your only choices were to jump to another league or hold out. Basically, you were putting your professional life on the line, and owners did not hesitate to use this, and other scare and muscle tactics, in their negotiations.

When I was eighteen years old, one of the things that Jake Brown had promised me was that he would see me into my pro career, help handle my finances, and be a friend to me even after I left the University of Cincinnati. Now he made good on his promise and entered into negotiations with the Royals front office. J. W. knew that we had leverage—for the first time all the rumors about the Globetrotters actually worked in our favor. After having lost Boozer, the Royals could not afford to let me jump ship as well. If I signed with the Globetrotters, their franchise was finished. If I had to play in Cincinnati, at least it would be on my own terms. After I returned from the Olympics, J. W. sat down with the Royals management and outlined exactly what those terms were.

In those days, such a meeting was unusual. Players didn't have agents or anyone else negotiating their contracts. J. W. was never my agent, mind you; he was my attorney and my friend. He didn't negotiate my salary—partly because there wasn't any serious money to begin with, and partly because management did not want to deal with a lawyer. They preferred to intimidate players.

Not this time. J. W. negotiated for me, and we all knew I had leverage. Soon the Royals and I agreed on a contract: three years, with a base pay of about thirty-three thousand dollars a year. J. W. also negotiated a pair of clauses into the deal, each of which was then unique to the NBA: the first provided me with a percentage of the team's gate receipts—this boosted my annual take to around fifty thousand dollars. The second, a multipart clause, was even more impressive. I could not be cut from the team. My money was guaranteed and had to be paid for the full three years, regardless of whatever injuries I might suffer. Moreover, I could not be traded without my consent—a fact that would become important years later.

The average working salary in the United States at the time was just over five thousand dollars a year. Stamps were four cents, bread just twenty, and a brand-new turbine-drive Buick convertible, complete with tail fins, went for just less than two thousand dollars. The day I signed my contract, I became one of the highest paid players in the league, and also the most protected. The Royals advanced me about fifteen thousand dollars on my salary.

I took care of my mother's debts and gave her the security that allowed her to spend more time with her gospel choir. Yvonne and I also put a down payment on a Tudor-style home in the neighborhood of Avondale at 3604 Eaton Lane. It was an integrated, upscale area, secluded and relatively wooded. Our home had three bedrooms upstairs, as well as a basement, which I fixed up with a friend of mine, Jimmy Thompson, to use as an entertainment room. There was a kitchen, a dining room, a living room, and a little sitting room off the dining room. I have fond memories of Yvonne and I spinning records in that place, in the basement, dancing together.

Armed with her master's degree, Yvonne returned to teaching. Sometimes I'd sit at the kitchen table, helping her keep class records. She told me that the children in her class used to use her full name at every opportunity: "Mrs. Oscar Robertson, may I sharpen my pencil?" "Mrs. Oscar Robertson, may I go to the rest room?"

I was only two hours away from the shotgun shack on Colton Street in Indianapolis where I'd grown up, but I had entered an entirely different world.

BEFORE THE SEASON started, a national sports magazine asked Celtics playmaker Bob Cousy about my chances. Cousy answered, "West could be the best. And Oscar could be a Royal letdown." Jimmy Thompson told me about the line, but I didn't think anything of it. If the franchise had been one of the league's bottom-feeders up to now, there were also indications of change. The draft that season had been surprisingly bountiful—including one of my Olympic teammates, Bob Boozer, who had finished his contract in the rival league. The two of us, along with returners Twyman and Wayne Embry, infused the Royals with a solid talent base.

Before we started our preseason workouts, head coach Charley Wolf called a special team meeting. Unlike the one George Smith had called when I started at Cincinnati, I attended this one. My arrival brought a lot of publicity with it, and the Royals were concerned that veterans might have had problems with this. I didn't say anything. After a few practices, the guys understood I was there to do my job. Besides, there wasn't time to worry about jealousy. Wasn't time for anything besides basketball, really. The exhibition season was upon us. Fifteen games in sixteen days, none of which players were paid for, although I seem to remember that tickets were sold.

On October 20, 1960, more than eight thousand people—the largest crowd in Royals' history—came to the Cincinnati Gardens to watch my regular-season debut. Our game against the Lakers was also notable for the introduction of my Olympic co-captain and supposed rival, rookie Jerry West. The large photo on the front of *The Cincinnati Enquirer*'s sports page the next day featured me, driving for a layup, and scoring with my right hand.

I had a triple-double that night, scoring twenty-one points to lead the team and amassing twelve rebounds and ten assists. The *Enquirer* called it "perhaps the finest performance in four seasons, as (the Royals) rang up more points than any one Cincinnati team in history." Of me, a columnist said: "His superb faking and generalship thrilled the fans, and there is no doubt he will be one of the greatest."

So I began my initiation. There were eight league teams back then, and we played seven games in as many cities in ten days. We'd get up early in the morning, get onto a bus or go to the airport, and hit a city. At the arena, we had to tape our own ankles before games, because there weren't trainers for anything other than serious injuries. Dolph Schayes and Bob Pettit were among the guys I know who broke their wrists and still kept playing. I'd estimate that eighty percent of the league played with charley horses, jammed thumbs, and pulled muscles back then, and the only thing the trainers offered for relief were freezing sprays of ethyl chloride.

After games, you went back to your hotel for a good night's rest. The next day at the airport, you waited for your flight, then fell asleep on the plane, cramped in those little airplane seats. We flew on rickety little DC-3s; any gust of wind shook them back and forth, and if we were playing in California, we'd have to stop six or seven times along the way. Guys received eight dollars a day in meal money, and the Royals always booked us into cheap, fleabag hotels. We'd arrive in the dead of night, get to our rooms, and discover the beds were too short. I used to have to put a suitcase rack at the end of the bed for my feet.

Back then, most teams did not have more than two black players, in part because of road travel. Three black players were too many to deal with. Teams avoided rooming a black guy and a white guy together. When Bob Boozer and I joined the Royals after the Olympics, this could have caused problems, as the team already had Wayne Embry. But Wayne was such a congenial man that management could room him with white players without anybody getting upset. So that freed things for Bob Boozer and me to room on the road, although every once in a while Wayne and I bunked together.

Over the course of the season, you played each team about twelve times, so you got to know everyone else's plays and they knew your own. We could have switched jerseys and run one another's sets to perfection.

When I think back on it all, I have to say that it was a good life. You really got to know everyone—your teammates, your coaches, other players, everyone. And you got to do it while playing basketball, the game you loved, against the best players in the world.

My on-court adjustment process went fairly easily, I think. The game was faster, the players stronger, but nothing overwhelmed me. The pro game involved thinking a lot, processing the different things you had to do, while at the same time being able to make decisions and react. Charley Wolf moved me to guard, my natural position, giving me the ball and control of the team. I responded in kind. I was a rookie, but in my mind I wasn't a young basketball player anymore. I had confidence in my knowledge of the game, and if a teammate ran a play wrong, I was going to let him know about it. If a ref blew a call, I was going to say something. Every city and game presented both new obstacles and excitement, and I wanted to take on all challenges, wanted to topple them all.

Jerry West liked to tell reporters that I never was a rookie. Jerry always felt that he had had difficulties adjusting to the professional game, but that I handled the ball with the confidence of a proven pro from the very beginning. Ed Jucker, my coach on the University of Cincinnati's freshman team, used to remark on the difference between the boy he had coached and the man I became. "He was like a stagestruck kid in college. Overwhelmed by it all. His wife deserves a lot of credit. She's really loosened him up."

During my first trip to Philadelphia, Tom Gola, a top defensive player, held me to fourteen points. Afterwards, he told reporters, "O's a pretty good player, but he's certainly no all-pro, and he has a long way to go." The remark was picked up by the wire services and spread coast to coast. A week later, Philly came to the Gardens. I scored forty-four.

When we visited St. Louis, the Hawks sent a defender into the backcourt to hound me. "We haven't picked up a man back there in years," Hawks guard Paul Seymour said. Other teams tried different things, sagging in their defense, hoping to keep me from driving and rebounding. One game I astounded my teammates by challenging Wilt Chamberlain, driving at him, attacking the basket, and scoring right over him. "If you're not confident," I told reporters, "you've got no business playing the game. That shot just won't go in."

We played so many games, traveled so much, that a trench mentality set in. Dark humor was evident. I remember being in the airport once, waiting for a plane. A confused fan came up to me. He knew I was an athlete, but couldn't figure out how he recognized me. When he asked who I played for, I deadpanned, answering with the name of a hockey team: "The Chicago Black Hawks, of course."

Our lineup of new faces played as an aggressive, cohesive unit and won five of our first six games. A month into the season, we'd played five home games and attracted more than sixty percent of the Royals' total audience for the previous season. Now, for the first time we traveled to Boston Garden. A lot of hype accompanied our matchup.

For a decade, Boston's Bob Cousy had been the league's definition of a point guard. Hell, he was an NBA all-star when I was still in junior high school. At six feet one, Bob all but created the model for tough, flashy floor generals. He was a consummate floor leader, always pushing the fast break, passing the ball behind his back and whipping it through his legs, finding the open man or crease. If you played off him, he was deadly with that antiquated set shot of his. By contrast I was the new kid on the block, six five and strong, solid and not flashy, all control and economy of movement, the first guard to really use his size and body to take defenders where he wanted to go. Where Bob was the grizzled, cagey white veteran, the leader of the defending world champions, I was the young black stud, leading a squad of upstarts. How would Cousy respond? How would I?

Six hours before game time, people were lined up for tickets. While Bob drove to the Boston Garden in a gray 1960 Cadillac and, in order to avoid fans and admirers, entered the arena through a "secret" entrance, I packed up my gym bag and walked to the arena from my hotel. A reporter from *Sports Illustrated* was on hand to cover the event. I refused to talk to him, beginning a ten-year boycott of any *Sports Illustrated* press men. Instead, the reporter focused on Cousy, who admitted to looking forward to the game. "Pride?" he said, minutes before taking to the court. "Of course, it's about pride. I've thought about this game all week long and talked to myself about it. 'Better get yourself up, Bob. Better be at your best, Bob. Oscar's coming to town to play in *your* arena before *your* crowd for the first time.'"

What the reporters—and I guess Bob—never really seemed to understand was that he was not really in competition with me, not in the traditional man-on-man way. I never guarded Bob. Arlen Bockhorn usually guarded him. I took the Celtics' bigger shooting guard, either Sam Jones or Bill Sharman.

It's been written that Bob never made more than thirty-five thousand a season when he played. Maybe he had issues with my salary. Maybe the problems we had in later years were due to nothing more than our being in the wrong place, on the wrong sides of the fence. I don't really know.

The Celtics did not play well that night, according to game reports. We pulled away from them in the second quarter, and withstood a late run to take the game 113–104, for our franchise's first win in the Boston Garden in six seasons. Cousy played forty-five minutes, scored twenty-seven points, and had seven rebounds and seven assists. In forty-six minutes, I scored twenty-five points and had six rebounds and seven assists. Afterwards, Bob said I played as though I'd been in the league for ten years.

But Bill Sharman, who had guarded me for a good part of the game, marveled over my ability. "He has three or four fakes all in the same move. He's bigger than most men you usually have to guard in the backcourt. He is a big man with the moves of a really tremendous little man, and he is always ready to whip off a pass that will lead to a basket if a teammate gets free."

We may have won that game, but the Celtics were a far superior team that season. Jack Twyman averaged twenty-five a game for us. And Wayne Embry was solid, turning in more than fourteen points and eleven rebounds a game. But beyond that, we didn't have much. Guys like Arlen Bockhorn, Larry Staverman, and Win Wilfong were decent players; they had singular and specific skills. One could hit outside shots, another hustled and defended, but they weren't exactly names that would be celebrated in the annals of basketball. Compare that with a Celtics team that had Hall of Famers at all five starting positions—Cousy, Sam Jones, Tom Heinsohn, Bill Sharman, and, of course, Bill Russell. Three of these players were named among the top fifty players in basketball history. They had a great defender and floor leader in K. C. Jones coming off the bench. Their coach, Red Auerbach, is to this day considered the best professional coach of all time. It goes without saying that we weren't going to beat them consistently.

The real secret behind the Celtics lay in one man. Forget about the stories of magic leprechauns in the rafters of Boston Garden and how the cramped visitors' dressing room and psychological games created some sort of Celtics' mystique. The fact is, no matter how good the players surrounding him were, no matter how competitive his coach was, Bill Russell *was* the Celtics' mystique. He was the truth, a genuinely great player. Bill was six feet nine, 220 pounds, with long, gangly arms; you could watch him play and think he wasn't doing anything much. Meanwhile, he'd dominate the game.

Bill Russell was a great player and true competitor. On defense he clogged everything up in the middle for Boston. He was so gangly and quick off the ball that he could double-team and trap you at a moment's notice or jump out to help a defender on a pick and roll. And when you beat your man off the dribble and thought you had a free lane to the basket, here came Bill, not just blocking your shot, but making sure to keep the ball in bounds, control it, and pass it out to start a fast break the other way. He took pride in stopping people, and mentally he was one of the toughest, most hard-nosed players in the league. His defense carried Boston in the playoffs and, I believe, was the reason they won championships.

I've always thought that this country doesn't often understand or accept the greatness of certain people. Bill was not one of the sheep, wasn't even a member of the flock. Race has always been one of the key problems in America, and Boston has historically been a particularly segregated and racially divided, troubled city. Bill was not treated kindly in Boston, even though he was the star of the Celtics.

Jackie Robinson had demonstrated beyond any doubt that a black athlete could play baseball intensely, intelligently, and with heroic dignity. Thanks to his success, other black athletes followed him into the game. But basketball had integrated more slowly. Though there had been a few Negro players in various eastern leagues as far back as the 1920s, in 1950, Earl Lloyd, Chuck Cooper, and Nat "Sweetwater" Clifton became the first three black players in the NBA. Bill Russell joined the NBA in 1956 and in many ways became the league's first black superstar. He was the acknowledged core of the Celtics, the league's most valuable player five times, a twelve-time all-star, and had more playoff MVPs than anyone could shake a stick at. But the game was owned and refereed by white men. Most of the players were white, the men who wrote about the game were white, and the vast majority of the paying audience was white. So Bill Russell had trouble getting endorsements that far-lesser white athletes easily procured.

When Bill would drive from Boston back to his home in Louisiana in the off-season, he had to wonder where he could eat on the highway, where he could stop. If he drove a Cadillac, the cops would stop him. "Where did you get this car?" they'd ask.

Anyone who knows him knows how bright and funny Bill is. But over the years, the press portrayed him as brooding and gruff. One year, though, *Sports Illustrated* actually managed to pick him as their Sportsman of the Year. Usually, they picked golfers.

Between the grind of the road, our collective inexperience, and the fact that the Cincinnati Royals weren't all that good a team to begin with, we faltered. By the all-star game, I'd missed a few games with a twisted ankle, and we'd long slipped from first place in the Western Division and were sinking fast. This did not stop fans from voting me into the all-star game, the only rookie to start.

The night before the game, Bill Russell was in a restaurant with a friend, cutting into a steak. A man came up to his table, asked for an autograph, and put a menu under Russell's nose. Bill signed and the man took a long look at the menu. He said something and walked away, a disappointed look on his face. Bill's eyes followed him with amusement.

"Did he think you were Chamberlain?" his dining partner asked.

"No. Robertson."

That year at the all-star game, I started for the West, along with Gene Shue, Clyde Lovellette, Bob Pettit, and Elgin Baylor. The team from the East started Wilt Chamberlain, Bob Cousy, Tom Heinsohn, Richie Guerin, and Dolph Schayes, with Bill Russell coming off the bench. All-star games were one of the few times that Wilt and Bill actually got to play on the same squad, but they rarely were on the court together.

With me throwing passes to Bob Pettit and Elgin Baylor, we jumped ahead and led 47–19 at the half. I made all five of my shots in the first half (most of them patented fallaway jumpers), and was voted the game's most valuable player—an honor which back then people used as the measuring stick of the best all-around player in basketball. I must have really played well, because they gave me the award even though I sat out the second half. Afterwards, the entire locker room seemed to be abuzz with my performance. A reporter asked Detroit Pistons coach Dick McGuire if he thought he'd ever see the day when another guard could compare with Cousy. A former point guard himself, McGuire was regarded by many as the second-best playmaker in basketball history, rating just behind Bob. Dick told the reporter, "O is better than Cousy ever was. O is the finest player in basketball."

Amid the bustle of reporters, Bill Russell found his dining partner from the night before and laughed: "Now you know why that man was so annoyed. That number fourteen is quite a rookie, isn't he?"

On January 14, 1961, Elgin Baylor and I put on a show at the Los Angeles Sports Arena. Elgin was the first real high-flier in the league. His aerial dynamics predated Connie Hawkins, who passed the torch to Julius Erving, who was the forerunner of Michael Jordan. Elgin and I each scored forty-five points and broke the old arena record in a nationally televised 123–114 shoot-out. Not long after that, our team got into another scoring war, this time with the Philadelphia Warriors. Wilt nailed us for fifty-three. I scored forty-two on them. My all-star performance, followed up by such an explosion of points, brought more attention my way, and with it, a singular honor.

In 1961, though, there weren't any competing around-the-clock news channels. Network and local news existed, but television's reach was still limited. There wasn't any Internet, no personal computers, and the average attention span had not yet been completely destroyed. Even the most serious of reporters did not have to worry about watering down their coverage or appealing to demographics. *Time* and *Newsweek* were the country's highest circulated news magazines at that time. They still are. *Time* was one of the magazines that set the tone for a national dialogue on important issues. When anything made it onto the cover, it mattered.

A reporter from *Time* visited Cincinnati and scheduled interviews with me. When we met, he told me that his magazine was planning to do a cover story on the NBA. They'd commissioned an artist to do a painting of me and were planning to use it for the cover. He was shocked when I didn't react, or show any excitement, but dealt with him in the usual staid manner I used on the other dozen or so reporters who, every so often, flew in out of nowhere and bothered me.

The publication date was February 17, 1961, four years after Dr. Martin Luther King Jr. first made the cover, two after Harry Belafonte, and a little less than two years before Dr. King was declared *Time*'s Man of the Year. It was the first time a basketball player made the cover of *Time*. The February 17 cover indeed featured a painting of me. Russell Hoban, a noted African-American artist, painted the portrait, and I assume he used a still photo of me as his model. It's a beautiful painting, one of dancing colors. I am in action during a game, underneath the basket, shooting the ball. Around me abstract players are leaping. The air seems to swirl. I've been told that as he worked on the painting, the artist told a friend that it was curious; if you took the basketball out of my hand and replace it with a sword, you'd have the classic stance for a soldier. I've always appreciated that.

The piece began:

> In almost every way, Cincinnati's Oscar Robertson is a pure product of the sport of basketball as it has developed in the U.S. The game was invented in 1891 in Springfield, Mass., by a gym instructor named Jim Naismith, who wanted to give his bored classes a switch from the daily grind of calisthenics. Today basketball is played with eager enthusiasm and improving skill by some 50 nations from Chile to China, but it has remained a distinctly American game. Its virtues are obvious: any number can play, indoors or out, in all seasons. It requires nothing more than a ball, and a basket that is much the same whether it hangs from a backboard in Madison Square Garden or a barn door in Kentucky. This season an estimated 150 million Americans will watch games played by some 20,000 high schools, 1,000 colleges, and swarms of amateur teams composed of players ranging from scurrying schoolboys to gimpy grandfathers.

In the course of four pages, I was the focus for a piece that went on to explore the growing popularity of basketball. The writer reported my life story and singled me out as an exemplar of the best of basketball. However, in doing so, he also made a special point of noting that I was indicative of a new generation of players. "Gone is the day of the glandular goon who could do little more than stand beneath the basket and stuff in rebounds."

Thanks to Wilt, Bob Pettit, Bill Russell, Elgin Baylor, myself, and others, the league was changing. It was evolving much the same way that the face of all major professional team sports would evolve during the 1960s, the way that Jim Brown's dominance altered the face of professional football, and Hank Aaron and Willie Mays changed the landscape of baseball.

Indeed, African-Americans took over professional sports during the 1960s, even as the struggle for civil rights raged; and I've always believed that we, as players, affected that struggle, helped it. Bear with me for a moment.

I will never forget when my wife phoned me in Boston and said she was going to march in Selma, Alabama. This was in 1965. Martin Luther King Jr. and hundreds of marchers were planning to protest racist voting laws by crossing Selma's Edmund Pettus Bridge. I paused before responding. I asked her who was going. She said that Terry Embry (Wayne's wife) and a lot of people from Cincy were going to Selma for the march. I said okay, and they got a charter and flew down.

On March 7, 1965, police attacked the marchers. Yvonne wasn't hurt, thank God, but the brutality of the attack was severe enough that it prompted Lyndon Johnson to sign the Civil Rights Voting Act into law.

I knew Dr. King and did a lot of things to support the struggle. But in those days it was extremely difficult for a basketball player to be a public figurehead of the struggle, no matter who you were. It didn't matter if you wanted to be a public figure. It didn't matter if your heart and sympathies were with the marchers. Dr. King and everyone else knew the ramifications of picking a man like me. My career would be over; it was that simple. No owner was going to have on his team an outspoken black man making political statements. You can't compare this to modern-day players who refuse to step forward and take political stances because they are afraid of losing endorsement money from a soda company. The fact is, back then, if you stepped forward and spoke out, your livelihood was cancelled. I believe that once the movement had gathered momentum, there were specific venues with which Dr. King and others asked people to be involved—I seem to remember that Bill Russell went down to see Dr. King, specifically because he was asked—but otherwise, they wouldn't ask you to do it. It just wasn't thought of to use athletes for political purposes. Not until Muhammad Ali got involved with the black Muslims in the later part of the decade did any of that really happen.

We were players. The only thing we could do was play. The only place we could make a statement was on the court.

Having said this, there is no doubt in my mind that the black man's proficiency on the basketball court and baseball and football fields had its impact on the civil rights struggle. Competitive sports occupy a special place in the American heart. I'd say that a solid majority of people who rooted for their favorite teams cheered whichever players got the job done for them, regardless of race. Yes, there were people who may have been happier if the white guy did the job better than the black man, who may not have wanted to have the black guy live next to them, or date their daughters. But if the black guy helped win a game, then, just as people accepted Bill Cosby because he was funny or Charlie Parker because he was a great musician, that black athlete was accepted, however gradual, grudging, or even conditional that acceptance might have been.

During the 1960s, when blacks took over professional sports—we did so not just as star players, but also as utility infielders, defensive specialists, and nickel-back safeties. We helped teams win, so over time we got jobs, and, over time fans accepted us. It's perhaps sad to say that this actually represented a step forward. But it did. And it was an important step, I think. One that, in some significant way, affected what came later, made it possible.

Looking back on things, I think it is safe to say that my appearance on the cover of *Time* represented a small step in this direction.

The scantest breezes had blown when I'd been in high school. It had gusted a bit during my college years. The February 17, 1961, issue of *Time* magazine, I believe, was a weather vane, pointing toward the idea that those winds of change were truly beginning to gather momentum.

I averaged 30.5 points a game my rookie season, which topped the team in scoring and made me one of three players—along with Wilt and Elgin—to average more than thirty points, the first time that three players had averaged that many points over the course of one season. I was second on the Royals team in rebounds at 10.1 a clip, and first in the league in assists (9.7 a game). Cincinnati improved from nineteen wins to thirty-three that season. We weren't a playoff team, but we seemed headed in the right direction. Our home attendance increased from an average of fourteen hundred a game to more than five thousand two hundred. For the first time in the club's history, fan annual attendance broke the hundred thousand mark—a figure that not only helped triple the previous year's box office take but also accounted for a huge chunk of the league's twenty percent jump in attendance.

CHAPTER NINE

The Triple-Double
1961–1963

IN 1961, THE NATIONAL Basketball Association expanded, adding the Chicago Packers to its ranks. Soon to change its name to the Zephyrs, Chicago had the worst record in basketball. Only their center Walt Bellamy provided a bright spot, averaging 31.6 points and nineteen rebounds, while also leading the league in field-goal percentage. The 1961–1962 season was also notable for the Boston Celtics, whose sixty regular-season victories marked a first in league history. And then you had Wilt: the phenomenon of all phenomena. In his third season in the league, Wilt, age twenty-four, *averaged* more than fifty points and twenty-nine rebounds a game for the Philadelphia Warriors, records which stand to this day. (In his wonderfully named autobiography, *Wilt: Just Like Any Other Seven-Foot Black Millionaire Who Lives Next Door,* he revealed that even those numbers were misleading: "Late in the season, I realized I was creating a monster. I was averaging almost fifty-five points a game then, and I realized if I did it for one season, everyone would expect me to do it every season. I started passing off more, and let my average drop to just above fifty.") That season, Wilt played in all but eight minutes of eighty games. Because of overtimes, he actually averaged 48.5 minutes a game—more than were possible during a regulation contest. And, of course, on March 2, 1962, he did something that will never be matched. Perhaps you've seen the picture: a sheepish Wilt Chamberlain looking at the camera, holding up a piece of paper with the number one hundred scrawled across it. That night, as the Philadelphia Warriors defeated the New York Knicks, 169–147, Wilt Chamberlain became the first and only person in the history of professional basketball to hit the century mark in a single game.

Numbers start to give you some idea of how dominating Wilt Chamberlain was, but they really don't do the man justice. It's impossible to overstate his dominance—he led the league in scoring his first *seven* seasons. The NBA literally changed the rules to try to stop him. They expanded the lane, even instituted a no-dunking rule for a while. In 1968, Wilt got bored with scoring and told his teammates and the press he was going to lead the league in assists. Then he went out and did. And what makes the whole thing truly amazing is that nobody could say it was an aberration—it was the third time he'd finished in the top five in assists.

Today, it's hard to imagine just how low basketball was on the sports totem pole. The NBA was a second-rate league. In 1962, even the best teams were drawing small crowds. Most teams played a third of their home games away from their actual cities, in small regional venues—Wilt's hundred-point night, for example, was played in Hershey, Pennsylvania, in front of a paltry 4,124 people—and the Warriors led the league in attendance that season. But news of his hundred points spread and added to the legend of Wilt Chamberlain—for years afterwards people came up and told Wilt that they were at Madison Square Garden the night he hit his hundred. Almost by himself, he made the league a curiosity, made it interesting. People heard about Wilt scoring a hundred, averaging fifty a night, and they wanted to see the guy do it. Without him, the NBA might have lost the small television contract, which it so badly needed back then. I believe Wilt Chamberlain single-handedly saved the league.

The Boston Celtics were a great team, however, and great teams will beat a great player every time. The rivalry is remembered as Wilt versus Bill Russell. In truth it was Wilt against the Celtics. Over the years, Wilt's teams played against Boston in forty-nine regular-season games, met routinely in the Eastern Conference playoffs, and met twice in the NBA finals. It's probably the biggest rivalry in pro basketball history. Usually, Wilt outscored and outrebounded Bill, but the Celtics came away with the title. It happened in the 1962 playoffs, with the Celtics putting an end to Wilt's fifty-point, twenty-rebound season, one of the greatest of all time.

Of course, the 1962 season was a pretty big one for me too.

WHEN ANNOUNCERS mention my name nowadays, usually they do so in conjunction with the term *triple-double,* a shorthanded phrase for one of basketball's seminal accomplishments. The year was 1962. I was all of twenty-three. Over the course of the season—my second in the NBA— I averaged double figures in three areas: points, rebounds, and assists (hence the term *triple-double*). No player in basketball history had ever done this. No one has done it since. Some people look at it as one of the holy grails of sports, an accomplishment on par with Ted Williams's .400 batting average.

The truth is, I didn't realize what I had achieved; I never looked at stat sheets. Actually, it took almost twenty years for anyone to figure out what I'd done.

Statistics were tracked, obviously. But basketball didn't occupy the place it now does in the national consciousness. And no one was looking at individual season averages in points, rebounds, and assists, to see if all three were double digits. But when a young buck named Earvin "Magic" Johnson brought ShowTime to the Los Angeles Lakers during the early 1980s, newspaper reporters met with the team's stat crew and started to talk about how, every now and then, Earvin hit double figures in scoring, rebounding, and assists. Soon, an enterprising researcher was combing the

NBA's archives, searching to find out how many people had achieved triple-doubles. He kept digging and finally discovered, quietly, amid reams of statistics and a bunch of numbers that nobody had bothered to crunch . . .

Oscar Robertson

Season	Team	MIN	FGM	FGA	PCT	FTM	FTA	PCT	REB	AST	PF	DQ	PTS	RPG	APG	PPG
61-62	Cincinnati	79	3503	866	1810	.478	700	872	.803	985	899	258	1	2432	12.5	11.4	30.8

There's a story attributed to baseball legend Willie Mays. When Jose Canseco was honored in the 1980s for being the first man to hit forty home runs and steal forty bases in one season, Mays said, "If I'd have known that would be such a big deal, I would have done it a few times myself." That comes close to expressing the bemusement I feel about all the attention on my triple-double season. According to the NBA statisticians, I lead in triple-doubles, with 181, far outpacing Magic Johnson (138), Wilt Chamberlain (78), and Larry Bird (59). I can't say that if I'd have known the importance of the accomplishment, I might have had more, because I played hard every night I took the floor. And anyway, an assist is much easier to get today than it was in 1962.

Jason Kidd is by far the best point guard in today's game. He's also something of a triple-double fan. Indeed, when he entered the league with the Dallas Mavericks, Jason chose number thirty-two in honor of the triple-double, saying it reminded him of what he wanted to achieve every night he took to the floor. After a few seasons, Jason was traded to the Phoenix Suns, where he was also thirty-two. When he joined the New Jersey Nets, thirty-two was taken. Jason settled for five, the sum total of three plus two.

Jason has told interviewers that if there was one question he could ask me, it would be how I managed to sustain those averages over a whole season. I think, in actuality, he's referring more to an idea than an average. I also think that when an announcer brings up my name and the phrase triple-double, he's talking about the same concept: the idea of the complete player. The idea of excellence in all phases of the game.

And a triple-double season really translates into the idea of sustained excellence.

So Jason's question might be: *How were you able to sustain that level of excellence over the course of an entire season?*

I had certain natural gifts. I was six feet five. I was athletic. I was fast *and* strong. I was skilled. My success in the backcourt advanced the natural evolution of the game and helped popularize the strategy of having large, athletic guards bring the ball up court and run the offense. In addition to my size and my skills, I understood the game, both at the individual and the team levels. This is an important distinction. Basketball is a contest of individual skills, improvisations, and challenges. It is graceful and poetic and brutal, often all at once. At the core is an individual game and a simple idea: Isolate your man, beat him, score; don't let him do the same to you. At the same time, the individual exists within a team structure—one that has its own demands, challenges, and improvisational moments. In a team game, if you isolate your man, beat him, and drive to the basket, another defender will come to help. Every individual action brings a team response.

I've always thought you play the game of basketball against yourself as much as against any opponent. Every situation on the court has its own natural logic, a feel and rhythm. At the highest level of the game, you are playing your best and are up against opponents who are every bit as good as you, opponents who can do many of the things that you can do, and some things you can't. That game is mental as much as physical. Your thoughts are embodied in your instinctive physical reactions. I used to finger basketballs for hours at a time; I couldn't explain why, exactly. Rolling a ball just gave me a feeling that I could handle it—the feel for the ball came through my fingertips, and I knew that I could do anything with it. To truly comprehend the game, you must achieve that sense of control with a basketball, but you must also master the game itself. When you do, you know there's no challenge you don't have the skills to answer, nothing they can throw at you that you don't instinctively know how to counter.

This involves skills: being able to dribble left when the opening is there, making the open shot when it's time to do so. But even those things are predicated on the idea that playing the game correctly is more important than your own personal desires. The teams I was on put the ball in my hands. Roughly seventy to eighty percent of the time that we were on offense, I had the ball. Not so that I could shoot it every time or dribble between my legs and draw attention to myself—things I could have done if I really wanted to. Rather, coaches gave me the ball to orchestrate the game. I understood the game and could shoulder the responsibility for getting our offense going, getting guys the ball at the right time, and making the right choices and decisions.

Here's an example. Say I have the ball at the top of the key and am dribbling, keeping my defender at bay with my body as I read the court. Down on the right baseline, Jack Twyman is running toward a pick, set on the low block by Wayne Embry. Maybe Jack's defender is trailing him, which means, I hope, Jack will run past the pick, curl tightly around it, and pop out in front with his hands ready, so I can hit him with a pass in rhythm. I'm watching for this, but I'm also watching to see if the defender is going to aggressively overplay, or pop over Wayne's pick, and try to deny that very pass. If he does try to play aggressively, I'm trusting Jack to gauge this and react, perhaps fading to the corner for an uncontested jump shot, or perhaps he will slip backdoor and be available for slick a bounce pass and a layup. Maybe Wayne, after setting the pick, is going to be able to pop out for an open shot. Or maybe he will roll to the basket. All this is playing out in one, maybe two, seconds. Meanwhile, I've still got my own defender in front of me, looking for the first chance to reach in, ruin all our plans, and head the other way with the ball.

If I know the offense, if I understand where the guys on my team prefer to get the ball, as well as how the defenders like to play, then I'm going to be able to read all this, judge what's going on and make the right pass. Or maybe I'll decide that none of these options are worth a damn. Maybe I'm going to pass the ball around the perimeter. Maybe I need to drive and create some momentum. So you see, when I was running the show out there, I had larger responsibilities than my own statistics. If I played the game correctly, that naturally took care of itself.

More important than scoring, especially at the start of a game, was getting guys involved, giving everybody a feel and a taste, and seeing who was hot. Bill Russell said I was like a quarterback and a coach on the floor. I can't just dribble down the court and jack up a shot. If I do that, Jack

Twyman starts to wonder just why he's running himself ragged, fighting through picks down on the baseline. Wayne Embry might shake his head—he's down in the trenches pushing and shoving for position, and here this fool comes down and fires it up first thing? It starts a chain reaction. Jack would have been willing to run the play patiently all the way through to its logical conclusion—maybe this might mean shooting off a pick; maybe it would have meant getting the pass, concluding he wasn't open, passing the ball, and then cutting and running through more picks. Instead, he's seen that I'm selfish. That gives *him* license to shoot as soon as he touches the ball too.

Meanwhile, at the first time-out, Wayne Embry comes back to the huddle and starts complaining. Here he is down in the post, banging and swinging and getting the hell beat out of him. Why doesn't he ever get to see the ball?

Do you think either one of these guys is going to bust his ass to get back on defense when I miss and the rebound comes off and the Celtics are running a fast break in the other direction? Hell, no, they won't.

If you understand the game, you're aware of all this. You've got it under control. The guys you see. The defender running up behind you, who you can't see, but somehow sense. You understand who likes the ball in what spot, and make sure you get the ball to them from where they can score. You know which players need to get some touches early in the game, otherwise they might sulk and be useless to you for the next three quarters; which guys can't dribble on the perimeter, and make sure they never have the ball in a position where they have to. If you are only dribbling for your own benefit, you are selfish.

I used to start games out by sizing up a defense, testing it, getting a feel for its cracks and openings, what the guys playing against me wanted me to do, how I could do the opposite. Red Auerbach used to say that Bill Russell never knew when to double-team me or when to back off. I was adept enough with the ball to keep Russell guessing. And if I could do it to the greatest defensive center who ever lived, I could do it to anyone.

Once I realized what a team was trying to make me do, I'd exploit that. We might have had ten, even twenty, plays in our offense, but once I saw who was hot, what was working for us, I mined that vein until it went dry. To me that was the essence of pro basketball: Run a play until the other team proves it can stop it, and milk a hot player until his run is over. Jack Twyman was a deadly spot-up shooter. Part of the reason he busted his butt to get to his sweet spots was because he knew I'd find him. Wayne Embry's offense originally relied on short, rolling hook shots. But when I joined the Royals, Wayne saw how well I could drive and pass. He realized that one result of my penetration into the lane was going to be defenders collapsing on me. Which meant he'd be open for a lot of ten-foot jumpers. Wayne didn't have a smooth midrange jump shot, but he spent hours alone after practice working on it. "We always busted our tails to get open because we knew he'd get the ball to us," Wayne told reporters. "How he saw us sometimes, I'll never know." While he played with me, Wayne had the best scoring averages of his career.

He wasn't the only one. This is from Kareem Abdul-Jabbar's autobiography, *Giant Steps*:

There is an exact moment when a center, working hard in the pivot for a glimmer of an advantage, has the position he needs for the score. You've run the length of the court, established your ground, defended it against the hands, forearms, elbows, trunks, and knees of another two-hundred-and-fifty-pound zealot who is slapping and bumping and shoving to move you off your high ground. You need the ball right then. It's like a moon shot: Fire too soon and you miss the orbit; fire too late and you're out of range, but let fly when all signals are Go, and you should hit it right on. Oscar had the knack of getting me the ball at the right place and time. Not too high, didn't want to go up in the air and lose the ground you've fought for. Not too low, didn't want to bend for the ball and create a scramble down there. Never wanted to put the ball on the floor where some little guy could steal in and slap it away. Oscar knew all of this, and his genius was, whether two men were in his face trying to prevent him from making the pass or in mine trying to prevent me from receiving it, in getting me the ball chest-high so I could turn and hook in one unbroken motion.

A friend once told me a story about the great jazz bass player Charles Mingus. Mingus was known, among other things, for his improvisational skills and loosely structured bands. During the 1960s, he somehow got mixed up with the psychotropic guru Tim Leary. Leary was making a movie in Woodstock, New York, and Mingus agreed to act in it and score it. The first day of the shoot, they're standing around with their scripts. Leary says, "To hell with the scripts. Let's improv the whole thing." Mingus shook his head. "Look, man," he said, "The key to improv is having something concrete to go away from, and something to come back to." I bring this up because basketball is *not only* about set plays. Part of the beauty is the improvisational moments, the brilliance that can explode from out of ashes and chaos.

The fact is, you do need one-on-one skills; you do need to be able to isolate your man and break him down. You need to be able to create enough space for yourself to take a tough jump shot, to hit shots with a high degree of difficulty, to drive and dish to the open man. Whatever I was called upon for, I did. When you watch Kobe Bryant play basketball, you see a great offensive player. But you also get the sense that he grew up and learned to play as if there was a television camera on him at all times. His style is something of an extension of Michael Jordan's game, and Michael's game not only had flair, it was the *embodiment* of flair. Both play a spectacular, highlight-oriented game, cherished by the cereal-box crowd and the marketing executives of corporate America. There's nothing wrong with that.

But I had a different style—someone once suggested it might have been because I grew up in a time before television controlled everything. It wasn't flashy. At the same time, if you watch Michael Jordan's patented fadeaway jumper, or his back-to-the-basket fallaway, now that's Oscar Robertson's shot. If you pop in a videotape of Magic Johnson protecting the ball with his body as he runs a half-court offense, then isolating his man on one side of the basket, bulling and backing him down, and then spinning off his man, that's Oscar Robertson. My play influenced them. *And I did these things before they were around to watch them.*

Admittedly, I didn't do them with double-pumping flair and prime-time charisma. It wasn't because I couldn't do tricks with the ball. My coach in high school never allowed me to play that way. And if you wanted to review my game films, you'd find a few occasions where I might have swung the ball behind my back—freezing a defender for just long enough to allow me to feed the post, or drive. But I simply wasn't a person for doing tricks and showing off. I wasn't going to consciously hog the ball and keep shooting and shooting to see how many points I could score. Running up sixty or seventy points in a night wouldn't prove anything, first of all. More importantly, it wouldn't help our team win. Instead, I came out every night and provided our team with what one observer called a "utilitarian and crystallized ruthlessness."

Say I've caught the ball at the top of the key again. Say that the last time I caught it here, I made a bounce pass inside for a layup. Now the hours I spent as a child and teen and college student pay off: all the jab steps and first steps I'd practiced, my understanding of the game and other players. Depending on what I see from the defender, I might fake a bounce pass (the last possession should have set him up to the point that he should be worried about it). In a fraction of a second, I observe how his feet are set, the position of his hands, how far away he is when I catch the ball, and then make immediate judgments. If he's worried about another pass inside and sags into the post, I might just shoot in his face. I might jab step and shoot. The next time I might jab step and fake a shot; then, when he's off balance, drive. This might be followed by a jab step, a pump fake, and a quick crossover dribble. I'm not consciously thinking about this stuff. It's a dance, with each possession furthering my opportunity to exploit him and whatever uncertainties I have planted. If I'm on top of my game, just catching the ball and squaring up on my defender should be like having a cat on a string.

But it's possible the defender stayed with me through my fakes and the play hasn't worked out.

When I played, games were won from inside the foul line. You played to get fouled and to get people in foul trouble. Even now you can shoot all the three-pointers in the world and make a lot of them, but it's fool's gold; if you don't get to the foul line and inside the paint, you're simply not going to win. I square up on my defender and start toward my right. I've got my hip between the defender and the ball and have my head up. As I dribble, I read the court, maneuvering my way toward the paint. I dribble harder—giving one head and shoulder fake to my defender, then another. I feel his position with my body, and bump against his hip. His wrist and elbow are in my lower back. All this helps to determine my next move, the next bump. Two dribbles. A third. As I grind him down, I wait for him to commit himself in one way or another. If he's taller than me, he probably isn't as strong, fast, or as coordinated, so I take it for granted that when necessary I'll be able to spin past him. Smaller guys I'll simply wear down, using my strength and height on them, just backing them down, jumping over them, then crashing the offensive glass.

Dick Barnett made a statement that received national circulation and became the catchphrase description of my game: "If you give Oscar a twelve-foot shot, he'll work on you until he's got a ten-foot shot. Give him a ten and he wants eight. Give him eight and he wants six. Give him six, he wants four, he wants two. Give him two, you know what he wants? That's right, baby. He wants a layup."

It may not be flashy, but it's true. One of my favorite tricks was to spin by my guy with my arm out so fast he didn't know what happened. It used to piss off Alex Hannum, who was a Hall of Famer. "Someone is going to grab that arm someday and throw Robertson into the third row." Bill Russell was more philosophical. He called the move my *free foul*, saying, "I knew that whenever I guarded him on a switch, Oscar would be dribbling with one hand and trying to club me to death with the other. Oscar's free foul was in keeping with his attitude toward the game. He'd gobble his way up your arm if he could. He always wanted something extra."

Jerry Sloan was one of the best defenders of my era. Physical play and flopping were big parts of Sloan's repertoire. At six seven, he was long-armed and really physical and just a bitch to deal with; he'd get great position and crowd you, not so much as allowing you room to move, let alone make a first step toward the hoop. Then he'd let you bang into him and flop for the charge. Of course, this also was suited to the way I played, and we had some real wars out in Chicago: with me letting him get set, then making a fake. As soon as he reached for it, I'd drive right into him. My body was solid enough that some people said that crashing into me was like being hit by Jim Brown. I'd crash into Jerry and jump over him and release my shot. By the time the ball was in the net, several players would be on his ass and the ref would have blown his whistle. Refs didn't give flops often when I played. Instead I'd head to the foul line, and an upset defender would bounce up from the ground and start complaining. Next possession we'd do it all over again.

No flash was involved. No heat. No complicated terminology or superlatives. Just good, hard basketball and a concentrated, calculated effort. They play off you, you make the jumper. They crowd, you go around them. When it's time to pass, throw hard, precise passes that demand to be converted. When it's time to rebound, do so with passion and determination. It's not physics, but it works.

"If he couldn't pass, you could play him differently," Tom Heinsohn told a reporter, after I'd rung up the Celtics for a loss. "But if you double-team him for a second, you gamble. That calls for a pass, and he'll pass it." Bob Cousy felt the same way. "O's such a threat that you'd like to double-team him. But if you do, that means that there's somebody free, and he'll hit him every time. If you don't double-team him, he'll take his shot when he gets it, and he's a terrific shooter."

When the ball game was on the line, I was going to be aggressive. If the game was close, at the end of the game I was going to force the issue more. I was going to make them stop me. Sometimes I dribbled too much or got the ball stolen. I did miss a few big shots in key situations. But I wasn't afraid to fail. If the ball was taken away once, it didn't mean it would happen again. I'd worked hard enough and believed in my game. I knew that I'd make the right decisions with it. My teammates did as well. When push came to shove, they wanted me to have the ball as much as I did. That's what being a leader is all about. I wanted to win. I expected

everyone to be as dedicated as I was. If someone didn't live up to that ex-
pectation, he heard about it.

If the referee on the other side of the court blew his whistle and
called a foul on me for something that by all rights he was in no position
to observe, and if there was another ref five feet away and he saw everything squarely and did not call anything, you're damn right I said something. No longer the quiet, shy kid I'd been at Lockefield, I challenged the
referees. "What the hell's going on?" was my usual phrase. Without even
realizing I was doing it, I'd slap my foot on the hardwood and hit the palms
of my hands against each other, emphasizing my frustration.

Sometimes words failed, so I'd just tilt my neck and give a long hard
stare. Guys dreaded that. But I didn't have patience for teammates who
messed up our plays. If we're running a pick and roll, and you have a chance
to roll toward the basket, and you don't do it, we miss our chance. So why'd
we run the play in the first place? Either you should do it right, or we
shouldn't call the play, or you shouldn't be out there. That there's a right
and a wrong way to play basketball is my point, and I don't think there's
any point being out there playing if you aren't going to do it the right way.
You aren't helping anybody.

Wayne Embry actually got into his first NBA fight because I was so
demanding. To understand just what a feat this was, you have to know
Wayne. At six feet eight, 250 pounds, he was a wide-trunked eagle of a
man, with such a huge wingspan and long hands that he ended up with
about the same reach as Bill Russell. Wayne was a lovely, funny man. He
played with as much desire and endurance as talent. Well, we were playing
Detroit, and Wayne was being held illegally by Ray Scott. The official
missed the foul twice, and both times Scott stole the ball on pick and rolls.
I slapped my hands together and said, "Dammitt, Wayne, how long are you
going to let Ray Scott mess up our plays?"

The next trip down the floor, sure enough, Ray reached and held
Wayne. And Wayne promptly turned and coldcocked him.

"I had to," he told a friend after the game. "You know what it's like
to have Oz on you."

(I think Wayne just wanted a little respect, was all.)

The stories go on.

Red Auerbach used to throw three waves of guards against me—Sam Jones (who had speed), K. C. Jones (a defensive specialist), and John Havlicek (a big, rugged player). Auerbach hoped they would wear me down by the end of the game. When Bill Russell took over for Auerbach, he said it didn't make a bit of difference who covered me. He let the guards decide who would guard me. They decided that whoever had the worst excuse had the job.

Frank McGuire had a similar thing happen to him when he took over the Philadelphia Warriors. A college coach for many years, he was still adjusting to the league and asked his players to work out individual match-ups for themselves until he better understood player matchups. Before their first game against us that year, the Warriors went around the locker room, deciding who would guard whom. Nobody wanted to guard me. Coach McGuire supposedly smiled and said he thought someone ought to be assigned to Oscar, "Just to make it look good." Tom Gola said he'd do it, " . . . but he's probably going to get thirty-six points off me." (According to Wilt, that's exactly how many I ended up with.)

There's the one about the college coach who gave his team a fire-and-brimstone speech before a game. "And remember," he said, "Robertson puts on his jock the same way you guys do." We went out there and beat them by twenty-five. Afterwards, their team dragged themselves back to the locker room. A guard told him, "I don't care what you say, that guy *has* to put his jock on different."

One NBA coach claimed I was worth sixty to seventy points a game. Bud Olsen, who rode the bench with Cincinnati for a couple of years, used to say I always had something new, something different. He'd sit on the bench and watch my moves and punch the guy next to him: "You see that? You see that?"

Even Wilt told his coach, Frank McGuire, "If I had my pick of all the players in the league, I'd take the Big O first."

My stats often get brought up in comparison with modern players. I think a true comparison is impossible, however, because of the changes made in the game. Three-point shots didn't exist in the NBA until the mid-1980s. If they had existed in 1962, I would have scored more points (I wasn't known as a long-range shooter, but if there had been a three-point shot back then, you can bet I would have been). Assists are also counted differently today. When I played, an assist was "without a dribble going to the basket." If I passed the ball inbounds to you, and you dribbled the ball once, that pass was not counted as an assist. I was the all-time leader in assists for almost twenty years, until the early 1990s, when Magic Johnson broke my record (Utah's John Stockton has since shattered that). But again, the rules are different now. These days, the rules allow you one dribble, but everyone knows that I can pass you the ball inbounds, have you dribble it the length of the court and hit a jump shot, and there's a fifty-fifty chance that I'll get the assist. If assists had been defined this way back in the early 1960s, I would have had another six or seven thousand.

Moreover, Magic had a far better situation when he was with the Lakers. With a minute or thirty seconds left, Magic Johnson could look right or left and see James Worthy on one side, Byron Scott on the other side. In the same situation, I looked to my left, and there was a guy who couldn't hit free throws. I looked to my right, and there was a guy who couldn't go to the basket. You can't pass to a guy who can't shoot free throws or take the ball to the basket at the end of a close game. So I had to pull up and look for the trailer.

Of course now we've gone from one extreme to another. Where it took more than twenty years for people to even know that I had a triple-double season, these days everything is a stat. We didn't keep steals in those days. Loose-ball rebounds are given to somebody now. It used to be a team rebound. If a power forward gets eight rebounds, he's an all-star now. If you only got eight rebounds when I played, you sat on the bench.

DURING THE TAIL END of the 1962 season, Wayne Embry twisted his ankle and had to miss five games. One game was at home, against the Detroit Pistons. Two of the Pistons starters, Bailey Howell and

164 ★ OSCAR ROBERTSON

Ray Scott, played the entire fourth quarter with five fouls apiece. Nobody on the Royals could do enough to make either man pick up their sixth and eliminating foul. We were up by eight in the fourth quarter, but then the Pistons started to come back. Two field goals by Howell late in last forty-one seconds finished us off, 119–118—meaning that a guy who should ordinarily have been out of the game a long time ago ended up beating us. Without Wayne, we didn't have the frontcourt to win that game.

When I had to sit out with a messed-up ankle, the Royals inevitably lost by twenty-five points or more. We finished with a 43–37 record that season and made the playoffs, but got bounced in the first round. That summer, our front office made another in what would become a tradition of draft mistakes, acquiring Ohio State's Larry Siegfried, then losing him to the American Basketball League, a fledgling rival league, which had taken up the old moniker of the ABL and which was founded by Abe Saperstein.

I wasn't around to watch that happen. As soon as the season ended, I packed my bags and headed for Camp Pickett, Virginia. I'd been sworn into the army during the regular season, at halftime of a televised game against the Celtics. I spent my whole off-season in the Army Reserves that year. I wasn't thrilled about it, but being on reserve was much better than going on active duty. It was a seven-year commitment, but it only required active duty for six months, and you didn't get shipped overseas. In those days they were drafting blacks left and right and putting them on the front lines. Of course, the military denies it. But America has a history of offering black military personnel great peril and minimal recognition. My peril was Fort Jackson, South Carolina.

During a summer camp, I went in uniform with two white soldiers into a restaurant for some sandwiches. No sooner had we sat down than the manager walked over and said that I couldn't eat there.

"But I'm in the U.S. Army, in camp outside town."

"If you want to eat here, go on back to camp and get your general. Then we'll see."

When he said that, it was like a little gear clicked into place in my head. I remember saying to myself, "I can sit down and eat at the Cliff House in San Francisco or Berman's Steak House in Detroit. But this little jerk tells me I can't have a drink of water in the Virginia boondocks?"

Some things about this country were just insane.

AFTER THE 1962 SEASON, the Philadelphia Warriors moved to San Francisco and became part of the NBA's Western Division. That meant someone in that division had to shift to the East. Cincy was the natural choice to balance the league because it was geographically closest to the other Eastern Division teams. So the Royals moved into the same division as Red Auerbach, Bill Russell, Bob Cousy, and the four straight titles of the Boston Celtics. If we wanted to play for a championship, now we had to go through Boston. With a starting lineup of me, Wayne Embry, Bob Boozer, Jack Twyman, and Adrian Smith, we went 42–38 and finished third in the East.

However, in April 1963, just as the team was preparing for the playoffs, Tom Wood, the owner of the Royals, passed away. The Wood estate wanted to sell its interests in the Cincinnati Gardens and the Royals in a package. Louis Jacobs, a Buffalo-based concessionaire whose fifty-million-dollar family company, the Emprise Corporation, had their fingers in the pies of many major-league sports franchises, was the prime candidate to buy up everything, especially as Lou Jacobs already owned eighty percent of the Gardens.

A second candidate soon emerged, however. Jake Brown, my lawyer and advisor, decided he wanted try to buy the team. J. W. teamed up with Warren Hensel, a Cincinnati booster and a huge basketball fan. They agreed with the Jacobs family on a deal where Jacobs could keep the Gardens, but J. W. and Warren would purchase the Royals.

Jacobs agreed to make the bid to the Tom Wood estate on behalf of Brown and Hensel. In a matter of weeks, the bid was accepted, and Brown and Hensel began to take charge of the Royals.

Warren Hensel could not stand head coach Charley Wolf and fired him. On the basis of Jack Twyman's recommendation, he hired red-faced Jack McMahon away from the college ranks to be our new head coach.

Just as it looked like the Royals had their new leadership in place, however, the Jacobs side of the negotiations began stalling. Laborious conferences took place regarding the Gardens' lease. Soon the NBA representatives demanded to see the Brown/Hensel agreement. For some reason, Jacobs wouldn't show it to them. The Jacobs people then became cold to Brown and Hensel and refused to answer their calls or letters. J. W. told me that if the deal had gone through as agreed upon, he and Hensel would have made a million dollars each out of the franchise. I'm sure Jacobs realized that and changed his mind. In any case, Jacobs lobbied with NBA president Maurice Podoloff and several other owners—arguing against his own deal. He didn't even tell his own attorney, Bro Lindhorst, that he was trying to sabotage the deal.

This was all happening while we were in the playoffs. And wouldn't you know it, we upset the Syracuse Nationals in the first round, and flew straight from Syracuse to Boston.

Two nights later, we played the Celtics in game one of the series for the Eastern Division title.

During the series, the ownership of the Royals would change twice. Pepper Wilson, our general manager, would make half a dozen phone calls at one point just to figure out who his boss was.

The back and forth and confusion lasted until training camp of the 1963–64 season, when Lou Jacobs finally ended up the owner of the Royals, and for all intents and purposes, the franchise lost its last chance at having ownership that actually cared about winning and losing.

Our team couldn't be worried about that. We had the four-time defending world champions to deal with.

During the regular season, whenever the Celtics came to Cincinnati, Bill Russell and other players used to come to my house. Yvonne would cook a big dinner for them. Then both of our teams would go and try to beat the hell out of each other. Out on the court against the best players, it doesn't matter if they are friends or not. If you don't play hard against Bill Russell, he will embarrass you. Same thing with Wilt. And with me. Our friendships always took a backseat to our game.

That year the Celtics were all balance and experience. They had won fifty-eight games with no player averaging more than twenty points. Thirty-four-year-old Bob Cousy had announced that this was his last season. They had all the talent and motivation in the world, and all odds-makers figured they'd beat the hell out of us.

That first game in Boston, it looked like the oddsmakers were right. At the low point, we were down twenty-two. But we came back to a 135–132 win that shocked the Celtics. Boston coach Red Auerbach complained constantly about the officiating. All the papers said that I was carrying Cincy on my back. Twenty-four hours later, we ran onto the court for game two in Cincinnati. We were down nine in the first half, made a run, faded in the end, and got blown out, 125–102. Two nights later in the Boston Garden, beneath the majesty of their championship banners and on the fabled parquet playing floor, we beat them by five, 121–116. The Royals, the undisputed underdogs of the series, had a two-to-one lead. And two of the next three games were on our home court.

We had a four-day break to rest and practice and work on our plays. We wasted no time. The day after we got home, our team walked onto the floor of the Cincinnati Gardens for practice. The floor was covered with sawdust and hay, and we had to step over giant piles of elephant shit.

While we'd been taking down the Celtics on their home court, the circus had come to Cincinnati. Lou Jacobs had neglected to inform the team's management—even during all of their negotiations—that he had booked the Gardens for the circus. For the duration of the playoffs. With no chance for rescheduling.

Our practice—and the series—moved to tiny Schmidt Fieldhouse at Xavier University, a venue with about one-third the capacity of the Gardens.

To say that we felt unsupported by the front office would be very kind. The whole team was furious. We'd worked all season to be in the playoffs, to get to the point where we had a chance to beat our biggest rival and make it to the championship. We had a chance for a huge home-court advantage, twelve to fourteen thousand fans screaming obscenities at the Celtics and pressuring the refs into calling things our way. Instead, the Cincinnati Gardens would be alive with trapeze artists and tightrope walkers. We'd be in some little fieldhouse that I didn't even know how to get to.

I played as hard as I could, but Boston took the game easily, 128–110. Days later they finally won at home, 125–120, and moved up to a 3–2 lead in the series.

Two nights after their home victory, I would not let us lose. In the friendly confines of Schmidt Fieldhouse, the Royals scored a 109–99 victory, forcing a seventh game in Boston.

On April 10, 1963, the day of the game, the case of Mississippi Governor Ross R. Barnett was passed onto the United States Supreme Court. The highest court in the land would hear about Barnett's efforts to block the admission of James H. Meredith, a black man, to the University of Mississippi.

Sam Jones arrived hours early at the Boston Gardens and spent time in the darkened, empty arena, practicing and shooting. Bob Cousy arrived through his usual secret entranceway, not knowing if this would be the final game of his professional career. The game had been sold out for several days, and it was as crazed an environment as you could expect. At the half, Boston led 68–64, but we were in striking distance and felt good. Cousy started the second half by nailing a set shot. In less than five minutes, Boston flew to an 86–72 lead, then extended it to 98–82 with a lot of help from six-foot-four Celtics guard Sam Jones, whose early practice paid off— he hit jump shots, off-balance drives, one-handed layups.

Sam Jones, K. C., Bill Russell, Cousy. If a player had on a white-and-green uniform and was anywhere near me, the guy was pushing, shoving, holding, or just pounding on me. I think it was Auerbach's gentle way of trying to wear me down or make me lose my cool.

In any case, I started leading us back. One possession after another. One trip to the foul line after another.

With a few minutes left in the third quarter and Cousy resting on the bench, we'd whittled a twenty-five-point lead down to nine, 98–89.

But when Cousy got back onto the court, he had a second wind and took control. It seemed like he hit every shot he took and dished out key assists, each one more spectacular than the other—a length-of-the-court bounce pass to Sam, a behind-the-back flip through the lane on the full run to Russell.

Boston outscored us 27–9 and took a commanding 123–98 lead.

We fought back with a 17–2 run, but it was too little, too late.

Final score: 142–131. The Celtics were on their way to yet another NBA championship.

Cousy finished the game with twenty-one points and sixteen assists. Russell had twenty points and twenty-four rebounds. Sam Jones was their real star, though; he ended up with a career-high forty-seven.

I ended the night with forty-three points, including twenty-one out of twenty-two free throws. No other Royal had twenty.

"Let me tell you," Bill Russell said, "They shocked the stuffing out of us in that first game. We had a twenty-two-point lead. Imagine. And they beat us. And they kept fighting us all the way. That Oscar—I've just seen too much of him, that's all."

"Poor Sam was so happy to be out of that series," Bob Cousy told reporters, "he almost cried."

Afterwards, reporters, fans, and players alike blamed our loss on the circus debacle and the ownership chaos. The truth is, we had the opportunity to beat Boston. We couldn't do it. We simply didn't have the right players on the court to beat the Celtics. A lot of the Royals were gun-shy about playing them; it was almost as if they couldn't go forward and play aggressively against the green-and-white Celtics uniforms. Moreover, we didn't have the bench necessary to beat them; we needed an infusion of a couple of players and a couple of stouter hearts. Sure, the confusion in ownership and the mismanagement of the Gardens might have thrown us off. But at the end of seven games, the Celtics were the better team. They went on to beat the Lakers in the finals, winning their fifth straight title, and sending Bob into retirement with a final victory parade.

I was dejected after we lost the series. Coming close and then ending up short can sting a lot more than never having a chance.

On April 12, 1963, two days after our loss, Martin Luther King was arrested in Birmingham, Alabama, for defying a court injunction and leading a march of African-Americans toward downtown Birmingham. The marchers were halted after four and a half blocks, but not before more than a thousand shouting, singing black men and women had joined the demonstration.

The same day, in Clarksdale, Mississippi, firebombs were thrown at a Negro leader's home where representative Charles C. Diggs Jr. of Michigan was staying. Two young men were arrested. They admitted to throwing the bombs and said they were "just having fun."

———————

THAT SUMMER I joined a group of basketball players and coaches on a kind of goodwill ambassador trip behind the Iron Curtain. We played exhibition games in Yugoslavia, Poland, and Romania. Even a game or two in Egypt, if I remember correctly. One night there were seven of us out to dinner. I was sitting there with Red Auerbach, Bill Russell, Bob Cousy, and a couple of other players. Red used to tease me all the time, and I really liked him, so I'd send barbs right back. All of us were at a table, sitting there, and Red's smoking one of his damn cigars, baiting me, and he asked if I would like to play for the Celtics.

"Hell, no! What the hell for?"

"You young punk, you!" He had a big grin on his face.

"If it weren't for Russell," I said, "you guys wouldn't be crap."

Bill was laughing at me, and Red was egging me on, and we were all having a good time. I didn't think anything of it at the time.

It wasn't until much later that I remembered Bob Cousy at the table that night. He was sitting there listening. I don't remember if he was laughing or not.

CHAPTER TEN

Union President, NBA Royalty
1963–1968 (Part One)

W HEN THE 1963 SEASON ENDED, Maurice Podoloff, the only commissioner the National Basketball Association had had so far, stepped down, replaced by the league's publicity director, J. Walter Kennedy. The Chicago Zephyrs relocated to Maryland and became known as the Baltimore Bullets. The Syracuse Nationals, meanwhile, moved to Philadelphia, filling the gap that had been left when the Warriors had left for San Francisco the previous year. These shifts were indicative of a definitive change in the league. No longer were franchises located in towns like Fort Wayne, Moline, Oshkosh, Waterloo, Rochester, and Syracuse. Now every team was located in a major metropolitan area, with the two smallest franchises in St. Louis and—you guessed it—Cincinnati. The smallest arena in the league now seated ten thousand. During the upcoming season, for the first time in league history, the total attendance would exceed three million fans. A contract was signed to televise the all-star game in prime time.

In Cincinnati, we had our own reasons for enthusiasm: a welcome infusion of frontcourt talent, in the form of one Jerry Lucas. The great forward from Ohio State, and my teammate on the 1960 Olympic team, had spent two years in the American Basketball League as the property of the Cleveland Pipers. But like so many teams and leagues that started up with grand hopes, the Pipers ran out of cash—in their case they went belly-up before playing so much as a single game—and Saperstein's fledgling ABL folded in 1962. Lucas ended up sitting out for a season before getting his shot in the NBA.

At six feet eight, 220 pounds, Jerry was a great athlete. Now he had to make the transition from pivot to forward, which required speed and leaping. But when he was a boy, he used to invent memory games, and he'd developed a photographic memory. Jerry was a Phi Beta Kappa student in college, and he understood how to apply his smarts to the game: how to lurk on the opposite side of the court and wait until a shot went up, at which point he could judge its trajectory and arc and immediately position himself for a rebound. He was tricky, physical, and bull-tough, a consummate team player. A three-time college All-American and two-time player of the year, Jerry had played center in college. He may have shot the ball in a peculiar, over-the-shoulder fashion, but he also set college records for shooting accuracy and understood the pick and roll as well as anyone I played with. With his back to the basket, he'd led an Ohio State squad featuring John Havlicek (a young guy named Bobby Knight was a reserve) to the 1960 title. A fan favorite throughout the state of Ohio, he was regarded by many as the best rebounding forward the game had ever seen.

Of course, if Jerry wanted to play in the NBA, he didn't have much choice either—Cincinnati held his rights. I know that guys in Cincinnati's front office still remembered some of the nasty things Jerry had supposedly said to *Sports Illustrated*. General manager Tom Grace certainly felt he'd been burned when Lucas went to the Pipers. But grudges didn't matter. Our franchise simply couldn't afford not to have this guy.

The day Tom Grace and Pepper Wilson finally swallowed their

pride and signed Jerry, our team became dangerous. Wayne Embry wasn't a traditional center, but he provided us bulk up front. Jack Twyman may not have held the scoring role he once did—something he wasn't happy about—but as a team player in the best sense, he refocused his efforts on the defensive end. Adrian "Odie" Smith and defensive hawk Arlen Bockhorn rotated in the starting lineup opposite me at off-guard. Tom Hawkins started as our small forward. And with Bob Boozer, Jay Arnette (an underrated, leaping six-foot-two speed merchant), and Harold "Happy" Hairston, we had unprecedented depth coming off the bench. For the first time since the franchise was in Rochester, the Royals front office had filled the roster with talent. We were a legitimately balanced squad, with each player capable of handling his responsibilities. Without Lucas, we'd taken Boston to a deciding seventh game. With this lineup and depth, according to various preseason magazines, we were favorites to dethrone Boston.

Jack McMahon was like a lot of coaches of that era; he was fiery. On the sidelines, he would yell and moan until he was red in the face. He also came in and, like many coaches, immediately decided we needed to play better defense and try to run more. He was a former player himself; he knew not to beat guys over the head for their mistakes and wasn't above going out to a bar with some of the players after a game, so he kept things on an even keel. Our training camp was on some army base, and Wayne Embry was named team captain. It was a good thing. Wayne was the type of guy who would tell you exactly what you needed to hear and do so in a way that avoided upsetting anybody.

On September 27, the day of our first exhibition game, the Jacobs family and their Emprise Corporation put an end to all ownership questions with the announcement that Jacobs had paid four hundred thousand dollars for forty percent of the Cincinnati Gardens and had also retained fifty-six percent ownership in the Royals. Warren Hensel—who never had owned much of the team, despite his involvement—was out. Bro Lindhorst, the Jacobs's lawyer, would take over as executive vice president, despite Hensel's many protestations that he had a written contract and was legally entitled to run the team. None of us could worry about it—as players we knew the front-office situation was bizarre, but we had a season to prepare for. We hit the road for an exhibition schedule-slash-barnstorming tour, playing night after night in dank high school gyms in small towns like Huntingburg, Indiana; Fort Dodge, Iowa; Chillicothe, Ohio; and Quincy, Illinois.

Things did not start off well. Jerry Lucas was accustomed to being a star and having the ball, and he had problems adjusting to an offense that did not revolve around him. It takes any player a while to adjust to a new offense and system, but because there was so much excitement and hype surrounding Jerry, I think the transition affected him even more. Where he'd set college records for shooting accuracy, now he was being asked to play for long stretches without the ball and to rely on someone else to set him up. Because Jerry took pride in his shooting percentage, I think he became self-conscious at times. Throughout the exhibition season and into the pre-season, the chronic knee condition that would bother him throughout his career began to show itself. Never the most mobile player to begin with, Jerry was reluctant to shoot open fifteen-footers and instead drove to the basket and picked up cheap offensive fouls. He and I had problems finding offensive rhythm together and establishing any kind of chemistry.

And since we played a good number of preseason games against St. Louis, Jerry's problems were further magnified. Night after night he was matched up against Bob Pettit, a Hall of Fame player who gave everybody fits.

The one place where Jerry's game was unaffected was on the boards, and I think this is the source of what became a long-standing misperception. Even if Jerry was tentative in our offense and unsure of where to move, once a shot went up, he was relentless, a rebounding demon.

Back when Syracuse had a franchise and Dick Barnett was their star, there was a story that players complained about not getting any passes from Dick. Supposedly, Dick answered, "If you don't like it, get the ball off the backboard." Somehow this story got applied to Jerry Lucas and me. Only now reporters claimed that Jerry had complained about not getting any passes. Now, the story went that I told him, "Then go get it off the back-board." Soon the word was out: Oscar and Lucas don't get along. The truth was, we'd played together and been friendly on the Olympic team but didn't know each other all that well—not yet. I passed the ball to everyone in our basketball scheme.

In any case, what at that time was the largest opening-night crowd in Boston Garden history showed up for Jerry's professional debut. At power forward, Jerry was more than ready for them and totaled twenty-three points and seventeen rebounds. Though I hit a crazy fifty-foot hook shot toward the end of the first half and managed to throw a bounce pass *through* Bill Russell's legs at one point, we were down fourteen with a little more than six minutes left to play. A run of nine straight free throws, one of my trademark baseline jumpers, and a Wayne Embry layup that I set up closed the gap. With twenty seconds left, we were down a point when Bob Boozer hit a long shot from the baseline. Sam Jones countered with a long jumper.

Seconds remained on the clock as we came out of the time-out and immediately mangled our set play. Somehow, amid the chaos, I found Bob open for a fifteen-footer. With the crowd screaming, he drilled it. Sam Jones missed a wild shot as the buzzer sounded, and we celebrated 93–92.

In the NBA, you really can't ever attribute too much significance to one game. The real mark of a professional team comes on a Tuesday in February, when you are in the middle of an eight-game road trip and find yourself in an arena you can't recognize, playing against a team whose name has blurred into all the others. But it was obvious that Lucas was going to remove a lot of pressure from Wayne Embry. He provided our lineup with a third major scorer, improved our rebounding, and immediately solidified our frontcourt and our defense. I was also encouraged because the word on Bob Boozer had been that he'd lost confidence in his shot during the 1959 Pan-Am Games. If the offensive skills he'd shown at Kansas State were back, we matched up with the Celtics extremely well—especially as Bob's combination of strength, height, athletic ability, and energy made him a perfect foil for Tommy Heinsohn, who was renowned for tricks like pulling on your jersey or strategically, slyly, shoving his elbow into your ribs. Bob played Tommy better than about anybody in the league, which we'd need if we were going to get past them in the playoffs.

If opening night was any indication, and Bob was going to give us scoring *and* defense, were we going to cause some real trouble?

Of course, there were growing pains. In San Francisco, Jack Twyman—who was so anxious to contribute that the previous game he'd volunteered to guard Elgin Baylor—fractured a bone in his hand. In Cleveland, Lucas and Happy argued over whether Happy should have passed the ball. They started yelling at each other on the court and kept at it in the locker room after the game.

Despite our big win in Boston, we were trying to find ourselves; the Celtics, meanwhile, were destroying the league. With Bob Cousy retired, the rest of their team seemed determined to show that they could play without him. John Havlicek, Tom Heinsohn, and Tom Sanders were splitting time at the forward slots, and K. C. Jones had stepped smoothly into the point guard slot. The only guy in their top six who didn't average at least ten points a game was K. C., and he was too busy playing defense and setting everyone up. With guys like Frank Ramsey, Clyde Lovellette, and Jim Loscutoff coming off the bench, the Celtics were still loaded, and they started the season on an unbelievable winning streak. Less than two weeks into the season, they were 7–1. It stretched to 12–1, then 17–1.

Meanwhile, McMahon shifted us into an offense that featured two post men, thereby clearing the middle for my penetration and also allowing Jerry to play with his back to the basket, a position in which he was more comfortable. At 10–8, we went on a tear. Against Philadelphia I had thirty-eight points and sixteen rebounds; Lucas had twenty-one points and a club record thirty-one rebounds. The next night Jerry broke his own record with thirty-three rebounds and twenty-five points. I chipped in twenty-nine points in twenty-two minutes, and Jack Twyman, out there with a cast on his hand, had seventeen points. It was our fourth straight road win, a club record. We were starting to play together and get to know each other, gaining confidence. After a fifth straight win and then a loss against Los Angeles, we went back to Cincinnati for our second game of the season against Boston. Rising to the challenge, I played all forty-eight minutes and had a triple-double as we handed them their second loss of the season, 118–108.

As the second month of the season progressed, Boston continued to lead the NBA with an incredible 22–3 record. Slowly, however, we were gaining on them. From 10–8, we'd run off to an 18–10 record, and then 21–12, the second-best record in the league. Still, we trailed them by five and a half games in the Eastern Division.

Our season turned on Sunday morning, December 15, when our general manager phoned Bob Boozer's home. The phone call represented the culmination of two years of simmering emotions. I think it also ended up costing us that season's NBA title.

There are different accounts of what happened. But one thing that's not in doubt: This story begins with Tom Grace, executive director of Tom Wood's insurance companies. Now, Tom Grace was a smart businessman, but he wasn't a basketball guy. He didn't play the game, nor was he raised on it. He'd become the team's executive vice president in 1959, when Tom Wood took over the Royals and the Gardens from the Harrison brothers.

During the first three of Tom Grace's early years, two of Cincinnati's number one draft picks had turned their backs on the Royals: Bob Boozer headed to the ever-powerful Peoria Caterpillars, and Jerry Lucas went to the Cleveland Pipers. This all but crippled the team's playoff chances and also irreparably damaged Grace's reputation, in that he had been unable to sign and deliver the players general manager Pepper Wilson had drafted. Ownership gradually gave Pepper more control. Around the league, meanwhile, our front office was viewed as a nice bunch of guys who could not successfully order an egg salad sandwich without having the chicken jump to another league.

By 1963, however, Bob had returned from the land of caterpillars, and Lucas was on board.

There was no question Jerry was going to start at power forward—he was that good. Jack McMahon gave Tom Hawkins the nod at the other forward spot. This meant Bob was going to come off the bench to play.

Bob wasn't thrilled about the situation. He went to Grace and said, "It looks like I'm the fifth wheel on a situation that is going nowhere."

From here on in, there are a number of opinions as to what happened.

Tom Grace once told *The Cincinnati Enquirer* that Bob was a malcontent. Jack McMahon and others felt Bob could not accept that Tom Hawkins had beaten him out for a starting job. Hawkins started at forward because he was fast and finished well on the break. In addition, McMahon did not exactly have confidence in Bob and would sometimes put Jack Twyman in ahead of him as the first man off the bench.

Logic says that the team traded Bob for basketball purposes, although press reports also said that the cash-strapped Royals convinced the Knicks to throw in some money—fifteen thousand dollars—as part of the deal.

However, in an interview done in the early 1970s, Tom Grace gave other reasons.

"Bob and I had become good friends. He asked if I could do something and I agreed. I pointed out to him, though I had lost whatever control I had of the Royals, I could get Ned Irish over with the Knicks to take him."

There. Bob Boozer asked to be traded. Didn't he?

"I never talked to Tom Grace about the deal," Bob told me. "Despite all the hype about Lucas, I was playing as sixth and seventh man and kicked in fourteen, seventeen, and eighteen points in the three games just before the trade. I'd recognized the situation: Lucas and Twyman were going to play. I went to Coach McMahon and told him I'd play in whatever spot they needed me. Coach told me he really appreciated my attitude. He even told the press, 'He's our key man off the bench.' But there had been reports in the papers saying Tom Grace regarded me as a malcontent, which was total bull. It was a political situation, and they traded me."

Whichever side you choose to believe, the end result was that Pepper Wilson called to tell Bob he'd been traded to the Knicks. Bob left for New York, fuming the whole trip at Jack McMahon, believing that the coach should have gone to bat for him and made sure he stayed with the club.

Now, I don't believe for a second that Bob asked to be traded. He loved playing in Cincinnati and knew how close we were to a championship. I also think that anyone who would claim that Bob was unhappy here is just plain, flat-out wrong. It's a deal I never understood. But it also illustrates the reason your favorite NBA player constantly tells the local newscaster, "It's a business."

When the season's in full swing, it doesn't matter if you understand the trade management just made. Doesn't matter if you agree. You've got another plane to catch. Another game to play. And immediately following the trade, we played great ball, beating the Knicks decisively. The Celtics came into Cincinnati for another showdown. (Before the game, Bill and the gang stopped by my house for dinner.)

At one point during the game, Bill Russell had me trapped on the baseline. I went into a crouch and pump-faked. He stood there. I stayed in my crouch for a moment. Russell, confused, hesitated, and I shot from the crouch and scored. On the way back up the court, he laughed, "You've got to be shitting me."

It was only the fifth Celtics loss of the season, but the fourth at our hands, and even Red was getting frustrated.

"We tried something new on them," Auerbach said. "I told the boys to stretch their fingers out wide with their hands way up on defense, figuring every little bit helps. But you know what that Oscar did?" Red shook his head in disbelief. "He shot through their fingers."

———————

IN EARLY 1964, Jack Twyman came to me. Jack was part of the inner circle of the National Basketball Players Association (NBPA), a fledgling union advocating players' rights. Playing conditions at that time just weren't appropriate for a professional league. Players didn't have health insurance. We always stayed in second-class hotels. Teams refused to send their trainers on the road trips. Players didn't get paid for preseason. And after the all-star game, you didn't even have twenty-four hours before the season started back up. Jack came to me because drastic changes were necessary. He wanted to know if I'd take over the job of the Royals' team rep to the players union.

The history of the problems between players and owners was long and complicated. Bob Cousy had helped start the union in 1954. That year, players openly threatened to strike on the afternoon of the all-star game. An immediate meeting with league president Maurice Podoloff led to various improvements concerning contract and playing conditions, and an agreement was made to start an unofficial pension plan, in which teams matched the players' contributions. The owners agreed to the legitimacy of the players union, and the players agreed to further negotiate matters of conflict. The game went on as planned.

But the league's promise wasn't kept; there was virtually no headway in making the unofficial pension plan official. Whenever union leaders tried to meet with Podoloff, he stalled. Whenever he made a public statement on a labor matter, it was a lie. This happened for six, seven years. More than a few owners thought they were doing players a favor by having us out there, playing in front of people. Some players were signed for five thousand dollars—the same salary a guy would get for delivering mail. If an owner did not like a player for personal reasons, they got rid of him. Meanwhile, we were busting our asses up and down the courts every night, running our bodies into the ground, then traveling and living in pathetic conditions. It reached a point when players could not help but view what Podoloff and the owners were doing as anything but cold, calculating delays and lies. Keeping us at bay, patting us on the head, and paying us with pennies, even as they kept cashing checks written in our sweat and blood.

All-star games were the only time when a significant number of owners and players gathered in one city, so negotiations usually took place before the game. In 1963, though the union had rules and regulations, it was still emerging as an organization. Tom Heinsohn was the second NBPA president, and Larry Fleisher, after a long "meeting" with Tom at Jim Downey's Bar on Eighth Avenue in New York City, had just agreed to be our counsel. The all-star game that year was in Los Angeles, and one of our demands was to have Larry included in the meeting. The owners refused. They said he wasn't a player, and they did not want any outside people in the negotiations—especially a lawyer. Never mind that we told them he was an elected official in our union. Never mind that *any* business negotiations should involve a lawyer. Never mind that owners sometimes insisted on being on hand for the players' meetings. Our union had to fight with them tooth and nail just to get our own elected official to sit in on negotiations with them. But we fought and we clawed, and we came away from the 1963 game with the promise that when 1964 came around, Larry would be involved with the negotiations.

In September 1963, Podoloff stepped down, replaced by Walter Kennedy. At the time, Tommy Heinsohn and Larry Fleisher told Kennedy they wanted to meet at the all-star game and discuss the pension plan—a plan to put money away for players when they reached retirement age, or in case they were injured and had extraordinary medical expenses, as was the case with Maurice Stokes. In November, Kennedy relayed Heinsohn's request to the owners. They turned it down. The players got a letter from Kennedy saying that he'd inherited Podoloff's files and correspondence. Supposedly, letters show that in 1962, Podoloff had forwarded Tommy Heinsohn a specific pension plan. Kennedy says that the plan never was accepted, nor rejected, and ownership was not going to meet with the players until they get a response.

What Kennedy didn't know was that Tommy had repeatedly tried to meet with Podoloff, but had continually been brushed off.

The all-star game that season was in Boston. Walter Brown, president of the Celtics and the host of that year's festivities, had assembled the largest collection of basketball stars in the game's history. The original Celtics of the 1920s were going to be on hand, as well as young old-timers from the 1940s and 1950s, plus the game's current top twenty stars. The league had worked strenuously to set this up and had managed a real coup: Television cameras would be broadcasting the story to viewers across the nation, live and in prime time. The commissioner and owners saw it as an opportunity for professional basketball to step into the limelight, for the league to prove it was a first-rate enterprise. All weekend there were meetings, with league and television officials doing whatever they could to make sure the night would be spectacular.

The morning of the game, Tom met with Fred Zollner, owner of the Detroit Pistons, who represented the owners in whatever pension plan dealings there might be. While no lawyers for either side were on hand, John Kerr of the Philadelphia 76ers, the Knicks' Tom Gola, and San Francisco's Guy Rodgers—the union's pension plan committee—sat in on the proceedings, during which a compromise was made and an agreement reached. If the league's players voted to accept the plan, its implementation would be taken up at the next owners' meeting—possibly in February, more likely in May. This was accepted by the four players at the meeting, and it looked like all was well.

Except none of this had been done in the presence of Larry Fleisher—which we'd fought to have.

Larry heard about the agreement and asked to see a contract. Tom told him nothing had been signed. That afternoon, Larry called Walter Kennedy three times, wanting to discuss this. Each time, he was told that Kennedy was in owners' meetings, ostensibly to discuss changes to the league's constitution. Walter Kennedy never so much as returned his phone call.

As all this was going on, a snowstorm was ravaging the Midwest and sweeping up and down the East Coast.

I'd been on hand for the birth of my first child, Shana, in 1960. Now my wife was expecting our second. But Wayne Embry, Jerry Lucas, and I had been voted into the all-star game. There was no maternity leave in those days. I didn't like it, but there was nothing I could do.

Wayne, Jerry, and I set out for Boston on Monday, the day before the game, but impossible landing conditions in Boston forced our plane to detour into Chicago's O'Hare Airport. There, we were told, there was an eight-hour backlog of departing flights. A few reporters, as well as the Royals publicity director, were on the same flight. Now we all were stranded. Bailey Howell soon joined us. Detroit's all-star forward also had been detoured into O'Hare, although, admittedly, Bailey was as concerned with who was paying his per diem as he was with getting to the game.

All flights into Boston were eventually cancelled, and, after much wrangling, our group ended up on a plane to Washington, D.C., where in the wee hours of the morning, we checked in to a nearby hotel, just in time to get wake-up calls from the front desk.

We headed to the train station for the 6:30 express. All told, it took thirty-two hours to travel from Cincinnati to Boston.

But the same thing was happening to players everywhere. Bob Pettit, the Players Association's vice president, didn't get into town until the middle of Monday afternoon. Same thing with Elgin Baylor. My group took a train to Boston, but it did not arrive until 4:00 P.M. Hardly any players checked into our hotel until 5:00 P.M., four hours before the game's scheduled tip-off time.

We'd already had meetings and discussed plans to strike the game. With or without the snow and delays, guys were prepared to boycott the game, if that's what it took to get a signed deal for a pension.

Once more, player reps arrived. Tom Heinsohn, John Kerr, Tom Gola, and Guy Rodgers met with Larry Fleisher, Elgin, me, Bob, and the rest for a hurried meeting.

At about 6:00 P.M., Walter Kennedy heard a knock on the door of his hotel room. Tom Heinsohn and Bob Pettit demanded to see him. They said he had to meet with Larry Fleisher at 6:30, or else there wouldn't be a game.

Kennedy said he couldn't, but if it was important, they could meet in ten minutes. So a bunch of calls were made, and soon Larry, Tom, Bob, Bill Russell, and Lenny Wilkens were in Kennedy's hotel room, demanding a meeting with all of the owners. We wanted the promises of the morning—i.e., the discussed pension plan—put on paper, and we wanted that piece of paper to be signed.

Walter Kennedy was at a loss for words.

He assured the guys. In the course of the day, he had spoken to representatives of all of the clubs. It would all be taken care of.

He spent a while telling the guys this, making sure that everyone was on board, and that the game was going to go on as scheduled. Finally, Larry and Bob and the rest left the hotel room.

It's been reported that at 6:30 P.M., the players union informed Walter that we weren't going to play that day. That's a lie. The game was scheduled for a 9:00 P.M. tip-off. At 8:00, every player was inside the Boston Garden, half-believing that a contract was going to be signed, half-expecting to play, but also prepared in case something went wrong.

At 8:25 P.M. Kennedy came in. He waited until guys from the Eastern and Western squads all gathered in the same dressing room.

"We have a problem," he said.

Walter stood there and fidgeted, obviously uncomfortable, and explained that he'd met with the owners. Walter began to retell the owners' version of the entire history of our pension negotiations. He said that this afternoon, Fred Zollner went to the other owners and recounted everything that had happened in that first morning meeting. Based on that meeting—and on the assurances that Zollner gave during it—Kennedy said the owners felt everything was settled. They felt Fred, in conjunction with our committee, had reached an agreement. That was good enough for now. All documents would have to wait. There weren't going to be any more meetings. Nothing was going to be signed tonight.

Walter was sorry. He really felt bad about all this. But we had his word. This was all going to get taken care of. He understood our complaints. He was with us on the pension matter, on our concerns about having trainers with us on the road, and on other issues as well. Meanwhile, we had a game to play tonight. The place was sold out. A national prime-time audience was waiting. Walter kept talking. Legitimately impassioned, he kept on until finally, he was inspirational in tone, desperate in fervor.

We thanked him and asked him to leave.

Then we kicked everyone out of the room except for ballplayers.

The union leaders—Tom Heinsohn, Bob Pettit, and I—stood at the front of the room. We said, "Look. This is where we are. This is what we have to do. If you want to go out there and play, we will never get anything. If we go on the court on their promises, we will never have anything at all."

It was quiet for a while. Slowly one person spoke up, then another. Soon guys were remembering just how much the owners had stalled over the years. Some guys weren't so sure. Kennedy had said all the right things, hadn't he? But then hadn't Maurice Podoloff made promise after promise too? Was this new commissioner really different, or was he pulling a con? The energy of discourse rose through the room, with one person's anger feeding off another. Frustration poured out. How long had we been trying to get this thing resolved? But nothing was resolved. Hadn't we told them we wanted our lawyer in the meeting? Hadn't they said yes? Yet they made sure to have the meeting without him. Those guys didn't want us to have proper representation—then, when we asked for a pension contract, when we asked for basic rights, rights that we deserved, they could respond, "Sure, we'll take care of it, just not today." Plain and simple, they could not see far enough past their own bottom lines to understand that taking care of players was progress, a step toward the league moving forward. They didn't want to see it. Did not care about the forest, so long as they had control of the trees.

Every few minutes, Haskell Cohen, the league's public relations man, tried to bust in the room. The game was supposed to start soon, he'd say. Television people were getting nervous. If we did not come out, they were going to kill the game. The league would never be on television again. This would be the end of the NBA.

He left, and then Red Auerbach came in and threatened to fire his players. Bob Short of the Lakers threatened his stars, Elgin Baylor and Jerry West. If they didn't come out and play, Short was going to fire them. They would never play in this league again.

Introductions were scheduled for 9:00 P.M. It was 8:50, and we had to make a decision. Television executives were running back and forth between our locker room and courtside, where the commissioner and the other owners had gathered.

Finally, Walter Kennedy left courtside and came into the locker room.

"Larry can draw up the papers," he said. "Have them sent to my office tomorrow."

He left, and we had another vote. Five minutes later, Bob Pettit came out of the dressing room and notified the league president that the game would proceed. The network delayed the start of the game by fifteen minutes, without saying a word to the viewing public at home.

If we had had more time, we might not have played at all. I was still suspicious. We'd had similar promises from Podoloff. I told the press that if progress wasn't made, it was possible there wouldn't be an all-star game. "I know this," I said. "I won't sign my contract."

The game? Well, it didn't have anything close to the drama we'd just been through. Some of the anticlimax could be attributed to the snowstorm and travel fatigue. A lot more, obviously, originated in the showdown we'd just been through—guys simply couldn't get their heads into playing ball after that kind of drama. After all that planning, the league's big showcase night was crowned by a truly lackluster game. Midway through the second quarter, the game was tied when my East squad went on an 11–2 run. We led by ten at half and ended up taking the game, 111–107. For the second time in my career, I received the game's most valuable player trophy. I couldn't have cared less, to be completely honest with you. My mind was on happenings back in Cincinnati and Bethesda Hospital, where my wife was delivering a healthy baby girl, Tia.

Despite all the drama I just described, all-star games weren't sideshows back then, though that's what they've become now. The players come for all the parties before the game, and the league likes to busy itself with gimmick after gimmick: rookie games and guys dunking over chairs and the like. Then the game starts, and players show off and cruise. It's a big popularity contest, and that's a problem. Any time you get the fans to vote for players, you don't get a real all-star game. Fans pick guys they like. Which means the guys who dunk the most on the highlight shows. In 2003, they picked Vince Carter, even though he'd been hurt all year. They picked forty-year-old Michael Jordan, just to put him on the team. They picked Yao Ming to start over Shaq. Yao's got tremendous potential, but he's a rookie, and right now nobody could possibly claim that he's better than Shaq. Players don't like it, but the league tells you to be humble when things like that happen. I'll tell you what. If something like that happened to me, I'd say I don't want to play.

At the all-star game in 1963 in Los Angeles, a problem arose before the game started because Bob Cousy and I were on the same team, we'd both been voted to start, and we both wore the same number—fourteen. Some guy came in and told me that he was going to give me a jersey with the number twenty-four on it. This was right before the game. Everyone was in the locker room. I said, "Wait a minute. Twenty-four is Sam Jones's number." I turned to Sam, the great Celtics guard.

"Sam. Isn't this your number?"

"Well, yeah."

"Don't let anyone wear your number, Sam."

The equipment manager told me, "Well, Bob's on the team, and he wears number fourteen, so we gave him the number."

I said, "Put fourteen-X on one, with tape. Put it on my jersey," I said.

"When the game is over, I can take the taped X off and have the jersey."

It might sound petty, but it bothered me that they were going to take it upon themselves to make the decision and not consult me, or Bob, or anyone, just treat me like a stepchild and think I wasn't going to say anything about it. I mean, what did it matter if he had fourteen and I had fourteen? Everybody knew who we were. I'm a six-foot-five black man. Bob Cousy is a six-foot-one white guy. Nobody was going to confuse us.

One thing I learned about organized sports was that if you let someone take advantage of you once, they were going to walk over you whenever they could. Even on something small like this, I wasn't going to back down. If they thought I was, they had the wrong person.

Anyway, we both ended up wearing number fourteen throughout the game. So it worked out fine.

The season picked back up, and so did we. The Big O and Jerry Lucas led in scoring versus Los Angeles at home, with Arlen Bockhorn frustrating Jerry West into an awful shooting night and just eight points. In a matchup against a vastly improved Hawks team, I was in and out of foul trouble; we lost by one in a heartbreaker despite my scoring forty points. The box score shows that we got our revenge. In a game against New York that was played in Detroit (don't ask me why), I had eleven assists before halftime, on my way to eighteen, and we blew out the Knicks, our eighth win in nine games against New York. The next night we blew out the Celtics again. Two nights later we ran into Baltimore, winners of six straight. We beat them going away. Suddenly, we were riding our own hot streak. I could be proud of twenty-one assists against the Knicks. Put on a show in Philadelphia. Adrian Smith, my sly and dangerous partner in the backcourt, had sixteen points and ten assists, and we beat San Francisco, marking our twelfth straight win, enough to cut Boston's lead in the Eastern Division to one-and-a-half games.

One of the things you wish for as a professional athlete is the chance to play on a team with other talented guys. If I am going to play a pick and roll, I'd rather have Jerry Lucas out there, because I know that if they double-team me, I can pass to him with confidence that he'll score. If they play behind his pick, I'll be open. If they hesitate, we'll be able to read the situation and properly respond. We've reached a point in today's game where too many guys don't understand this. They may already be millionaires, but they think the way to make a name for themselves—to get the bigger contract, the shoe commercial, the endorsement gold—is through stats. And the way to get stats, they figure, is to hog the ball and play for themselves. The truth is, if the game's played correctly, by guys who understand how to play, everyone's stats are going to be better, and the team is going to win.

Prior to the 1964 season, I had routinely been in the top three in every statistical category, other than rebounding and blocked shots. But my performance that season was something else. I averaged 31.4 points a game, 11.4 assists, and 9.9 rebounds—missing another triple-double season by what amounts to less than a rebound a game. I also led the league in free-throw percentage and was among the leaders in minutes played. It was without a doubt my best season as a pro, and a huge part of that had to do with the guys I was out there with. Jerry Lucas topped the league in field-goal percentage, was fourth in rebounding, and averaged eighteen points a game, placing him fifteenth best in the league and good enough to net him rookie-of-the-year honors. Wayne Embry averaged just under eighteen points a game. Jack Twyman popped in fifteen and a half a clip. We were the highest-scoring team in the league, led the NBA in total points, points per game, field-goal percentage, and assists. We were second in rebounding. Third in free-throw percentage.

I wish I could say that it was good enough to get us a title, that we were able to keep winning at the torrid pace we set in February. But during the final month of the season, we came back to earth. Without any legitimate bench help to relieve our forwards, we just didn't have the legs to maintain the breakneck, high-speed offense. Though we still had high moments (mine included a game where San Francisco's coach Alex Hannum tried to guard me with six-foot-ten Wayne Hightower), our big men ground down. We finished the regular season with a 55–25 record, the second-best record in the league, and ended up four games behind Boston in the Eastern Division. It was the best record in Royals' history. We set a new home-attendance record and made it to the conference finals for the second consecutive season. But in the end, without Boozer, we had no answers for Tommy Heinsohn, and the Celtics took care of us pretty easily in five games, cruising with an average margin of victory of about ten points a game.

Jerry Lucas has said that he's thought that Royals team was one of the great teams in NBA history, and he feels it's a shame we'll never be considered an elite team because we did not win the title. I'd agree, but with a caveat: It's a shame we didn't have a chance to stay together and see if we *could* win the title.

Tom Grace disagrees. He's always claimed, publicly, that Bob Boozer wasn't playing enough, and the team needed to try and make some sort of move to get over the hump. It was one of Tom Grace's final big moves while in charge of the team, and he was criticized for years about it. And while I always liked Tom, I have to say, he should have been criticized. It was a bad trade. Cost us the championship. Instead, Boston won their sixth straight.

Nonetheless, on March 22, 1964, I was awarded the President's Trophy, the National Basketball Association's most valuable player award. It was a special honor because other NBA players voted on the award (you couldn't vote for a guy on your own team). I ended up with sixty of a possible eighty-five first-place votes, and 362 points on the scoring system (a first-place vote got you five points; second, three; third, one). Wilt Chamberlain placed second in the voting with nineteen first-place votes and 215 points. Bill Russell, who'd won the last three years, finished third with eleven firsts and 167 points. My margin of victory was the largest on record at that time.

I have to say, the whole thing was a complete surprise. I'd been first-team all-NBA for four straight years and was pretty much recognized as the best all-around player in the game, but no matter how well I'd played, I never really thought about getting the MVP. For one thing, I did not think about personal awards—I was a team player. I worried about wins and losses. More significantly, I didn't worry about the MVP, because it was impossible for anyone other than a center to get consideration for the award. For example, Jerry West never won the MVP. Not only because of the position, I think, but because Bill and Wilt were just too dominant. They were synonymous with the NBA back then, meeting in the NBA finals year after year, going at it in those battles that, even as you watched them being played out live, you just knew were legendary. In many ways, they were the league. And the players' voting reflects this dominance—nine of the ten MVP awards handed out during the 1960s went to one of them.

Obviously, I had a great individual season in 1964. Our team was a title contender, even if we fell short. I also had a significant role in the union's all-star game showdown. So I guess there are decent reasons that Bill and Wilt didn't have a clean sweep.

At the same time, losing a chance at the title ate at me.

———————

THAT SEASON represented a crux in my professional life in many ways, for it was a year of apexes, prophetic moments, and telling incidents. The best team in Cincinnati Royals' history was one that lost a chance at the championship because of our front office's bungles. The most valuable player of both the league and the all-star game moved to the forefront of the struggle for players' rights. Over time that involvement would result in a major lawsuit filed against the league. It would also lead to my testimony before the United States Senate and result in previously unknown legal freedoms for basketball players and unparalleled changes in the business of basketball. At the same time, inside the league's corridors of power, my union position would get me labeled as a malcontent and a troublemaker by the owners—and this label would cost me plenty. It would subtract years off my career.

Meanwhile, the NBA was starting, slowly, to catch on with the public. In 1965, a decent television deal finally got signed. ABC agreed to broadcast games on a weekly basis for six hundred thousand dollars a year, with the fee jumping to a million a season if the relationship went on for the contract's full five years. By highlighting big-city teams such as New York and Boston and stars like Wilt and Earl Monroe and Jerry West (a forerunner of a strategy that served NBC and Michael Jordan so well during the 1990s), the games started to generate interest—the ratings were respectable.

The league expanded to twelve teams in 1966. The next year, in 1967, another league, the American Basketball Association (ABA), announced itself with an expensive booze-filled press conference, and a red, white, and blue basketball. George Mikan, who ran the conference and became the new league's president, brought a certain amount of credibility with him because of his Hall of Fame career (he was the game's first towering center) and because of his business acumen. The ABA ran for a raucous, turbulent ten years and transformed the game of basketball in all sorts of ways.

When it started, the ABA was perceived as a rogue, outlaw league, with a wild, freelancing, playground style of game (they could only manage to sign guards and had few quality big men) and that colorful, twirling basketball (someone once said it should be on a seal's nose). Because the ABA did not have a television contract, they were dependent on ticket sales to stay in business. Their franchises tried everything and anything to get people in the stands. They introduced the three-point basket to the game, the dunk contest, and all-star weekend extravaganzas. Where the NBA was seen as a walk-it-up, pound-the-ball-inside game, the ABA was loose, flying, and freewheeling—all playground moves and three-point bombs. Teams may have folded, moved, or changed ownership constantly, but their front offices also set new standards in promotional creativity: giving out posters at games and thousands (if not millions) of red, white, and blue basketballs to children. They also delved into the realm of surreal and bizarre promotions. The Miami Floridians were the first to dress up pretty dancers in tight uniforms and have them perform dance routines, the Indiana Pacers had a cow-milking contest during one of their halftimes, and the New York Nets actually tried a Gerbil Night. The first five hundred fans received a free rodent.

The ABA came out of the gate aggressively. They stole the flashy young star, Rick Barry, from the San Francisco Warriors. They broke with all established protocols, signing Spencer Haywood while he was still an underclassman. Julius Erving went to the unheralded University of Massachusetts, so few knew just what an important and charismatic star he would become. But when the ABA signed him after his sophomore season, the league found a savior. Artis Gilmore soon joined Julius, along with skywalking David Thompson and high school phenom Moses Malone. Because they needed quality players, the ABA also took on Doug Moe, Connie Hawkins, and Roger Brown—players whose alleged connection with a point-shaving scandal resulted in being (wrongly) banned from the NBA.

The ABA wasn't entirely made up of stars—not even close. For all their coups and major signings, they also had to scramble to fill out rosters, and that resulted in a lot of eccentrics and way-outs, like Marvin "Bad News" Barnes, James "Fly" Williams, Art Heyman, and Wendell Ladner. A combination of three-ring circus and publicity magnet, the league seemed to make news every day, every week, including multimillion-dollar contracts, one after another. It did not matter if a contract announced at fifty thousand dollars a season actually paid only five thousand dollars of it that year. The announcement was what mattered to the ABA and the newspapers.

A lot of the ABA's bluster was smoke and mirrors. Their league did not have much money. Teams were constantly rolling the turnstile figures ahead. And if you took a microscope to their agreements, you saw that the big contracts were phantoms. Let's say a guy signed a million-dollar contract. He's going to play eight years and be paid a million bucks. Do the math and that comes out to $125,000 a season. But wait. In fine print, the contract states that $80,000 of *each year's* salary is deferred. So really, our supposed millionaire is only receiving $45,000 annually. That's for each season, for eight years—during which time, you can bet that other players salaries will have jumped ahead, inflation will have come into play, and there will have been a cost-of-living increase. But he's signed and sealed; his money is set. Once he completes his eight seasons, incremental, regular payments will begin. But even then, depending on the terms, the bulk of a player's contract might be strung out over as many as twenty-five years. One guy, Joe Caldwell, jumped to the ABA, played for five years in the league, and was in court fighting about his contract well into the 1980s.

Having said this, the ABA gave guys a choice. Until they came along, if you wanted to play professional basketball, the NBA was the only serious game in town. If the NBA had been fair in the way they ran their business, that would have been one thing. But NBA contracts had a clause known as the reserve clause that effectively bound a player to a team for life. The only way a player could leave was if he was traded; when a contract was up, the only team he could negotiate with was the team that held his contract. If your team presented you with a ridiculously low new contract, there wasn't much you could do about it. Even if you were one of the best players in the game, your hands were tied. The salaries weren't so high that you could afford to miss a year. So long as you wanted to play professionally and also eat, you had to make a deal.

Such was the case in 1965. My original contract had ended. At this point, I'd been first-team all-pro for five straight years and won the MVP award. I visited with Jake Brown, talked with him about how things were going, and figured out a basic outline for what I wanted. J. W. had done my first contract with the Royals, and we always wrote my contracts. But aside from that first deal, I'd sat down with management and handled my own negotiations. Tom Grace, who I'd never had any problems with in negotiations, was out as the Royals vice president. Instead, about three weeks before the season started, I sat down with general manager Pepper Wilson.

I asked for a ten-thousand-dollar raise.

Royals management countered with an insultingly small offer, for basically the same amount of money I'd played for the previous season. Take it or leave it, I was told.

At the time, Wilt Chamberlain and Bill Russell were the two highest-paid players in the game—Wilt had signed a contract for one hundred thousand dollars; Bill Russell, befitting their rivalry, for a single dollar more. I wasn't seeking that kind of money. Rather, I based what I asked for on what I thought I contributed, what I thought my value was to the team. When we sat down to negotiate, Pepper told me that my income compared to the Royals' gate was high. I answered right back that Wilt played on a team that wasn't much more solvent than the Royals, and he managed to get paid top dollar. I said I wasn't asking for his salary level; I'd taken into consideration the team's overhead when I made my request. At the same time, I told management, I am in the same position as the guys who owned the team. Running a team is a business for them. Well, my business is playing. I'd performed as well as any player ever had, and the team needed to pay me accordingly. If they couldn't, then they shouldn't be in business.

I was told the matter wasn't up for negotiation.

If there was another league (this was a couple of years before the ABA formed), I might have jumped to it as soon as I left the office. Instead, I did what I could do, which was to hold out. I didn't call them. They didn't call me. It was a cold war, and it stretched for days. For a week. Two. "Listen," one anonymous Royal told *Sports Illustrated*, "they can cut me twenty-five percent and give it to Oscar if it means bringing him back. That's how important he is to us." It's probably a good thing that the guy did not identify himself or re-peat that sentence around the front office. They might have done it.

I called one of the reporters I knew in New York and said I wanted to be traded.

The way the Royals front office dealt with negotiations angered me more than their ridiculous contract offer. At this point in my career, I said, I deserved respect, not ultimatums. They had refused to negotiate. They'd come to the table with a crazy, ridiculously low offer and refused to budge. They were the ones putting pressure on me. If I want to make any deal at all, if I want to play ball and help the team, now I'm the one who has to cave. On top of this, management started leaking untruths in the press, in-flating my demands and publishing my salary. In one statement, manage-ment would say it was unethical to discuss contract negotiations in the press. In the next sentence, the same general manager would discuss the details of my existing contract.

Look, if you ask any of my friends, they'll be more than happy to tell you how frugal I am. Believe me, they'll pile on the stories. Art Hull has al-ways said that I was the tightest guy with a buck that he'd ever seen. He once watched me spend an hour looking around for a nickel that I dropped on the carpet. He loved telling and retelling that story, but always was quick to add, "On the other hand, Oscar's generous to a fault with his time, which is often much more valuable. If I asked Oscar to come over to the house and help me move out a piano, he'd be over and spend hours tugging and bending and hauling, maybe risking a shoulder injury."

I wasn't going to be bullied or blackmailed by the Royals management. I told the press I was negotiating a barnstorming tour. I said I was going to play locally, out on the West Coast, maybe in Florida. It wasn't true, but the Globetrotters were still around so there had to be some money to be made in touring. Why not find out?

"They don't seem to want me to play," I told reporters. "They don't seem to care. Maybe they figure they will penalize me. Maybe that's their strategy."

Five days before the season opened, I came to contract terms with management. I signed for about seventy thousand dollars, various bonuses based on the gate, and the use of a car.

Two seasons later, we went through the entire standoff again.

That year I ended up missing training camp and the entire exhibition season. The press in Cincinnati started to heap abuse on me. *Greedy* was the word they chose.

When I sat down with Pepper Wilson that year, I said, "If I am greedy, I learned from you."

Management just looked at me. What could they possibly say? Who is greedier—the guy who wants to get paid what he is worth, or the team that indentures its players through perpetually unfair and rigged contracts and refuses to pay those players what they are worth?

The truth is, management in Cincinnati wasn't very effective. Before I ever came into the league, they had a chance to draft Bill Russell, and they chose not to do it. They whiffed on Willis Reed. They had the number one draft picks for two straight years—Bob Boozer and Jerry Lucas. Those guys signed with other leagues; hell, the only reason they ever came to the Royals and made us a decent team was because the ABL folded and they had nowhere else to go. In 1967, when the ABA first formed, the first pick of their draft was a six-foot-nine forward named Mel Daniels. Mel ended up being one of the best players in the ABA. I believe he won their MVP award in the league's second year, and I know that his jersey was among the first to be retired by the Indiana Pacers. Well, guess what team had Mel's NBA rights? Guess what team he abandoned so he could join a league that, at that point, did not even exist?

Reporters always called Pepper Wilson one of the most popular general managers in the league. Pepper was a nice man, but maybe all the other general managers loved him so much because he couldn't make a good draft pick, couldn't swing any shrewd trades. If I gave you a list of the players Cincinnati drafted while I was with them, you'd have to be a hard-core basketball fan to recognize any of them.

By contrast, the Celtics would reload and restock. Tom Heinsohn's gone? Here comes Don Nelson. Sam Jones is retiring? Here comes John Havlicek. Here comes Jo Jo White. Some of it was luck. One year Tom Wood was sitting next to Red Auerbach at a draft meeting in New York. Boston had won the title again, so naturally they had the bottom choice. Auerbach turned to Wood and said, "What am I going to do? This is a pretty frail group left. . . . There's some kid from Ohio State here with a funny name—Havlicek—what do you hear about him?"

Wood told him, "All I know is that our scout claims he's a better ballplayer than Lucas, but we've already got Lucas. So it doesn't make any difference."

"Well," says Auerbach, "he's only six four and awfully short for the pros. I guess I've got no other choice. What the hell. I'll take him."

So help me, that's how the Celtics stumbled onto Havlicek.

If you look at professional basketball and how a team builds a winning franchise, it's pretty simple. You have to restock your team with good draft picks, and you have to make key trades. The teams that don't, don't win. Flatly put, we could not do it. After we traded Bob Boozer, we traded other key players. We got rid of Tom Hawkins. Fought with Happy Hairston. Management kept bringing in guards to replace me when we needed forwards and centers. We got rid of one forward, Bob Love, because he had a speech impediment. The team thought he was dumb, so they traded him to Chicago. Of course, he became a superstar there. We had one pick, Larry Chaney, from Arkansas, who wasn't married. But we drafted Dave Zollner, who was married. Larry Chaney was a far better player, but we kept Dave, because he was white and was married. That's how the Cincinnati Royals did things. We played almost a third of our regular-season home games in

Cleveland because Lou Jacobs owned the arena there and wanted to sell hot dogs in Cleveland. That's what mattered to our ownership.

Our front office wanted it both ways. On the one hand, you weren't going to receive proper medical attention if it meant missing a game. On the other hand, when it came time to negotiate a contract, they were more than happy tell you that your numbers were down. Clearly, if you're playing injured, of course your numbers are going to be down.

In the end, what the Royals wanted was that you help the team win, but always under their terms. They wanted you to do well, but not too well.

If you want to number-crunch it, there can be no doubt of what I accomplished. Over the course of my first five seasons in the league, I had one triple-double season (1962) and was a fraction away from it a second time (1964). If you consider my totals for all five of those seasons, you'll find that for five years of basketball, I actually averaged a triple-double—it comes out to 30.3 points, 10.6 rebounds, and 10.4 assists. After I'd averaged a triple-double for five seasons, the Royals hadn't wanted to give me a ten-thousand-dollar raise. For my first six seasons, I still averaged a triple-double—but I had a holdout that season as well. Check the numbers through my first eight seasons, and I'm only a fraction away. Eight seasons.

As for the Cincinnati Royals' records: In the 1965 season, we finished the year with a 48–32 record. In the 1967 season, we slipped to 39–42. The next season, when I missed training camp, immediately pulled a hamstring, and missed some games early, we were 39–43.

It's not easy to show up at training camp each season and know in the back of your mind that you are on a team that is only good enough to go to the second round of the playoffs. The competitor inside of you thinks that you are going to get it done this season—this is the year you will play for the title. Every player in sports thinks that way. But to win you also have to have good management. If they don't acquire the right players or make the right trade at the right time, you won't win championships.

If you are coaching a track team and considering a runner who runs a hundred meters in twelve flat, you can't take him. He's not going to win.

When I was with the Cincinnati Royals, our front office loved twelve-second sprinters. I felt I was playing at the top of my game. I thought I was doing exactly my job, being a professional, all-pro guard. So eventually I thought, *Well, if the guys running this team can't see the forest through the trees, what can I do about it?*

My way of dealing with our mediocrity was to go on with my job, to take care of my own business. After a while, I started to find my own challenges inside the game, personal goals and ways to keep myself focused. Then when the road trips and home games ended, I went back to Eaton Lane, spent time with my wife, played with my kids. I rarely said one word to Yvonne about the Royals. She was busy with our kids and other problems. She still understood my predicament. "He doesn't voice these things, even to me," she once told a reporter. "But I have the impression that he's competing against himself now, even more than against another player or team. Just to see how much better he can be, how he can do something a little differently and still do it well. Just to keep accomplishing and improving."

CHAPTER ELEVEN

The Sixties Continued
1963–1968 (Part Two)

I'M OFTEN ASKED WHAT I THINK of today's player's salaries. Well, when I played, I made a top salary. I had to fight for it, but I made it. And as the president of our union, I was fighting for all player's salaries. After everything we went through, how could I possibly complain about the salaries guys make today? It's true that today's average NBA player makes more than two million dollars. It's also true that guys at the end of the bench have million-dollar, multiyear contracts. And if you ask them, *Are you worth it*, I'd bet that most of them will answer, *Yeah, I am*. In years past, players strove to win championships. Now you hear more and more players say, "I got mine"—implying that they don't care about anyone else, then proving it with extravagant lifestyles. But whether I agree with those guys or not, I'm never going to complain about a player making money. The fact is, the only reason a guy coming off the bench is worth millions of dollars is because some owner out there is willing to pay him.

Right now, the league is in something of a flux, and finances are a big part of it.

During the 1990s, David Stern and the NBA rode Michael Jordan's popularity. But it also utterly aligned itself with corporate boxes and white-collar ticket holders. While there's no shortage of charismatic young guys who can jump and dunk, nobody has captured the public's imagination the way Michael did. Nor are there any rivalries like Magic's Lakers against Bird's Celtics in the 1980s, or Michael's Bulls against Isiah Thomas's Bad Boys. Meanwhile, in its drive to accrue television money and ticket revenues, the league has abandoned free television in favor of cable deals. They've priced out most people from seeing a game—except corporate America.

In the last two years, professional basketball has seen two major trends: one, an influx of European players who coaches and commentators say are extremely well versed in the fundamentals and understand the game; two, the hyping of physically gifted high schoolers who eschew college for a chance at the pros.

Kids want to dunk and shoot from deep and dribble through their legs a hundred times, and there's nobody out there who is willing to teach them the right way to play or instill better habits. AAU and high school coaches don't do it. They're too worried about getting traveling teams together and playing in the best invitational meat-markets. College coaches are too busy promoting themselves and signing shoe contracts so that television cameras will capture their genius. Half of the coaches, whether it's on the high school or college level, are afraid that talented kids will leave if they discipline them. Indeed, so many college programs have such small graduation rates and are so thoroughly corrupt and embroiled in scandals that it's impossible to argue that kids shouldn't jump straight to the NBA.

Watch an NBA game tonight. You'll see players who can't make a reverse pivot. Can't make a crossover dribble. And the NBA's answer hasn't been additional coaching for these young guys. Rather, it's been to welcome top-notch high schoolers with open arms and shoe contracts and their own commercials.

The best players get to sit on the bench for three years or so, and if they have the work ethic and commitment (like Kobe Bryant or Jermaine O'Neal), they'll work hard and begin to figure things out for themselves. The rest? A developmental league was started for all the teenagers and college kids who make the leap before they're ready. But that's not a real answer, it's a cosmetic fix. The league's only a few years old, and already there are complaints that its coaches are like AAU and college coaches—more concerned with winning games and promoting themselves than with helping young players learn the game.

The result is something akin to Starbucks. Once Starbucks has put one of their coffee shops on every corner in the neighborhood, they go to another neighborhood. Once they've got the fifty states covered, they go overseas. Well, now the league's going overseas for players. Because those guys are being taught the game, for one thing. And then there are the marketing reasons. Why do you think the NBA went overboard welcoming Yao Ming? He's a good player right now. He's got potential, sure, but he's far from great. Even Yao knows this. But the NBA's thrilled to have an in with China.

Maybe I am coming from a different mindset. The current NBA is a multi-billion-dollar business. Teams travel in their own private planes, with luxury seats and individual DVD players set up for each team member. When I played, the job wasn't a routine one. But there was a routine to it, especially traveling. You grew accustomed to it.

On a typical trip, I'd lose all concept of what day it was. Say the team started off with a road game in Milwaukee. The plane left early in the morning on the day of the game, maybe 9:00 A.M. We'd check in to a hotel, then play the game, then head back to the hotel at around 11:00 P.M. The next morning, we'd take a bus and ride for hours, arriving directly at a Chicago hotel. The team checked in and rested before going to play the game and then headed back to a hotel. Afterwards, I'd hit a music club before the team's midnight curfew. The next morning, we have to get up early again, because we're flying to Portland, where we'll have a day off. Not a full day off, because we'd still work out that afternoon, shoot some, and talk about Portland's defense. That night I might grab a paper and go check out a band or one of the entertainers I'd met over the years, like Dizzy Gillespie,

Sam Cooke, James Brown, the Temptations, Smokey Robinson. I'd go to see them perform, and maybe head backstage afterwards to say hello. And then back to the hotel before curfew.

Most nights in the hotel room, I'd flip the television on and watch until I fell asleep. Wayne used to wonder how I could watch so much crap on TV. I used to ask him how he could sleep as much as he did. Then Bob Boozer might come by for some soul talk.

The next night, we'd play in Portland. After just a few trips up and down the floor, I knew who'd been out past curfew or whatever. I know whenever I let myself get hooked by a late-night movie on television, I sure felt it the next day.

You learned to adjust to life on the road, because your nights and days were turned upside down. Maybe breakfast would be at 1:00 P.M. Dinner might be after the game, as late as 11:00 or midnight. It took me years, but I finally learned to sleep on a plane. You simply had to get some sleep whenever you had a chance. I also learned about the art of packing light. I could get ready to go to Los Angeles for a week right now in fifteen minutes.

Our next game would be in Los Angeles, but since we'd arrive in that city at noon, there'd be no shoot-around. Maybe we'd have a team meeting. We'd play the game. Whenever we stayed in Los Angeles for a whole night, one of my old high school teammates, Norm Crowe, was happy to take me in and give me a home-cooked meal. After a while, I knew people in every city we played. Most of them were friends from my years at Crispus Attucks. I was always reluctant to bother them though—I never wanted to be an imposition, for one thing. For another, I had my own travel routines and did not want to break them. And most of the time, we went back to the airport right after our game. From Los Angeles, we then flew to Houston for our next game. The flight would take off at 12:30 A.M. and be in the air through the night. With time changes and everything, we'd arrive at about 6:00 A.M., go to the hotel, and get a little rest. Then it was time to hit the arena, loosen up, and play the Rockets. It wasn't uncommon, in the middle of a long road trip, to forget exactly who you were playing, what city you were in. Suddenly, your mind would go blank and you'd have to think, "What day is it?"

Every city was its own adventure. The courts weren't like today's lacquered, standardized basketball courts. There were screws sticking up out of the old Cow Palace floor in San Francisco. Boston Garden's parquet was noted for, among other things, its dead spots. Celtics players used to lead you to them, and when you dribbled on a dead piece of wood, they'd be waiting; the ball would bounce low, or spring off to the side, and a Celtic would pounce. After a while you knew each court's idiosyncrasies and adjusted, much in the same way that pitchers track hitter's ballparks and the nooks and crannies of different fields.

Finally the game against Houston would end, and it would be time to head back to the airport, back to Cincinnati, flying all night, touching down at the break of dawn.

A grand total of five games in less than seven days, while also flying across the country and back: a typical road trip.

"Everything happens while he's away," Yvonne used to say. If the furnace broke down, I wasn't there. If the dryer detonated, I wasn't there. The year's most paralyzing snowstorm was bound to happen when I was out of town.

Our three healthy daughters were born in 1960, 1964, and 1969. I was playing in the all-star game in Boston when our second child, Tia, was born. Yvonne did an excellent job raising our kids. For a significant portion of the year, she did it alone. I wasn't there. If they needed disciplining, it was up to her. There wasn't much point in trying to catch me up and fill me in on things. Yvonne faithfully went to every home game, leaving the kids with a sitter. Our afternoons at home were casual. I couldn't do much during the season. I had to conserve my energy for the games. As often as not, on the day of a game, I'd have a noon meal or just sit back in my den, watch TV, and let the girls climb all over me.

I'm not complaining, mind you. Basketball provided my family with financial security. It allowed Yvonne and me to raise our daughters safely. The game gave me a lot of opportunities, knowledge I would never have gotten otherwise. I got to meet Princess Grace and different kings and queens. I've been all over the world. If it weren't for basketball, I would still be in Indianapolis doing menial tasks. Maybe I would have gone to a small college and gotten through. I'll never be ungrateful or unappreciative for what I achieved through basketball. Having said this, there was a price. The game exacted its toll in all sorts of ways.

More than earning money, meeting princesses, or visiting exotic locales, my reward was a simple fact: I played against the best generation of players, ever. It's true that a good chunk of my career was spent on teams that had no chance to win a title. It's true the road schedule was a physical and mental grind. But every night that I went out onto the court, I was out there playing with and against some of the best players who ever lived. There's nothing a competitor wants more than a challenge, to match himself against someone who's every bit as skilled and talented as he is. That's what kept me going every night.

We ushered in the modern era of basketball. You wouldn't have the game of basketball as we know it without us. We were cornerstones in building the game and the way it is played today. Today's player, whether he knows it or not, wouldn't be where he is without us.

We had Bill Russell and Wilt, the two dominant players in the history of the game. Jerry West was the best clutch player I ever saw, the best shooter, and one of the best competitors. His biggest talent, perhaps, was emerging at the right moment to take advantage of a well-timed pick or pass. Jerry hated to lose so much that you could see it transform him. Jerry and I were friends, but our rivalry was intense.

People always ask who was better: Magic Johnson, Larry Bird, or Michael Jordan? But they forget that those three never played against one another in matchups. Wilt Chamberlain played against Bill Russell. I guarded Jerry West. Our rivalry was especially entertaining, both to watch and to be a part of, because I played with such efficient and calculated focus, while Jerry was a great shooter. Bob Ryan, the renowned basketball writer for *The Boston Globe* has said that I developed more different skills than any other basketball player he ever saw, whereas Jerry may have had more desire.

America looked at Jerry fondly. Playing in L.A. with Wilt and Elgin on his team meant playing with a great cast. Nowadays, I regard Jerry as a basketball genius for what he did as the general manager of the Lakers. And the genius definitely has his work cut out for him in building the Memphis Grizzlies into a contending club.

It also must be said that Elgin Baylor took a backseat to no one. You could not stop Elgin from driving to the basket. Animal, vegetable, or glowing green radioactive minerals couldn't stop him. You sure couldn't outjump him, or hang in the air any longer than he did. Elgin was the first player in league history to score seventy points in a game. Elgin was the first and original high flier—the first man to show tremendous hang time and aerial dexterity. He was just unstoppable.

There were other great players as well. Bob Pettit was about the hardest-working rebounder the game's ever seen. Nate Thurmond was a gentle man off the court, but he intimidated everybody in the league. You didn't go into the paint when Nate was in there. There were all those great Celtics teams that I couldn't get past—Cousy and Heinsohn and Sam and K. C. Jones. There were guys like Chet Walker, Hal Greer, Rick Barry, and high-flying and always hustling Billy Cunningham. If you looked at Jerry Sloan today on the sidelines, coaching the Utah Jazz, you'd have no idea just what a tough, physical defender he was. We used to have wars; I brought the ball up, and he did all he could to keep me from scoring. How about Willis Reed? Everyone knows about his inspirational performance in the 1970 finals, when he gave those twenty-seven meaningful minutes on one leg to lead the Knicks to the championship. But how many people remember his feathery, left-handed jump shot, the commanding presence he was when healthy, or that he was the first player to be named the MVP of the all-star game, the regular season, and the playoffs in the 1970 season?

If the first half of the 1960s was spent bringing professional basketball to public legitimacy, the second half of the decade saw a broadening of the game. In part this was a natural extension of the rise and acceptance of the black professional athlete. In part it had to do with the widespread popularity of and technical advances in sports broadcasting and the natural ease with which basketball can be followed and appreciated on television. Consider the decade itself—a time of upheaval: nonviolence movements, campus radicalism, peace marches, the Twenty-fourth Amendment ("The right of citizens of the United States to vote in any primary or other election for President or Vice President, for electors for President or Vice President, or for Senator or Representative in Congress, shall not be denied or abridged by the United States or any state by reason of failure to pay any poll tax or other tax . . ."), and the 1964 Civil Rights Act. A decade of political assassinations and the rock revolution, of Vietnam, the women's liberation movement, youth culture, and drugs and experimentation in every shape and form. On any given day, you could turn on the news, read the paper, or just walk down a city street and get the sense that society itself was unraveling. I think this was reflected in the game of basketball too. Players like Bill Russell, Jerry, Elgin and the rest emerged at a time when talents and abilities were directed toward winning as much as they were to personal accomplishment. When society started moving in a different direction, and the health of the game was not necessarily at stake, creativity became a more distinct part of the game. I'm not saying, mind you, that guys didn't show flair when I was growing up. My brother Bailey was colorful; there were tons of guys at the Dust Bowl with playground moves to spare, and if you ever watched Marques Haynes dribble, you would know that there's nothing being done now that wasn't done fifty years ago. But those moves were for the playground.

As the 1960s progressed, this changed. The game and its players evolved. The ABA's reputation as an outlaw, playground league had its role in opening up the game. But be it ABA or NBA, now there was a new breed. Earl Monroe, Connie Hawkins, Walt Frazier, and Pete Maravich were guys who played with a distinct flair and personal style.

Earl led the way in many ways. Known alternately as "Black Jesus," "the Pearl," "Magic," and "Black Magic," Earl was a tremendous athlete and stunningly creative with the basketball. Bill Bradley once described him as "the ultimate playground player." It was a challenge to play against him. You never knew what he was going to do, and you had to be on your toes because you didn't want him to embarrass you. When you played against the Pearl, it brought out everything in you, and personal challenges like that were why you played the game.

Connie Hawkins was pure electricity. At six eight or six nine, he had these long arms and the largest hands you ever saw. He could palm the ball and wave it in front of you, doing all kinds of loops. The Hawk was one of the best leapers anybody ever saw, really a prelude to Dr. J. and Michael

Jordan. There was nothing either of them could do in the air that Connie couldn't. By all accounts he's the best playground player to ever come out of New York City and could have had a chance to be one of the all-time great players in basketball. He was thrown out of college and banned from the NBA for years for having a friendship with a known gambler, Jack Molinas. He lost the formative and prime years of his career to that scandal; I've always thought was wrong. Instead, he spent time with the Globetrotters, then in the ABA, where he was their first MVP. When he finally made it to the NBA in 1969, knee problems had slowed him up some, but he was still a force. He'd hang in the air and palm the ball and move it in these swooping loops that people loved. It was the Globetrotter in him.

On the floor, Walt "Clyde" Frazier was one cool basketball player and a great floor leader. Nothing flashy, mind you; he just played within himself and ran the Knicks. The Knicks had a loaded team in the late 1960s and early 1970s, featuring one great basketball player after another. He cemented their whole team with his easy, loping grace and his icy ability to read the court and run the show. Willis Reed, a Hall of Fame player, said, "It's Clyde's ball. He just lets us play with it once in a while." He's publicly said that he looked to me as a floor leader and tried to copy me. Off the court, Clyde was the embodiment of a different type of cool: broad-brimmed velour hats, wide-labeled crushed-velvet jackets, and a celebrated reputation for Rolls Royce sedans and nightclub prowling.

I couldn't possibly list that era's breakthrough and flashy players without including Pistol Pete Maravich. Pete came along at the tail end of the decade; in 1970, he broke my all-time collegiate scoring record when he played for his father, Press, at LSU. At LSU, his dad designed an entire offense that revolved around one player. Everyone else on the team fought just to get a shot here and there. That's not good basketball, and it shows in LSU's records while Maravich was there. They never made it to the final four. Didn't come close. When he came out of college, the Atlanta Hawks paid him more money than the rest of the team combined. That, in addition to his flashy style of play, created some problems for him with his teammates.

Pete had a great shot, and he could score. But he had defensive troubles. He could make a flashy pass, but he wouldn't always make the right pass. I remember once when Pete was on a fast break. He bowled the ball the length of the court to an open teammate. The man stood there and watched the ball roll out-of-bounds. Then he walked up court staring at Pete. I can understand why the guy did that. When you bust your ass to get open, a guy's got to throw you a pass that allows you to score. Otherwise why work so hard?

In some ways his style and story represents a cautionary one, especially given the tone and tenor of today's game. If you are going to work on dribbling and shooting and being flashy, you better be able to play all facets of the game. Too many young guys think that highlights are the game, or that the Nintendo version of basketball is actually the real thing. If you honestly believe you are going to shoot sixty shots a game, well, for your sake and your team's, you better be a complete player. You better be able to rebound. You better play some defense. Learn to pass the ball. Learn to get someone else in the game. The only way to win any games that matter is to make the rest of the players better. Pete never won a championship, not at any level. He was a reserve player on Larry Bird's first Celtics championship team, and it's really too bad that his knees gave out and he had to retire during that season. I didn't know him, but I always heard this haunted him somewhat. Pete had a hard life as an adult. He died playing pickup basketball a few years back.

Television doesn't show highlights from my era much anymore. The history of the game is for some other time, some other channel. When ESPN Classics does show a game from the 1960s or 1970s, the camera shots may not be as clear as they are now, but that doesn't mean the game is any better today. Conventional thinking among basketball fans is that basketball has become faster. Not true. The guys I played with could compete with today's players.

Players like Kevin Garnett, Tim Duncan, and maybe Dirk Nowitzki— six-foot-eleven and seven-footers with coordination and agility and the skills to play all five positions—probably represent the next step in the evolution of the game. I will concede that today's modern athletes certainly have the better diet. They also do a lot of weight training—although I don't know if you need to be able to lift five hundred pounds to play basketball. But find today's newspaper and check the box scores. Maybe the Dallas Mavericks average a hundred points a game. The scoring was much higher in my era than it is today. And that's without the three-point rule.

I played against some of the greatest defenders in the history of the game—Russell, Chamberlain, Nate Thurmond, Walt Bellamy—but still the scoring was a lot higher than it is today. Some so-called experts will tell you it's because of the coaches and athletes. I've seen basketball analysts say that principles of help defense are more advanced now and take advantage of all the athleticism. I say that's bull. If Jerry West was on his game, you couldn't stop him. I don't care what defense you were in.

Every modern coach has ties to the history of the game and uses strategies and defenses that are decades old. Everyone knows that Tex Winter is the guru of Phil Jackson's Triangle Offense, which Michael Jordan and Shaq swear by so faithfully. Well, Tex was Bob Boozer's head coach at Kansas State. Pat Riley learned about defense and winning hard from Knicks coach Red Holzman. And Tex and Red weren't doing anything new, either. They were coaching based on principles that had been around for years and years.

And if the athletes are so much better right now than ever before, shouldn't they be better on both ends of the court?

The difference, to me, is the quality of basketball skills and the level of basketball knowledge that we had back then. Plain and simple, ours were better.

It's something of a cliché to say that modern television and broadcasters are in love with the dunk. Commentators think that because a guy can dunk a ball, he's the greatest thing ever. Producers like to show the same dunk on highlight clips and video packages, edited quickly so the move is repeated four and five times.

I don't want to sound like some dinosaur: "In my day, we knew how to play, to dunk; we had to walk uphill both ways to get to the basketball court, and then when we dribbled, the ball rolled down the hill." Dunking's been part of the game for a long time. Many players I knew when I used to play at the Dust Bowl could dunk a ball. Gus Johnson tore down rims more than thirty years ago. I could list guy after guy who was a great dunker. It never meant anything to me but two points. A lot of them never dunked because it embarrassed a defender, and he'd take it out on them the next play. I rarely dunked, but I did do it once in a while in practice, just to show people I could.

But if you can dunk a ball, you are now the greatest player in the world. Gone by the wayside is ability to make a play or think about the game of basketball. Street lingo today translates "skills" as the ability to dribble the ball behind your back or off your knee. But knowing how to run a good fast break is a skill. So is busting your hump and getting out on the wing and filling the lane at the proper angle. Teams don't run the way we did anymore.

Knowing how to rub off a defender when you use a pick is a skill. Knowing how to feel a defender with your body and read the court to see where help is coming from is a skill. Knowing how to stay in control, pace yourself, and not use all your energy too early or give away all your tricks, that's a skill. Setting solid picks and knowing how to get yourself open from them; knowing how to hit a guy with a pass the exact moment he frees himself and how to get him the ball in a place and at a time that allows him to shoot in rhythm; getting position low on the post; boxing out; playing solid man-to-man defense while also knowing where the ball is—those are skills. Certain players in the game today have them—Jason Kidd and Tim Duncan are two, off the top of my head. But most younger players don't, not by a long shot.

Shaquille O'Neal is one of the greatest players of all time. He's big, strong, and fast. Shaq's go-to shot is a dunk. There's no doubt he would have gotten his share of dunks on Bill Russell. There were times he'd get position close to the basket, and there's nothing anyone could do about that. Bill was six nine, and he had long enough arms where he might have been able to front Shaq. He might have been able to deny him the ball from the side. He was smart enough and competitive enough that he could have played against him. Bill could exploit anything, make you rely on the weakest parts of your game. Shaq doesn't have much of a jumper. He has a jump hook but doesn't have the kind of full hook that would be unstoppable. (Hell, his jump hook might be unstoppable if he shot it more.)

And on the other end of the court, I doubt that Shaq could have defended Wilt Chamberlain.

———————

LONG AFTER MAURICE Stokes's bank account had been drained and his workmen's comp had dried up, he remained paralyzed in a Covington hospital bed, his therapy and treatment running thousands and thousands of dollars a year. Jack Twyman had declared himself Maurice's legal guardian and took on all of the responsibilities. One thing he did was contact sports writers from across the nation, most of whom joined in the cause. Pat Harmon of the *Cincinnati Post* wrote a column that brought in donations. My friend Milt Gross wrote a column about Maurice in the *New York Post* that brought in more than three thousand dollars. Cliff Keene of *The Boston Globe* knocked out a story, and a family sent a check for five hundred, which, their letter said, usually went for Christmas. Jerry Tachs—the same *Sports Illustrated* reporter who had caused me so much grief with his story when I was at Cincinnati—wrote a feature that brought in more than twenty-five thousand. Jim Murray at the *Los Angeles Times* and Bob Broeg of the *St. Louis Post-Dispatch* wrote pieces, both of which brought in thousands of dollars.

During the off-season, Jack also endured years of fund-raising lunches. Once he received a donation of two thousand cases of tomato sauce, delivered to a Cincinnati warehouse. The next week of Jack's life was spent as a new entrant in the wholesale food business, with the proceeds going to Stokes. Howard Cosell even brought Jack onto his ABC Christmas special in New York, which helped a lot. The big financial breakthrough, however, came via a soft-spoken man named Milton Kutsher. A huge basketball fan, Kutsher ran the Monticello Hotel in the Catskills in upstate New York—the same hotel that an NBA scout had wanted me to work at when I'd been recruited for college. Every year starting in 1959, Kutsher brought together thirty-five NBA all-stars, at their own expense, and held a giant fund-raiser basketball game. During the first ten years, the game at Kutsher's along with the columns and pro-

grams by the nation's sports media raised more than one million dollars, all
of which went toward paying Maurice Stokes's medical bills.

I'd first met Maurice at a dance at a place called Castle Farms here
in Cincinnati, back when I was in college. I'd seen him play a few times. I
did not know the man very well, but after his accident, I used to visit him
and cheer him up whenever I could. It wasn't the easiest thing, to see an
athlete of his ability in that situation. But like everyone else, I kept hoping
for the best. Soon enough I became involved with Kutsher's games, taking
on the responsibility of getting players to commit to playing, helping to
arrange their trips to and from the game, and maintaining the event's annual momentum. When Jack Twyman fell out of favor with Cincinnati
management and coach Jack McMahon, he retired from basketball in 1966.
I saw Maurice more and went out of my way to see that visiting players in
Cincinnati would take time and drop in on Maurice, making him feel welcome and cared for in the players' fraternity.

While Maurice was in the hospital, he regained some movement in
his upper body and began a series of arm and chest exercises to develop his
upper-body strength. With the help of a speech therapist, he also did a lot
of reading. History and poetry were his favorites. After Martin Luther King
died, Stokes had this put into writing:

> There are a great deal of people who get upset about the death
> of a great man. I have to admit that I used to be one of those
> people, but no more. He has left so many great memories that
> it makes one feel rather good whenever his name is men-
> tioned. You don't have time to remember any of the bad
> things that happened, if you remember the good things he left.

During the summer of 1965, everyone was up at Kutsher's for the
Stokes game. Tom Heinsohn met with Larry Fleisher and said he was going
to retire from basketball, which meant the Players Association would need
a new president. The two of them talked with Jack Twyman. At the time,
despite Walter Kennedy's locker-room promises at the all-star game, there
still wasn't any pension plan (the Kutsher's game was Maurice's pension).

Playing conditions were still dismal. It was obvious that there was a long and fierce fight on the horizon. Whoever was going to take over the union would have to be intelligent, dedicated to the players' interest, and willing to spend an enormous amount of time for the cause. It needed to be a star, the men agreed, a premier player, someone who played so well that the league couldn't punish him. Someone who would also impart courage to other players who were somewhat timid and insecure about their futures. Since there were more and more black players coming into the NBA, it also followed that the new head of the union should be black.

The three of them took me aside. I told them I was honored and flattered they'd asked.

For the next eleven years, whenever Larry called me and said, "O, hey, we need a meeting," I was there. Negotiations with the league were annual or semiannual; sometimes they were hectic and sometimes they were icy. Few and far between, sometimes they were protracted, drawn-out affairs, held through countless meetings over a stretch of seven or eight months. Between 1965 and 1976, I attended every one I could, though my term as president ended in 1974. If our union needed a meeting, I was there as well. It did not matter how much time it took, or whether I had to pay for the ticket out of my pocket. ("He was the worst guy in the world for billing the association for travel, telephone, or anything else," Larry once told an interviewer. "He spent big money of his own and spent free time on off days during the season.") The way I saw things, it was part of the job. If I wasn't willing to do this stuff, why should anybody else?

Larry used to say that I had the one great talent necessary for an effective labor negotiator: always distrust the other side. On one occasion, the league made an announcement of major consequence. Larry was four thousand miles overseas and could not be reached for comment. Knowing the first person the papers would contact would be me, he waited until he could get a paper, skipped to the sports page, and read a story that interviewed me for my reaction. "Oscar said word for word what I would have said." Larry and I shared one basic core understanding: When owners dealt with players, whatever they attempted was against our interests. That was our starting point. The league could prove that this was not the case, but we proceeded from that basic distrust.

By 1967, I understood the role of the media, as well as the necessity of using the press to get my message out to people. I realized that if we were going to get our side of the story out to people, I had to do it. This became essential when we got sick of waiting for the league to make good on their promises and went head-to-head with ownership again. Looking back, the issues seem obvious. We wanted a hospitalization and medical plan. We wanted an exhibition schedule that lasted ten games instead of fifteen. We wanted to be paid for these games. We wanted an end to regular-season Saturday night and Sunday afternoon back-to-back games. We wanted to establish a set schedule, limiting the number of regular-season games to eighty-one. We wanted the creation of an actual all-star break, as opposed to a schedule that had the regular-season games resuming on the day after the all-star game.

Most importantly, we wanted to end the reserve clause, which any rational person could see was patently illegal.

In truth, I believe the league with the red, white, and blue basketball, the ABA, presented a sufficient threat to ownership to compel them to change their thinking on most of the player-treatment issues. The changes may have been made grudgingly, but we did obtain a shorter schedule; we did get paid for exhibition games; we did get trainers on the road and an end to some of the excessive scheduling practices. Not because these things were wrong, but I believe because there were owners who were worried that key players would jump leagues if they felt they weren't being treated humanely. They were probably right about that.

As for the reserve clause, that war would rage for years.

AT THE TIME, there was a tremendous gap between the contributions of black players to the game and the public's acceptance of us outside the game. Matters such as our insurance and pension plans never registered as something the average fan cared about, let alone the idea that the black man scoring all those points and doing all those spectacular things deserved them. In this sense we were very much akin to the jazz performers in Las Vegas during the

1950s, who were allowed to play on the stages but could not stay in the hotels.

I have mixed feelings now when I watch a basketball game and see all the shoe commercials. On the one hand, a sneaker doesn't make you jump any higher or play any better. So it's more than a little disturbing to see black players peddling these $100 and $150 sneakers and promoting crass materialism. Perhaps more than anyone, inner-city kids thrive on basketball, and I think there's something vicious about equating basketball talent with expensive shoes.

Having said this, those commercials also can be seen as an indication of how far things have come. When I was playing, black athletes were never hired to do commercials or endorse products.

If the idea of an endorsement is to sign up the best players or the guys who were popular or charismatic, it naturally follows black players should have had offers. But about the only offer I had was a how-to book on basketball fundamentals that came out in 1964 (*Play Better Basketball*, it was called). Besides the book, I can remember only one other: Late in my career, I lent my name to an insurance company that recreated my childhood love of the game for a commercial. As for TV appearances, I did Curt Gowdy's *American Sportsman* show, going fishing with marine biologist Jack Casey and ABC. I also filmed an episode during the first season of *Greatest Sports Legends*. That's about it. Wilt showed up on Johnny Carson sometimes. Maybe Bill Russell every now and then. That was it for national appearances by black basketball players.

Converse sneakers were big back then. But they never used a black player to endorse their shoes. Same thing with Adidas. They would give you the shoe to wear for free, but that was all. I think Rick Barry was the first player Adidas paid for an endorsement. He didn't get much money, but there were posters of him in every sneaker and department store. Recently, Converse wanted to re-release their All-Star sneakers, with a retro campaign that used the legends of the game. When they contacted me, I said I did not want to be involved. When I was a star, they never came to me or asked another black person for an endorsement.

Some friends have told me that it's time to let bygones be bygones, that Converse has been through untold bankruptcies and ownership changes and is trying to right its corporate ship. Surely, my friends say, the people who run the company now have nothing to do with Converse's policies in the 1960s. If I were to associate myself with them, couldn't it be seen as an example of how far things have come? Couldn't it be an opportunity for me to have a measure of closure on an issue that's bothered me for so long?

I don't think so. For one thing, they didn't want me when I was in my prime, so why should I do it now? For another, I have serious reservations about the way shoe companies target children to sell wildly expensive sneakers that don't help anyone jump better. On top of that, a part of me thinks that until black men own the companies selling the sneakers and clothes, the guys in the commercials are still playing the role of those jazz musicians in Las Vegas, back in the 1950s.

And there's also a final, more prosaic reason: I never liked playing in new sneakers. I kept all my sneakers for a long time and wore their soles to the nub. The fact is, the Converse shoe couldn't take all the turning, twisting, and stopping in my game. Adidas either, although I wore those for the majority of my career with the Bucks. Spalding was the best sneaker I ever wore, and I don't know if they make sneakers anymore.

———

WHEN YOU GREW UP in an all-black neighborhood in Indianapolis as I did, you had to prove you weren't a criminal. When you came to college the way I did, you had to prove that you were actually there to go to class and weren't some slacker on the take. And because I was successful, because I was quiet and reserved, people accepted me. They did it grudgingly, and still whispered to themselves when I wasn't in the room, but they accepted me. I married an African-American woman, but her skin color was very light and, sad to say, that helped the way people looked at us. In every endeavor, I had to prove myself. Through sports, I gained entry to different venues, met various types of people.

My wife once said that a person of color may not be an activist, or walk in marches, but he or she simply cannot sit on the sidelines. You can never be passive because these misconceptions affect you all the time. They affect you no matter how high up as a black person you go, no matter how educated you are or how much you acquire, or how much freedom you feel you have. When you feel that perhaps you have attained a level where it doesn't affect you so much, there's always some little thing that knocks you off your feet, reminding you all over again.

When Yvonne took our child to a camp, she'd be the only black child there. We enrolled her in Cincinnati Country Day School. She was one of the only black children there. She'd be in a vacuum, the same way that Yvonne and I were in a vacuum. If we walked into a good restaurant in Cincinnati, people would initially look at us with that faint expression of distaste. Then it would dawn on them, they'd say among themselves, "Oh, that's Oscar Robertson." And the expression changed. After you've seen that a dozen times, it's worse than being refused admission to the restaurant in the first place.

When Yvonne and I first moved to Avondale and onto Eaton Lane, the area had been integrated. Over time the demographics shifted; more black families moved in, and soon the whole neighborhood was black. Every once in a while a story circulated that my family was about to move into a white neighborhood. I believe "exclusive" was the word the papers used. The stories were false, and there was no need for anyone to panic. The fact is, Yvonne and I first moved into an integrated neighborhood precisely because I didn't want to live where I wasn't wanted. No way were we going to create extra problems for our kids.

My wife is a cultured and educated woman. She is an avid reader, collects fine art, is active in any number of cultural organizations, and also draws and paints (though she never sketched me—says I can't sit still long enough for a rendering). My mother wrote spiritual music and is a renowned singer. She's recorded and toured with the Beck Jubilee Singers—a group that in some circles is held in the same stature as the Mormon Tabernacle Choir. Mom's sung on national television and to a sold-out Madison Square Garden. My brothers were all strong family men. As for me, I used to come home after practice and shoot hoops on a basket and backboard that I'd nailed above my garage. Sometimes I would shoot by myself, just to work on my stroke, but lots of times neighborhood kids would come around, and I'd play with them, especially my friend Odell Owens.

One of my oldest and closest friends was Adrian Smith from Kentucky, who came straight out of Adolph Rupp's all-white basketball factory. I'd known him since 1959. We used to relax at one another's homes all the time, and our wives used to trade recipes. All of which is to say, mine is a family of decent people. We had—and to this day have—no problem with anyone who has no problem with us. My attitude was, *Don't worry*. If you don't want me living next to you, don't worry, because I won't. If you don't want me to socialize with you, don't worry.

There are a lot of fine, just, and large-hearted people of every race and color in Cincinnati. The fans in Cincinnati were classy and supportive to me. Having said this, the city has always been known as a politically and socially conservative one, and you can see the ramifications of this conservatism in all sorts of ways. Look at the history of professional sports here. Every major black star that played in this city ended up getting traded. Frank Robinson is the first and best example.

One of the best-hitting outfielders who ever lived, Frank played in Cincinnati in the late 1950s and early 1960s and won the National League most valuable player award in 1961. Frank was an outspoken guy, a civil rights advocate who had many threats made on his life. In 1965, Reds general manager Bill DeWitt traded Robinson to the Orioles with outfield prospect Dick Simpson in exchange for pitchers Milt Pappas and Jack Baldschun. DeWitt defended the deal by calling Robinson "an old thirty." Well, the next season, Frank was the first Triple Crown winner since Mickey Mantle—leading the American League with 49 HR, 122 RBI, a .316 batting average, a .637 slugging percentage, and 122 runs. Frank was named the American League's most valuable player that season, which made him the first man in baseball history to win the award in both the National and American Leagues. How's that for an "old thirty"? It was the worst trade in Reds history.

But that was just the beginning with the Reds. Look at every talented black player the Reds have ever had, like Vada Pinson and Bobby Tolan. Something's always wrong with them. Take a look at the great Big Red Machine that won two World Series and dominated the mid-1970s. Tony Perez at first base, Joe Morgan at second, Dave Concepcion at short, George Foster in left field, Cesar Geronimo in center, and Ken Griffey in right. The only players who were written or talked about were Pete Rose and Johnny Bench. The papers hardly ever mentioned the rest of the team. Understand, I know Johnny Bench. I like Johnny Bench; he is a great player. And I know Pete Rose. A great player. I am not criticizing them. I am using this as an example to explain the mindset of this city, this area.

When Johnny Bench was inducted into the Baseball Hall of Fame, the city had a rally. I think Johnny was voted in unanimously—as he should have been—and the city rallied behind him, which they should have. A street was named for Pete Rose. When Frank Robinson went in, I don't think the city even sent a representative. Finally, Frank came back to Cincinnati for a small ceremony. But the man played most of his career here.

The Royals always had a hard time in Cincinnati. One thing people always said was that our fan base was as much from downstate Ohio, Indiana, Kentucky, and West Virginia, as from the city. They argued that in the dead of winter, people didn't want to deal with the ice and fog and sleet to see the Royals play. They noted that for all the Ohio players (short list: me, Twyman, Embry, Adrian Smith, Jerry Lucas, George Wilson, Arlen Bockhorn, Tom Thacker), the Royals simply never caught on here, and there was no way of changing this.

They also said that Cincinnati fans were unbelievably stingy—the joke was that vendors at Crosley Field had to pry the money for peanuts and popcorn out of the hands of each Reds fan. People pointed to the Bengals, saying that when the team first started playing here, even though interest was off the charts, the team could not sell out a 28,000-seat stadium.

These excuses are ridiculous. When the Royals were a title contender, we drew. If our front office had put a first-rate team out there and promoted us the right way, people would have come. Instead—and you have this in a lot of Midwestern cities—you have front offices that want to get in the big game but don't want to pay the cost. We didn't get the right players and did not pay them enough, and our teams weren't successful, and that's why fans did not come. When it comes time to pay a player, management justifies lower salaries by saying, "Well, this is Cincinnati. It costs less to live here and is a good place to live." Well, Boston is a good place to live too. So is Los Angeles. So is Houston. And New York. And New Orleans.

When I played for the Royals, there were some 162,000 blacks in the metropolitan Cincinnati area. I doubt if more than ten or twenty ever held Royal season tickets. Austin Tillotson once went to a bunch of games and counted the crowd. Over the course of weeks' worth of home games, he counted the number of black fans on two hands. That's inexcusable. But it's also typical. If management had cared about getting black fans interested in the team, the fact is, they would have done it.

However, if the economics of the city are so out of whack that black men can't get jobs and feed their families, then surely these men don't have the money to take their kids to see a professional basketball game. It doesn't matter if the tickets are the cheapest in the league; if you don't have money, you still can't pay for a cheap seat.

That's a much larger issue.

What I am talking about here is racism on an institutional level, and that poisons us all. It comes from the people who own banks, which refuse to give black small-businessmen loans. It comes from the country clubs that won't let blacks be members unless they are famous, and even then uses them as tokens. It comes from corporations that refuse to hire minority executives for their highest positions, yet rely on minorities for their revenue and rank and file. And, of course, it comes from the newspapers and media outlets that are selective in who they hire and how they gather information. It comes from the agendas of the news editors, journalists, and broadcasters. These things could change if the organizations and the people who ran them wanted change. The question is, do they?

———————

IN 1967, JACK MCMAHON was fired as coach. His replacement, Ed Jucker, had coached the University of Cincinnati to NCAA titles in 1961 and 1962. Ed Jucker was a college coach at heart, but that rah-rah stuff doesn't work in the pros. He used to tell us to "go out and make things hurt a little bit." He regularly forgot our names in the huddle. He once forgot Wilt Chamberlain's name, instead telling us to "stop the big kid." He announced that John and Tresvant would be our starting forwards, which would have been fine if they weren't the same guy. In college, if you make a mistake, the coach gets all over you, and Ed tried that with us. You can do that when you are a fifty-year-old man talking to an eighteen-year-old college kid. Not in the pro game. A good NBA coach says, "Okay, you made a mistake. Let's not do it again." Then they move on.

Before the season started, I had another fight with management about my contract and missed training camp in a protracted holdout. During the first week of the regular season, I pulled my hamstring. The injury flared and receded throughout the year, along with back and groin problems, and for the first time in my professional career, I was in and out of the lineup.

Wayne Embry and Jack Twyman had moved on, but we still had a decent club. Jerry Lucas and I remained the team's core. We played a third of our home games in Cleveland that season, others in Omaha, and there were rumors that Jacobs wanted to move the franchise. The team had no local television contract, and if your radio antenna was pointed in the wrong direction, you weren't going to hear our broadcasts. Midway through the season, Ed Jucker decided that I was taking too much abuse bringing the ball up court after baskets made by the other team, so he had other players handle that duty. But in the process it took the ball out of my hands, hurt our ability to get into our half-court offense with as little wasted motion as possible, and ignored one of the cardinal rules of basketball—playmakers want the ball. If I'm a coach in trouble and I have Michael Jordan, I tell the team I want Michael Jordan to have the basketball. Or Wilt. Or Oscar Robertson. I don't think Ed understood this. I never got the sense he really understood pro basketball, per se, because during his two-year reign as head coach, he also played our starting five almost exclusively, forgoing our bench entirely, running us into the ground by the middle of January.

Attendance for our home games fell to an average of 4,100, the worst in the league, and we finished four games below .500—missing the playoffs for the first time since my rookie season. I finished seventh in the league in scoring and third in assists. I was on my way toward thirty years old and playing for a team that seemed to be getting further and further from title contention. I was considered the greatest all-around player in history by my peers, but at the same time I was becoming the symbol of everything that had gone wrong with the Royals franchise. Local fans had grown accustomed to my solid style, and I believe they started to take my talent for granted. If I scored thirty points, had ten assists, and eight or nine rebounds, they said, "Ah, well, just another game for him." If somebody else scored fifteen or twenty points, the headlines would scream how sensational he was. I understood that I was being held to a different standard.

But now the newspapermen who had never liked me much anyway had their chance. Inaccurate and misleading stories began to appear. Where once I had been praised for my ability to control a ball game and make the right decisions with the ball, now a column was printed claiming that Norm Van Lier said I held the ball too much. Newspapermen circulated stories that Jerry Lucas felt he should have gotten the ball more. John Tresvant and Fred Hetzel believed that they were traded because I controlled the ball too much, though neither was ever quoted directly on the matter.

A New York writer named Phil Berger was covering the New York Knicks as a beat reporter in 1969 to 1970. In his book, *Miracle on 33rd Street: The New York Knickerbockers' Championship Season*, Berger, in a minor passage, wrote, "A writer traveling with Oscar said: 'Like every time you see a team in the locker there's always some noise between the guys on the team, "Let's go out there and give them a game," and this and that, just something that shows the guys know each other but between Lucas and Oscar there was none.' "

Of course, the claim that was reprinted the most, and came to be accepted as fact, was that Jerry Lucas and I did not like each other.

Let's set the record straight.

As far as hoarding the ball, my response would be a question for anyone who knows the slightest bit about basketball: Who would you rather have the ball, Oscar Robertson or Norm Van Lier?

As far as John Tresvant and Fred Hetzel's alleged complaints: The Royals had traded Bob Boozer, one of my best friends on the team. They'd helped Wayne Embry into retirement. Every time my contract came due, I fought with them tooth and nail for every dime. I was the last person they were going to listen to on player matters.

As for the book, the only paper that traveled with us was *The Cincinnati Enquirer,* and even that was sporadic. In 1968, the *Enquirer*'s sports editor had been promoted from his position as a beat writer. He had covered the Bearcats and Royals for the last ten years. I don't know if he had been one of the local guys who had fumed because I talked to New York reporters. I don't know if his problems with me were racial or based on something else, because he also wrote that the black players on our team hung out in our own clique, separately from the white players. (This was when we had three black guys on the team. Two of us roomed together— that's the clique. If Bob Boozer stopped by the room, I guess we became a gang.) I can definitely say that he was the first person to play up problems between Jerry Lucas and me.

But the *Enquirer*'s coverage of me soured well before my last season in Cincinnati. For example, in 1968, the Organization of African States circulated a petition asking people to condemn the Olympics for holding their Summer Games in South Africa, which at the time had a governmental policy of racism and apartheid. Along with senators, statesmen, people of business and culture, I signed the petition. There were hundreds of notable people on this list. Thousands of people altogether. But the story came out like this: "O Voices for Boycott." Now, I know that for a Cincinnati paper, I stood out as the most prominent local celebrity on the boycott list, but there was no mention in the headline or the story of any of the other people involved in the boycott. There was no mention of what I felt about this boycott. What came across was that I wanted to boycott the Olympics. Period. I'm an Olympic gold medal winner; I don't come to decisions like this lightly. The day the article came out, I called him and we had words. I told him if he did not print a retraction, I would sue him. From that point on, I never spoke to anyone from the *Enquirer.*

And there was no problem between Jerry Lucas and me. Newspapers created this rumor. Sometime around 1966 or 1967, a writer from the *Enquirer* printed rumors and unattributed, anonymous quotes about a problem. These got picked up and put on the circuit, and became fact of law. The truth is, Jerry was a great player, but he wasn't a great one-on-one player. He's said as much: "I've never been good with the ball, so there's never been any sense clearing out a side for me." And we played together for six seasons and ended up developing a rapport, especially on pick and rolls. During our final season together, 1968–1969, the two of us were healthy for a stretch and had the Royals playing well enough that Frank Deford and *Sports Illustrated* were speculating about our postseason chances.

Jerry and I were inducted into the Basketball Hall of Fame the same year, and to this very day he remains a good friend. Having said this, the whole time Jerry was with the Royals it was written that I didn't like him. I remain convinced that the papers did this because I was black and he was white.

After the 1967 season, for the third time in four years, I found myself at war with the Cincinnati front office. This time the dispute was over the meaning of a clause in my contract. The clause was supposed to pay me a percentage of the gate receipts in addition to my salary. The Royals brass did not feel that way. We could not settle the matter, so once again I did not report to training camp. At this point in my career, I was making around one hundred thousand dollars a season. Considering the team's weak attendance figures, the issue wasn't a matter of money, because even if I won, I wasn't going to be getting a fortune. Rather, I felt the wording dispute was a matter of principle. In the NBA, respect is measured by the figures on a player's contract, plain and simple. If I broke my leg or fell on my head in the middle of the game, would the league be taking care of me?

A few days before the 1968 season, I did not think I'd be playing in the league. The Royals, meanwhile, were making calls trying to find an available guard, and Ed Jucker had resigned himself to the idea that the season would start without me.

Finally, the deadlock broke; the Royals gave me a new three-year contract, which included an incentive clause that rewarded me with higher bonuses based on how far the Royals went in the playoffs. If the Royals did not finish higher than fourth during the regular seasons of any of these three years, I would make a total of just less than four hundred thousand dollars. If they made it to the finals for all three seasons, my salary bumped another fifty grand per year.

It would be my last contract with the Cincinnati Royals.

CHAPTER TWELVE

Moving On
1969–1970

"I'M WILLING TO MAKE a few mistakes—but not too many." And so Bob Cousy kicked off his first press conference in Cincinnati. Though there were flecks of gray in his trademark crew cut, the new coach of the Cincinnati Royals showed all the optimism and confidence he'd been known for as a ten-time first-team all-star and a five-time NBA champion. Once the highest-paid player in the league, Bob had retired from basketball in 1963, after which he'd grown a bit antsy for the game and had coached Boston College's basketball program into the NCAA tournament. Always a proud man, Bob had stayed in shape with a regimen of tennis and golf. During summers he ran a basketball camp, and he was more than happy to take to the court and hold his own against any college kids who might challenge him. So when Louis Jacobs's son Max approached him about coming on as a coach and player, Bob jumped at the six-figure offer.

A new regime was officially underway in Cincinnati. Max Jacobs was running the team for his dad. Ed Jucker was out. Pepper Wilson got his marching orders and was replaced by Joe Axelson, a guy nobody had ever heard of. Even the radio announcer was replaced. The new management team spared no expense in announcing itself. During the summer, billboards started appearing around town: COUSY IS COMING. The first practices of the season were like photo shoots, with newspapers and magazines running posed pictures of Bob standing, back to the camera, under the basket in his coaching sweater, a big "Cousy" on the back.

One day while all this hoopla was taking place, I was at my house with a friend, Jimmy Thompson. He'd taught me to do woodwork and was helping me with some remodeling. One of the team's commercials came on.

"Hey, Oscar," Jimmy's tone was joking, but he didn't look like he was amused. "You better watch out for Bob Cousy."

"What are you talking about?"

"Remember that article he wrote that you would be a Royal letdown? Cousy, he don't care for you."

I laughed Jimmy off. I did not know Bob except as a basketball competitor, but we'd always had a wary respect for each other. If there was any rivalry, it was a professional one, and I couldn't imagine that anything from those days would carry over. Cousy had proved himself as a player, and he'd had some success as a college coach. And we were never going to win under Ed Jucker. I figured it had to be a step forward. Because there was some overlap between our careers, and we were both floor generals, I thought we'd see eye to eye on a lot and would be able to talk basketball and strategy.

I never imagined that the worst year of my professional life was about to begin.

Although he was unfailingly polite with the press, Bob's competitive nature and self-assurance hadn't been softened by time. Calling everyone "Babe," Bob announced that he would remake the Royals into a fast, tough, running team, just like the Celtics had been in his heyday. In practice he told returning players we lacked discipline. He threatened guys he thought weren't working hard: Toe the line or else. Bob decided that Jerry Lucas was slow and out of shape. Four games into the regular season, Jerry was traded to San Francisco. Bob saw something in Adrian Smith he didn't like; Adrian went packing with Jerry. In exchange for one Hall of Famer and another ten-year veteran, we got Bill Turner and Jim King, two guys who couldn't crack our starting lineup. I didn't understand it, but didn't say anything. Our new starting line featured thirty-six-year-old Johnny Green at forward, thirty-three-year-old Connie Dierking, me and Norman Van Lier at guard, and Tom Van Arsdale at forward. It wasn't exactly in line with the stated commitment to rebuilding and youth, but I guessed they were going to rebuild in stages. Fine. Then Bob changed things further. Bob wanted Van Lier to handle the ball. Meanwhile, I'd be moving off screens and finishing plays.

The problem was that our new playmaker, Norm Van Lier, wasn't tall enough to see over the guy who guarded him. This not only delayed his passes but also made him susceptible to the pressure of double-teaming. Now, instead of having an all-pro guard for ten straight years running the show, we had problems getting into our offense. Still, we beat the Celtics twice in the first weeks of the season, and our record was 8–6. So I just went out on the court and did my job.

While all this was happening, a minor drama started to unfold between Bob and his former team. Red Auerbach may have retired as the coach of the Celtics, but now as their general manager, he was just as shrewd. During the preseason, when he'd read that Bob intended to coach *and* play, Red decided not to release Bob's name from the retired list. The local papers mentioned this delay as the supposed impetus for our two early wins over the Celtics, but Joe Axelson was the only one angry about the stall. Eventually, the two sides reached an agreement in the form of cash and Bill Dinwiddie. One month into the season, Bob Cousy, age forty-one, completed our youth movement.

We were in Cleveland playing the Knicks. The Knicks were going for their record-setting eighteenth straight win. With sixteen seconds left, they trailed by five. I fouled out. Bob rose from the bench, put himself in to replace me, and immediately threw the ball away. New York scored, drew a foul, and converted the free throws. Cousy turned it over again. New York ended up winning in overtime. The next time he wanted to play, he brought the wrong uniform. "It took me about eleven minutes of actual playing time to realize it wasn't going to work," he later told an interviewer. "I feared I was going to tarnish something that I had accomplished over thirteen years and that I was very proud of." After thirty-four minutes, spread over seven games, Bob Cousy re-retired as a player.

For all the hype about the team's commitment to youth and re-building, our veterans were getting the job done. Connie Dierking was our only other dependable scorer. But soon he broke his hand. Johnny Green may have been thirty-six years old, but he was the only guy down low getting any rebounds for us. He was out there so much that his ankle started giving him problems. Not long after that, Herm Gilliam was called to fulfill his reserve commitment with the armed forces. If all three had been available, we still weren't anything more than an average team. Without them, things started to fall apart. We were a team in flux, a mishmash of veterans and young guys without any cohesion or identity. If I had been handling the ball more, I could have settled things down, found open men, and made sure to feed players when they made it to their sweet spots. As it was, our guys were lost out there. I'd run off a pick and get open and expect to get the ball, and it just wouldn't happen. Maybe guys couldn't see me. Maybe they couldn't get the pass off. I'd been the all-star MVP for the third time the previous season, was putting in twenty-five a night, and could still score almost at will, but as things progressed and we began to slump, I became concerned.

Whatever my prowess as a scorer might have been, first and foremost I'd always been a playmaker. And we were a team that needed direction. Bob may have been intent on having a team play "his" style of ball, or the Celtics' style of basketball, or whatever it was, but at the end of the day, you've got to use what you've got. Concepts and styles are fine, but basketball is basketball. So long as there's a twenty-four-second clock, there are only so many things you can do on a court. We weren't getting anything out of our offense. I'd averaged ten assists a game through my career. It seems to me that if your goal as a coach is to have your team play unselfishly, and you've got a bunch of green players out there along with a guy who led the league in assists every year—a guy who holds the all-time record for assists—it might help the team to have that guy distribute the ball.

Something had to be going on.

Soon I heard a rumor. Every night after the game, Max Jacobs would call from headquarters in Buffalo. Before asking Joe Axelson whether we'd won or lost, he'd want to know the attendance count. Another rumor: the gate receipts were picked up every night, sent to Buffalo, and then money would be sent back to run the team and pay expenses.

We kept losing. It was hard to stay as focused. Soon a story in *The Cincinnati Enquirer* intimated that Bob wanted to install a running game that I didn't fit. We traveled to cities, and various guys told me they'd heard I was on the trading block. One night, we were getting blown out in Philadelphia. With nine and a half minutes left, Wally Anderzunas tapped my shoulder and said he was coming in for me. As I left the floor, the voice over the P.A. said he was coming in for Tom Van Arsdale. When I got home from the road trip, my wife and friends wanted to know what happened in Philadelphia. I had no idea what they were talking about. Turns out, the next day's *Enquirer* surmised that I had taken myself out of the game, and the beat reporter had written a story about it without talking to me. Stories soon followed about the bad feelings between the coach and me.

One day after practice, Connie Dierking came up to me. "Why don't you just go to Cousy and talk to him?"

Over the years a lot of people have asked me the same thing.

In life, sometimes you get into a situation where you let fate decide your course of action. I hadn't done anything to create this situation. So I figured why should I try to solve something I had no control over?

Kissing someone's ass in a situation like that isn't going to solve anything. I couldn't have lived with myself if I did that.

I knew that I didn't have any role in the team Cousy wanted. I could see that he had his own plans in mind, and nothing I could say or do was going to change that.

"Let me tell you something, Connie," I answered. "I have done nothing to Bob Cousy. I hardly know Bob Cousy. But you know what? He is going to get rid of you too."

And he did. A few weeks later, Connie was shipped out to the 76ers. When the all-star break came, I was the only starter left from last year's team. The newest incarnation of the Cincinnati Royals had dropped its sixth straight game and fallen to last place. I visited New York. Milt Gross called. He asked about friction and the team and the state of things. I chose my words carefully and said nothing more damning than, "It's an impossible situation." Milt brought up the Philadelphia game. "How can I take myself out of the game?" I replied. "The kid told me he was coming in for me, but maybe it would have been better if I had taken myself out." Milt asked if I thought I'd be traded. "I'd be foolish to think the possibility of being traded wouldn't come up," I answered. "I know the management's talked about it. I don't necessarily want to be traded, but if it happens, it is something I would have to live with."

I told Milt, "The way I see it is Cousy is trying to build for the future. He wants young players. I suppose at thirty-one he doesn't consider me a young player. I don't like it."

"There are two mammoth egos involved," wrote Milt in the next day's *New York Post*. "Oscar was a spectacular player but never played on a winner. Cousy was a spectacular player and played on so many winners with the Celtics that what is happening with the Royals must be galling to him." The column concluded:

> The theory consequently is being batted back and forth like rebounds under the board on which nobody can get a firm grasp. Is Cousy trying to mold his personnel to his Celtic concept or mold himself to his players?
> "We don't have a guy in the middle," says Oz.
> Sometimes it seems they don't even have Robertson.

IN A TOWN LIKE Cincinnati, only a few games were broadcast on television, radio reception depended on anything from the formation of the clouds to the position of your antenna, and the local evening news might show two baskets in a fifteen-second report. If you wanted information about the Cincinnati Royals, you read the newspapers. The *Cincinnati Post* was a small-circulation paper that relied on wire services for the bulk of its national and feature coverage. While it sent reporters to all home games and practices, the *Post* did not have the budget to send a reporter traveling with the team. As a result, *The Cincinnati Enquirer* was the sole source of consistent information and the paper of record—the main resource for fans who couldn't see or hear games for themselves, as well as for papers outside Cincinnati who picked up the *Enquirer's* stories whenever the Royals made larger news.

Whenever I've talked to sportswriters or any other reporters or journalists, all I've asked is that they be fair in how they cover me. If you see something, write what happened. I may not like what you write, but if that's what happened, I won't complain. Along these lines, I've always felt that if a reporter wants to know about something, he should come to me and ask. I'll answer any question. Again, it may not be the answer the reporter wants. But as long as he prints what happened and asks me about it, things will be fine. But the following piece of biased journalism from the January 26, 1970, issue of *The Cincinnati Enquirer* shows why racial problems and hatred have long dogged Cincinnati.

Robertson, Green Just Too Tough for Bullets, 129–122

With all the sanitation workers out on strike in Cincinnati, ageless Johnny Green looks like the best garbage man in town. And if Johnny is cleaning up in the back of the truck, Oscar Robertson has to be up front at the wheel.

Green and Robertson, the slightly elderly Frick and Frack of the Cincinnati Royals, brought a touch of vaudeville to the Cincinnati Gardens Sunday. And when it was over, the Baltimore Bullets walked off stage looking like rotten tomatoes.

Robertson scored 41 points and passed off for 15 assists, and Green came up with 19 points underneath the basket and

grabbed 12 rebounds. Not bad for a 36-year-old playing only
32 minutes with his fifth club in the last five years.

I understand that beat reporters have their deadlines to meet. I appreciate that you might get tired of covering a team night after night after
night and look for ways to be creative, and work current events like a union
strike into your stories and metaphors. Having acknowledged this, I ask the
following:

If Johnny Green and I had been white, would we have been compared to Frick and Frack—would that have been used to describe us? Sure,
it might be a fairly common way of referring to two people who are closely
connected in some way, friends or whatnot. But the *Random House Histor-
ical Dictionary of American Slang* cites the phrase as coming from Black English, and advises any user that, "Some care may be needed in using the
phrase, as it is said also to be a Black American English slang term for the
testicles." Whether the paper was consciously aware of the uses and roots
of a term like Frick and Frack is something of a moot point. It is a term with
racist overtones, as is the rest of the story. Moreover, these biases, whether
intentional or not, are so deeply ingrained into the structures of power that
to this day, I think, society is still trying to deal with them.

ON JANUARY 28, 1970, I arrived at the gate of the Cincinnati Gardens on my way to play the Bucks. The parking attendant showed
me an ad for a grocery store that was in the paper that day. The ad showed
the entire Cincinnati Royals lined up in the store. Except for me. "What's
the matter, Oscar, aren't you on the Royals?"

Two days later, we were in Boston and lost to the Celtics. I pulled a
muscle in my groin and couldn't run and had to sit out the last six minutes
of the game. On my way to the locker room afterwards, I had to crouch just
to walk without wincing. It took me a while to shower and get dressed, and
I was finishing up when a reporter approached. How did I feel about the
trade, he wanted to know.

He was told to leave. Even back then it was strange to hear you were traded from a reporter instead of your front office. I needed to make a call. Jake Brown said that, yes, it was true. The Royals had made a deal with Baltimore, bringing in Gus Johnson—a powerful forward with tremendous leaping ability, who once shattered a backboard during a game. Gus was my age, and he made about fifty thousand dollars less than I did. But there was a reason for that. His knees were all messed up, and his body wasn't going to last much longer. I knew they didn't care about Gus. He was toward the end of his usefulness, and eventually they would unload him. They just wanted me out of Cincinnati.

I figured if that's what they wanted, then it was time for me to leave. But I was going to go on my terms. J. W. and I talked for a while. The next morning, Bob called me at home.

"Babe, I know you've been unhappy with the team, so we've traded you for Gus Johnson." Isn't this a bitch. From all that has been written and said about me, he knows that I am not happy with the Royals.

"Yeah. I heard. You better come meet me at J. W.'s office."

"What? Why?"

"It's not so cut and dried."

"What do you mean?"

"We'll discuss it with Jake."

A few hours later, Bob Cousy, Bro Lindhorst, and Joe Axelson were scattered on the couches and chairs of J. W.'s office. J. W. asked them the terms of the trade. Joe answered: "Straight out for Gus Johnson, no other consideration."

"Well," J. W. smiled. "Unfortunately, Oscar doesn't want to go to Baltimore. And I guess you haven't read his contract lately. Oscar has the right of veto over any trade."

It was like a bomb exploded in there. Cousy, Axelson, and Lindhorst stared at each other. Then Bob met my eyes, squinting, a question in his eyes, as if he couldn't quite comprehend what he just heard.

They all began sputtering. "Oh, but he'll like it in Baltimore—and they'll pay a lot more money." "I thought you'd jump at the opportunity." "We're doing you a favor, sending you to a contender."

J. W. cut them off, addressing Lindhorst. "Would you go to Baltimore for fifty thousand dollars, Bro?"

That quieted them down. J. W. took control of the room, first telling the Royals front office that we didn't want to leave any avenue unexplored. Then he called Baltimore and laid out our terms, pulling a figure out of the air—three years for seven hundred thousand dollars, more than twice my salary with the Royals.

There was a pause on the other end of the line, and then Baltimore's front office said they would get back to us.

Cousy, Axelson, and Lindhorst looked like they were in shock. Axelson asked J. W. what they should do next.

"Well, you've already leaked that you've traded him," J. W. said. "So you better trade him. We'll get in touch with a few clubs and tell you where Oscar wants to go."

Axelson threw up his hands. "If he has a veto," he bellowed, "we can make a trade and still have to come back to you for approval."

My lawyer smiled again. "That's right. But we'll cooperate. We'll tell you the places he's willing to go, and you can go from there."

It really was an unbelievable scene. The three of them slinked out of there, shoulders low, heads down at their shoes. Once they were gone and everything had died down, J. W. asked me what my criteria were and where my first choice would be.

I thought about it before answering. "I need to think it over and talk to my wife."

WHAT FOLLOWED was a spectacle that was half circus, half media war. For the next two weeks, the *Enquirer* ran daily stories about my trade, or lack thereof, about my ingratitude, my selfishness, my fake injury.

In my opinion, the *Enquirer* writers were the mouthpiece for the Royals management's propaganda. Players from other teams were asked loaded questions like, "Don't you think the Royals play better without

Oscar?" Once, when a reporter intimated that I was faking an injury, Wilt responded, "Could you ask an intellectually honest question, please?" Finally, the newspaper completely abandoned commenting on my game and started attacking me as a person: "Bob Cousy had done everything possible to placate the Big O, whose mood is always the same, bitter. For years, Oscar privately has scorned the Royals management; he has ridiculed Cincinnati and its fans, he has knocked other players, both on his team and on others; he has never been willing to pay a compliment. He is, has been, and probably will grow old a bitter man, convinced that it all is a plot." Thanks largely to the newspaper and Bob Cousy, I would never play for the Royals again.

Meanwhile, the team went from a steady state of decline into a dull plummet. The Royals switchboard was flooded with calls, and a few old friends defended me in print, asking, "Why do they knock Oscar?" Jerry West, in his own low-key way, seconded the motion. Following the Lakers easy win over us he said, "I would say they might have missed Oscar just a tiny bit, just a tiny bit." Then he turned serious. "He's the guy who gives them direction. With a player like him, you just can't afford to take him out of there. Honestly, it's hard for me to imagine them trading a player of his caliber, because they don't come along every day. Personally, he is the best basketball player I have ever seen. I'm sure there are other reasons behind it."

On February 4, 1970, *The Cincinnati Enquirer* ran this story:

Oscar In Limbo

It was a tough weekend for Oscar Robertson, now in limbo. First the Cincinnati Royals broke his heart. Then Pete Maravich broke his college scoring record.

When Oscar told Baltimore he wanted $700,000, he put one foot in the basketball graveyard. Sunday night, when the NBA trading deadline expired, he put in the other foot.

By declaring squatter's rights on his Royals uniform, by not agreeing to go to Baltimore, Oscar has placed himself in a box and there does not seem to be a way out.

The Royals have indicated they consider him a six-foot five-inch millstone around their necks. And now the rest of the league knows his asking price. What is left? If he decides to play out his option, he will be 33 years old when he reaches free agent status.

The breakup of the shotgun marriage between Oscar and coach Bob Cousy started three weeks ago. The Royals had won seven of eight games to pull even with the .500 mark and then they lost games against Milwaukee and Phoenix. Oscar played lackadaisically in both losses.

Afterwards, sitting in his motel room after the Phoenix loss, Cousy muttered, "If he thinks he can call my bluff, he is badly mistaken."

Bob Cousy knew he had failed with Oscar Robertson. He was the only player on the team he could not reach. And the truth was becoming apparent. Oscar would not change, and if he did not, the Royals would never become a running team. While Oscar dribbled, the fast break died.

It killed Cousy to look on the floor and see Connie Dierking, a 33-year-old ballplayer who was washed-up eight years ago, giving 100 percent. He watched Johnny Green, 36 years old and a reservoir of determination, race up and down the court. He saw Tom Van Arsdale playing with a wrecked knee. There was Norm Van Lier with scarred knees, wrenched elbows, and a bruised body. And he looked at Oscar Robertson and saw a man who had played ten years without a floor burn.

Five years ago it would have been preposterous to say the C&O Bridge would decay. Five years ago it would have been preposterous to say the Royals would trade Robertson. But now the Royals were willing to do the preposterous. They were going to trade the best player in basketball to improve their team.

They needed an excuse. The economy provided the answer. Robertson's contract expires at the end of this season and Cincy was certain he would ask for a huge raise.

But Robertson's agreement with the Royals is the worst agreement since the one at Yalta. He vetoed the deal unless he got $700,000 from Baltimore for three years, which figures out to $2,845 per game, or figuring his career average of 40 minutes per game, the sum of $4,268.83 per hour of basketball.

The Royals traded Oscar because Bob Cousy does not think basketball is a one-on-one game. This is an argument gained from years of winning championships with the Celtics, who never had a star but always had a team. It is an argument gained from years of winning at Boston College, which never before had a winner.

The Royals would never lose if Oscar and one player from the other team could play one-on-one for 48 minutes. But basketball is not this way and the Royals with Robertson have never been a champion.

There are some people who say that Oscar Robertson should not be traded, that the city of Cincinnati owes something to him.

This is a curious argument, one which comes from people, judging from attendance figures, who are apparently not paying their way into the Gardens to see Oscar.

For these people there is an alternative. Someone should start an Oscar Robertson defense fund. If 30,000 put up $10 apiece the money will be there to retain the Big O. It seems like a small price to pay.

It all comes down to the fact that the Cincinnati Royals, for the first time, have a coach, an owner, and a front office who are determined to bring a championship to Cincinnati. For the first time they are willing to fight public sentiment, willing to fight against the easy course of action,

238 ★ Oscar Robertson

willing to fight for what they believe is right. The ballplayers are no longer running the Royals. It is a change for the better.

This piece was the last straw for me. Never mind that it contained cheap shot after cheap shot. Never mind that information was published about my contract negotiations that no reporter would have unless the front office leaked it. If the writer wants to disagree with how much money I make or the position I've taken as the head of the players union or what kind of jelly I like on my peanut butter sandwiches, I couldn't care less. The thing that burned me up the most was the idea that for ten years, I didn't hustle. I never got my knees hurt going after loose balls. Hadn't gotten so much as a floor burn. What you see here is a written campaign of character assassination. "All" I had accomplished for the Royals was make first-team all-pro ten straight years. Lead the team in scoring, also for ten straight years. I was all-time assists leader, all-time leading rebounder for guards, the only player in the history of basketball to have a triple-double season. I wasn't working hard enough? I was lackadaisical and responsible for all our losses? Ten years and I never did anything for the Royals?

Now, I know that Bob Cousy did not say those kinds of things about me, either to my face or on the record. But I also know that he—or anyone else in the front office—could have stopped the slurring in the paper. At the very least they could have stopped leaking information. Moreover, coaches often take a writer aside and talk to him, asking him to get off a player's back if the writer is consistently and unfairly attacking a player. I believe Bob Cousy could have done that. Did he agree with what the guy was saying?

This happened thirty-plus years ago. Time heals all wounds. But I have to conclude that Bob wanted this to happen.

As soon as I read that column, I called a press conference. It was the first time in more than a month—since talking to Milt Gross at the all-star game—that I spoke to the media. I announced that I would honor my contract and play the remaining twenty-four games of the season, but that I wouldn't play for Cincinnati the following year. I explained that I refused the trade to Baltimore, foremost because I didn't want to uproot my family during the season. I was lucky that I was in the situation where I could refuse the trade. If I hadn't had that clause in my contract, they could have sent me to Timbuktu and there wouldn't have been a thing I could have done.

I tried not to let things get to me. I kept going to rehab, working to get my pulled muscle back in shape so I could return to the court. One day I was having a Cincinnati Reds trainer named Marv Pollins examine my injury at Spinney Field, where they trained. Dick Forbes was sitting in the same whirlpool, two feet away. Dick had been a sports columnist with the *Enquirer* since before I'd signed to play ball at the University of Cincinnati. He'd had an accident and he was there, getting treatment. A friend, Clem Turner, also was there. I fell asleep in the whirlpool and started slipping down into the water. Clem Turner pulled me up and out.

A call came in for Marv Pollins. It was the Royals trainer asking if I was really hurt. Dick Forbes heard the whole conversation. So did Clem.

Marv answered that I was sitting right there with an injury that was real. He said I would be ready to play in about a week and a half.

Well, the next day's paper featured a report claiming I was ready to play, but didn't want to play because of Cousy.

I called Dick and said, "Dick, you heard what the trainer said. Why don't you write the truth? This is not true."

"I can't," he told me. "They won't let me. I can't afford to do it."

I disliked Forbes from that day forward.

For a long time I held a grudge. Are all journalists like this? Can you trust them?

Days later, Dick called me. He was writing a column and wanted my side of the story. I got angry. All of a sudden he was acting in official capacity and had put on his reporting hat. But when he'd seen facts for himself, right in front of his eyes, he couldn't do anything.

Dick wrote his column and described me in the whirlpool. While he firmly claimed, "Oscar Robertson has an injury, there is no fake about that," he also stopped short of writing that the trainer said I could not play, or that the Royals had called and claimed I was a liar.

To his credit, Dick also wrote: "It will do no good for the Royals to try and keep Oscar, particularly when he says himself he is leaving. But it is a shame what is happening. People come into town who don't know or understand Cincinnati, and in less than a year they are running an institution out on a rail."

In any case, between the public outcry about the paper's biased reporting and the team's losing streak (now at four), the situation was turning into a debacle. To smooth things over, the Royals front office called a public conference with boosters and the press. Cousy jokingly called the meeting "the last supper." One by one he disavowed his previous statements, claiming that the team hadn't shopped me around the league; they had initiated one phone call and that offer had been rejected. He claimed that his reason for trading me was my salary, and that he and I got along fine. "We've never had the slightest personality conflict as I have stated publicly and nationally. If we can't have Oscar next year, then we have to help the team and that is what the whole thing was predicated on."

Our next game was at home against the Knicks. Still injured, I sat on the bench in street clothes and watched as New York hit seventeen of their first twenty-one shots. We trailed only by six at halftime but ended up losing by forty-three. The most entertaining thing about the night was that some fans behind me had made a big banner, which they stretched out over the heads of six or seven people. It said, "Please Stay Oscar." The national press got hold of a photograph of me sitting with that banner behind my head. *Newsweek,* AP, UPI, and all the New York papers picked up the soap opera. I kept to myself, not showing anything at all.

The next day, the Royals lost to the Celtics, 130–117. It was our sixth straight defeat.

Finally, on February 22, I put on my white-and-blue Royals jersey. The Gardens were as packed as they got that season; over 9,500 fans stomped and clapped through the whole game. They cheered us on while we snapped our losing streak, beating the Pistons 127–119. In my return to action, I played forty-four minutes, scored twenty-eight points, had fourteen rebounds, and eleven assists. A win and a triple-double still didn't impress the *Enquirer*: "Robertson's timing looked off and the layoff obviously affected his conditioning, although he showed no signs of the groin muscle pull (sic) which sent him to the sidelines shortly after the Royals attempted to trade him to Baltimore"—but nothing short of my head on a platter would have at this point. Anyone else with an opinion offered praise, be it Clem Haskins ("You couldn't tell he missed twelve games. Not on his performance tonight."); Jerry Sloan ("He looked good, he always does. He could play on one leg and look great. There isn't anybody better, is there?"); even Bob Cousy ("He made a couple of drives to the hoop today that were as fast and strong as I have ever seen him make.").

I think that at this point things between the team and me had gotten so bad that they had to improve. Maybe both sides were looking for a reason for the circus to end, and my return provided it. Management and I never officially spoke. We were entering the final month of the season, and though I'd gotten tired of dealing with management and their hired sharks, the game itself never stopped being fun for me. I played through the final month, sometimes inspired, other moments just driving on autopilot, wanting the year to be over.

On March 20, 1970, I put on Cincinnati's jersey for the final time. My old teammate and friend Jerry Lucas scored thirty-one points and twenty-five rebounds as the San Francisco Warriors beat us, 118–111. In defiance, I did not shoot during the final nine minutes of the game. Cousy was asked about "the situation."

"Leave me alone, will you, babe? I pass. There's one game left. Leave it go. I pass."

We finished the season 36–46 and for the third year in a row didn't get a playoff berth. I led the team in scoring, averaging 25.3 points, 8.1 assists, and 6.1 rebounds per game, and had my tenth straight all-pro season. But there had to be one last slight. Instead of risking humiliation by letting the players vote for the most valuable player, management gave the award to Johnny Green. Nobody had ever heard of a front office naming the MVP before. Johnny and I were friends. I truly was happy for him.

I told him, "Johnny, don't worry about it. I know what these people are trying to do. You just go ahead and play. Forget about them."

THE LAKERS HAD Jerry West. The Knicks said, "Well, we have Frazier." Phoenix was immediately interested, and, eventually, almost every team called to talk about trade possibilities and bidding prices. But an idea had been forming in my head, gathering momentum.

I wanted to stay on in the Midwest. I liked the change in seasons. I wanted good schools for my children. I wanted them in a good neighborhood. I told J. W., "I just might like to play in Milwaukee." "If I can get you a three-year contract for seven hundred thousand dollars," J. W. asked, "is that a deal?"

IN 1968, R. D. TREBILCOX of Whitefish Bay, Wisconsin, had been one of forty-five people who suggested that the state's new entry into the National Basketball Association should be known as the Bucks. On his contest entry form, Trebilcox wrote: "Bucks are spirited, good jumpers, fast and agile." R. D. won a new car for his efforts, and soon afterwards the team mascot—a male deer with massive antlers—was unveiled, as were team colors of forest green and crimson.

Bucks owner Wesley D. Pavalon, thirty-seven, was the youngest owner in the league. Alternately referred to as an eccentric maverick; a wonderboy millionaire; a glorified, fast-talking carny barker; and "the Jewish Howard Hughes," Pavalon had made his fortune through a trade and technical institute known as the Career Academy, which did business through franchise schools and mail orders. Known to work all night, making long-distance calls across the planet, sleep all day, and then arrive at his office at 4:00 P.M., Pavalon was a huge basketball fan. He readily admitted that his team's big break had come through pure chance, when, on a spring day in 1968, during a three-way telephone hookup, NBA Commissioner Walter Kennedy flipped a coin, and Richard Bloch, president of the Phoenix Suns, called heads.

The coin landed tails, and Pavalon won the rights for seven-foot-two college superstar Lew Alcindor (the future Kareem Abdul-Jabbar).

Pavalon then secured the new star by outbidding the rival ABA in negotiations that over the years became legendary because the ABA's negotiator had a million-dollar check in his pocket and refused to offer it. Lew signed with the Bucks. With Flynn Robinson as the team's playmaker, Jon McGlocklin at guard, Bob Dandridge and Greg Smith as forwards, and the rookie Alcindor as its center, it took only one season for Milwaukee to spring from last place into the playoffs.

Over the years, Pavalon would develop an almost pathological fondness for his superstar center. Under his orders, Herman Cowan—Pavalon's executive assistant and the vice president and director of public relations for Career Academy—would take the rookie Alcindor under his wing, show him around, and get him on national talk shows. Cowan was the man behind the curtain for the Bucks. When he heard about my call, he quickly rounded up Pavalon and the rest of the Bucks execs into one room for a closed-door meeting. That afternoon, J. W. Brown was invited to Milwaukee.

It was the first time my salary was negotiated in a way that did not resemble a combination of dental drilling and secret service interrogation. Pavalon simply told Jake, "We want to pay Oscar what we think he is worth. Milwaukee had a fine season, used lots of young players, and all they need is Oscar to join with those kids." J. W., who was a brilliant negotiator, couldn't believe how easy it was. Later, he marveled, "There was no dickering. Oscar quoted a figure. Milwaukee said we are going to pay it because you deserve it. That was the end of the discussion on money."

Brown wrote out a deal memo in longhand on two duplicate pieces of paper: seven hundred thousand dollars for three years, a no-cut clause, an injury clause, approval on trades, and deferred compensation in case of a trade.

Cincy's hands were tied. If he wanted to trade me, Joe Axelson had to start dealing with Milwaukee.

The Bucks were going to offer their starting forward Bobby Dandridge for me and put a kid named Bob Greacen in Dandridge's place. Dandridge had just finished his rookie season, and he had an awful lot of potential. I wasn't about to go there if they messed up their starting unit. I told J. W. that if the Bucks traded Dandridge or Greg Smith (their other starting guard), there would be no deal.

Yvonne was unhappy about the prospect of leaving Cincinnati, but at the same time, this year had been so awful. It seemed like getting away could mean a fresh start. Throughout the whole soap-opera season, she had been her usual supportive self. But it got to her, seeing what was in print. Sometimes I think she was madder than I was about it.

She and I both liked the idea of Milwaukee. We grew up in the Midwest; our kids were born there. They liked having four seasons and the wintertime. I knew with Lew down there, my job would be easier, but it would be different. I told Yvonne, "Things are going to be different. It will be good."

The Knicks changed their mind about me and offered me a chance to line up with Bill Bradley, Dave DeBusschere, Willis Reed, and Walt Frazier. Maybe that would have been a great team, but it was too little, too late. Baltimore also made some overtures, and Phoenix tried to pretend that I hadn't nixed them. Finally, J. W. and I met and agreed to go to Milwaukee.

ON APRIL 12, 1970, Knicks fans got a treat at the Garden. Willis Reed outmuscled rookie Lew Alcindor and pushed him around the paint until Alcindor fouled out of the game. He walked back to the bench while fans sang "Good night, Louie," and the Knicks blew out Milwaukee, 132–96. With that game they took the Eastern Conference championship 4–1 and advanced to the NBA finals.

After the game, Pavalon told Alcindor, "Don't worry. We're going to get you some help next year."

Late that night, Milt Gross phoned in a very small paragraph to his copy desk at the *New York Post*. Slipping in before the paper's final deadline, its tiny headline read: "Oscar Robertson headed for Milwaukee."

Hours later, every sports page in America had the story.

FLYNN ROBINSON was a product of the University of Wyoming. Joining the NBA in 1965, he had originally been a member of the Cincinnati Royals but had missed his rookie season because of a heart murmur. His murmur cleared up, and he backed up Adrian Smith and me. At six feet three, Flynn was fast and could shoot. He averaged 8.8 points in fifteen minutes a game in his first year in the league, before he'd been traded to Chicago for Guy Rodgers. Flynn had become a regular with the Bulls and averaged almost sixteen points a game before Chicago traded him to Milwaukee. During the Bucks' inaugural season, Flynn had averaged 21.8 points a game and led the league in free-throw shooting. "He tore us up all year," Cousy said of the first of his two newest players. "It'll be nice to have him on our side."

Also coming over to the Royals would be twenty-three-year-old Charlie Paulk. Paulk was six feet nine, a former NAIA All-American at Northeastern State College in Oklahoma. Axelson claimed that he was the key to the trade, the strong power forward the team had always lacked. Cousy claimed Paulk could play the pivot, but also admitted he hadn't seen Paulk play, because Charlie had been serving in the Marine Corps for two years. In case this gave anyone pause, Joe Axelson then repeated that Paulk was a find and assured the press that Paulk's tour would be over just in time for preseason practice.

Yes, I was traded for a Marine who hadn't played ball in two years.

Yes, Bob Cousy was trusting Joe Axelson completely on basketball matters.

And no, Joe didn't know a basketball from a pumpkin.

I'd come to Cincinnati when I was seventeen years old. I'd spent my entire adult life here, met and married my wife in Cincinnati. My children were born and raised here. It was a lot to leave behind. But I was going anyway.

———————

THE FOLLOWING SEASON, Bob Cousy would get the running Royals he started. Amid dwindling crowds, the Royals started losing and kept it up all year. Rookie playmaker and star Nate "Tiny" Archibald would score forty-seven points in an early game in which the Royals would blast the Hawks. That would turn out to be the team's high point. The Royals would then begin losing. As crowds dwindled, Flynn Robinson barely made it off the bench. Charlie Paulk played a season or so for the Royals and was a modest contributor, at best. By March, the Royals were playing some home games in Kansas City. Charlie Mancuso—who managed the Omaha Civic Center—would be described by Cincy papers as "a sort of consultant for the Royals." Cincinnati would even play a home game in Las Cruces, New Mexico.

By the spring of 1971, the club's owner, Max Jacobs, had officially relocated the team's base of operations to Buffalo, going so far as to take the books with him. The Royals were playing some home games in Kansas City. The Royals had officially crashed, landing at the bottom of the league, finishing 33–49 with no playoff berth, and attendance at the Cincinnati Gardens fell into the toilet.

On March 30, 1971, the Royals traded Flynn Robinson for the number thirty-one pick in the draft. ("He didn't fit in," said Axelson.) On October 20, 1972, after a conditional trade to Seattle fell apart, forward Charlie Paulk was placed on waivers by the New York Knicks, ending his brief NBA career. The Royals finished the year 30–52 and missed the playoffs for the fifth straight season.

Before the start of the next season, what had come to be obvious was finally made official. The Royals were sold to a group of ten Kansas City businessmen—one of whom was Joe Axelson—for five million dollars.

The team played their last game in Cincinnati before 2,416 fans on March 12, 1972.

Being carried by my teammates, 1958.

Playing through an injury at the height of my career in Cincinnati.

Jerry West of the
Lakers and I in 1961.

Five of basketballs greatest stars in one corner: Wilt Chamberlain, me,
Lew Alcindor, Jerry West, and Elgin Baylor.

Lew Alcindor and I teaming up to get the basket against
Wilt Chamberlain and Jerry West.

Turning the corner past the long legs of Lew Alcindor, versus
Clem Haskins, 1971.

In action against the Knicks, 1973.

Being honored at my retirement celebration with my family looking on.

From left, Yvonne, Mrs. Jackie Robinson, and me.

At the dedication of the statue of me in Cincinnati,
endowed by J. W. Brown.

That summer, the Cincinnati Royals became the Kansas City–Omaha Kings. Kansas City's arena seated more than fifteen thousand people, and the Jacobs family controlled all the concessions there. Years later, Joe Axelson told reporters that before the 1969 season had even started, the team had commissioned a study on the matter. That explained everything. I was put through a year of hell because someone wanted to move a few more hot dogs.

Finally, on November 22, 1973, when the Kings had lost the fourteenth of twenty home games, Bob Cousy broke down and cried in the locker room as he announced his retirement. Later he admitted to a team executive that he was sorry he did things the way he did. He'd lost all control of the team. The Kings would remain in Kansas City until 1985, when crowd apathy and ownership problems spurred a move to the franchise's current home, Sacramento, California.

IN APRIL 1970, while my trade was being negotiated, Maurice Stokes struggled with pneumonia. His heart weakened from illness, he passed away. He was thirty-six. Shortly before his death, he dictated the following:

> There are aspects of life that everyone seems to take for granted. When the sun peeks over the horizon, it is the signal for the beginning of a new day. The beauty that the sun creates is something that words cannot describe. To me, one of the great satisfactions of living in the country is that you can get the real beauty of the sun, without the obstruction of the smoke.

CHAPTER THIRTEEN

Milwaukee, Lew Alcindor, and the Championship 1970–1971

PROFESSIONAL BASKETBALL had officially entered the arms race. During the second half of the 1960s, as the NBA was expanding from nine to seventeen teams—and NBA owners received a large entry fee every time a new franchise joined the league—the ABA was fighting an uphill battle to establish itself as a viable rival. Cities weren't willing or able to support two pro basketball teams, so the leagues raced and struggled for footholds in the most desirable markets. Whenever a talented player did become available, bidding wars ensued. To the delight of players and the chagrin of owners, salaries rose to unprecedented levels.

By the end of the decade, guys were switching leagues without a second thought; underclassmen regularly abandoned the college circuit.

Critics started complaining that the overall quality of play was diluted because there weren't enough good players to fill up two leagues' worth of rosters. The NBA's television ratings were down. The ABA couldn't even secure a national deal. Finally, merger talks began. During one negotiation, the reserve clause was raised. New York Knicks owner Ned Irish announced he would never give up the reserve clause. Ned had huge amounts of clout with the league—some said that the commissioner's office consulted him before making any major decisions. The moment he stormed out, negotiations were over.

When Joe Axelson and the Royals tried to trade me without so much as having read my contract, it reinforced everything I believed about owner arrogance, the need for players' rights, and the importance of getting rid of Ned Irish's beloved reserve clause. Since the Royals team I was on wasn't going to the playoffs and my professional basketball life in Cincinnati was coming to an end, I had time to concentrate on other issues. While the public venom between Cincinnati's front office and myself had settled into a cold war, I was working with Larry Fleisher, John Havlicek, Paul Silas, and Dave DeBusschere on a plan.

On April 16, 1970—four days before I was traded to the Milwaukee Bucks—the National Basketball Players Association and its president filed a class-action suit in New York District Court. We filed on behalf of fourteen players. As union president, my name headed the list.

In what became forever known as the Oscar Robertson suit, we claimed that any proposed merger between the National and American Basketball Associations would restrict player mobility and make pro basketball a monopoly. Our suit therefore claimed that any proposed merger constituted a violation of the Sherman Antitrust Act.

We called for the abolition of the player draft and the option clause that bound players to teams. From the lawsuit: "There can be no merger until issues such as free agency and 'freedom of movement' are settled."

At the time, the suit did not receive much attention. The playoffs were in full gear, and New York was abuzz with the Knicks, who were methodically grinding down the many talents of seven-two rookie Lew Alcindor and his Milwaukee Bucks.

We had bumped into one another at a Kutsher's summer benefit game a couple of years earlier. At that point, Lew was a college superstar and in the midst of his celebrated run of three straight national championships. So there would be no stain on his senior year of eligibility, he paid his way to Kutsher's like everybody else, and we took the court on the same team. "Once Oscar drove down the middle," Lew remembered in an interview, "I came in behind him. He got the ball and drove, and I cut the wrong way. Man, he yelled at me. He said, 'Listen, you've got to do it this way.'"

Alcindor continued. "What'd I do? I listened, man, that's what I did. When Oscar Robertson talks, you listen. And it helped me. The next time he drove, I cut his way. I didn't think I was open at all—and then the ball was in my hand, like magic. I said to myself, 'Well, well. You just met Oscar Robertson, and already he's taught you something.'"

The day after the Knicks eliminated the Bucks, Lew was getting ready to board a plane to Los Angeles. He glanced at a newspaper and saw a headline announcing that I'd been traded to Milwaukee.

———

IN 1970, Wes Pavalon's life was crumbling around him. His American Stock Exchange ticker symbol RRR was in the middle of a plummet from a price of fifty dollars a share down to one dollar, marking one of the biggest disasters in recent ASE memory. The empire was in shambles. And, as if this wasn't bad enough, his marriage was on the rocks. "The Bucks are my release," he liked to tell reporters. "They are my dreams come true. I'm not the Establishment guy in this town, and I don't go to opera and culture things like that. But I have given this city a performing art. I have given them the ultimate in basketball. Yes, a performing art."

Herman Cowan helped find me a home on Kenboern Drive, a cul-de-sac on the northeastern side of Glendale. It was a brick multi-level home, with cathedral ceilings and a fountain in the front foyer. When news came that I had purchased a home on Kenboern and was moving in, the neighborhood held a meeting and passed around a petition of complaint, arguing that I would adversely affect the property values.

Eventually, this petition reached George and Jane Preister, the family who would become my neighbors. George was an executive at the Falk Steel Company; Jane, a schoolteacher. Rather than sign the petition, Jane took a cherry pie over to Yvonne and welcomed her to Milwaukee. I was unpacking crates when I heard the doorbell ring. I wandered in to see what was going on, casually said hello, then left Yvonne and Jane to talk. Maybe a week later, I was mowing the lawn, and George Preister came over. We exchanged hellos. George and I would become dear friends and still are today.

It was an uncertain time all around; the majority of the neighborhood was worried about having me move in. I was unaware of this situation until George Preister and I had become very good friends. Then he told me the true story about the neighborhood.

Lew Alcindor was just a young colt at the time, seven two and 235 pounds, all of twenty-three years old, showcasing an Afro and mutton-chop sideburns, and throwing those beautiful, graceful skyhooks in from well above the rim. Lew could score, rebound, pass, play defense, and block shots—pretty much combining the individual talents in which Bill Russell and Wilt Chamberlain had specialized. His offensive repertoire was unstoppable, to the point that many people felt that he had surpassed Wilt (who admittedly was getting on in years) and become the best basketball player on the planet. By contrast, I was going to turn thirty-two in November.

The questions were many. Could Oscar Robertson transform the Bucks into a championship team? The answer was yes. How much gas did I have left in my tank? Between Lew's contract ($1.4 million spread over five years, roughly $280,000 a year) and mine, we accounted for a half a million dollars a year in salaries—far more than the combined salaries of the other three players in the starting lineup. Would player resentment be a problem? And as the Bucks played at the Milwaukee Civic Center—an arena known as the Mecca, but which had limited seating (10,746)—did such huge player salaries create money-flow problems? Could Coach Larry

Costello manage to keep the team together? Did I want to coach the team? Were there any black coaches at all?

Bucks management did their best to address these issues at an introductory reception and press conference for me, held at the Pfister Hotel. Team owner Wes Pavalon unveiled my new forest green jersey. Jon Mc-Glocklin already had my old number, fourteen, so Wesley unveiled what he called the appropriate number for me: one.

"I don't think Oscar realizes exactly how good Lew is," Wes told reporters. "And I don't think Lew realizes how good Oscar is. Until they play together, they won't be able to realize how great this thing can be."

Added general manager Ray Patterson: "I have to laugh when somebody says Oscar will have trouble working with Lew because he's used to having the ball all the time. Who would you rather have the ball all the time? The potential with these two guys together? It just scares you."

I was entering a new phase of my life. I'd played basketball in Cincinnati for the past fourteen years. Other than spending five or ten minutes on the same floor at all-star games, passing to Bill Russell and/or Wilt, I'd never played alongside a great center. Now, after four years of regular-season games that had meant absolutely nothing, I was being brought in for the specific purpose of leading the Bucks to a championship. I was ready for the challenge.

Eventually, I was introduced to the press in Milwaukee.

When they asked me about how I was expecting to adjust to Alcindor, I replied, "It won't be an adjustment; it'll be a pleasure."

Was money the biggest factor in your decision to go to the Bucks? "No," I said. "Lew is here, and it's a chance to play with a championship team. I think I can fit in well here. It's true there are a lot of kids on Milwaukee, but they got some valuable experience in the playoffs against a team like the New York Knicks. I know a little about that. It's like a fistfight. You learn your way around."

What about the groin injury that kept you out of twelve games? What about your feud with Bob Cousy? "Water over the dam," I said. "I'm not connected with the Royals anymore. I don't want to rehash it. There has to be a wrench, though—I lived and played there for so long. But I figure home is where the heart is."

The Bucks were coached by a workaholic. During twelve seasons as an NBA guard, Larry Costello had gained a reputation for toughness and thoroughness, and now that reputation had carried over into his coaching. Ever since 1968, when Larry had retired from the game and become the Milwaukee franchise's first-ever coach, players around the league had joked about his intense practices, with guys on other teams always telling us how happy they were not to have to do them. Larry was a no-nonsense coach on the sidelines, and during every game and practice, he had this pad at his side. Larry constantly sketched on that damn pad, coming up with this new tactic, that new play.

Lew Alcindor and I were of different generations. Where I had a traditional family life, a wife and three daughters, Lew lived in a luxury apartment complex called Juneau Village and had just a couple of years in the league. Both of us had key things in common, however. We both had reserved personalities, and, I think, we each felt isolated from the mainstream, middle-class world. We weren't close at first and did not spend time talking, on or off the court. But along with Larry Costello, we shared certain traits. What I think mattered the most was that we agreed that being as efficient as possible cut down our chances for errors. We had professional attitudes and approaches to the game. No nonsense.

"Each regards his game as a business, a complex occupation to be attacked with the precision and coolness with which an accountant surveys a ledger," wrote a *Sports Illustrated* reporter. "Both deal in basketball's essentials only, avoiding wasted motion and creating spectacle only by the uncluttered purity of their styles." During the season, we were dedicated wholly to basketball and wanted nothing more than to get the job done. This made it easier for everyone. You step on the court, and you know what is demanded of you.

I think this attitude was present from the first day of training camp and set the tone for the course of the season. The Bucks were one of the first teams with a full-time assistant coach who had only minor scouting responsibilities. This allowed Larry to run the most precisely mapped-out practices in the league; they were great workouts, with predetermined time allotments for specific drills.

Anyone could see that we were loaded that season. Between Lew and me, the team had two giant pillars on the same court, pairing skills and abilities that, in contrast to many superstar pairings, actually complimented one another. I'd never played with a dominant center, and Lew now had an outside threat to take pressure off him, make defenses play him more honestly, and make sure he was both fed and protected down low. Just the two of us would have been too tough for almost anyone in the league. But we also had Bob Dandridge, the athletic six-foot-seven forward who had a sweet jumper, ran the court all day, and showed all the skills of a future all-star. (Bob was coming off a rookie season where he'd averaged thirteen points and 7.7 rebounds. He'd go on to play in four all-star games.) Greg Smith, our other starting forward, had been around some and was a tenacious hustler. I knew if I set him up well enough he could provide some scoring for us. In the backcourt, Jon McGlocklin had been an all-star for the Bucks before Alcindor's arrival, and his rainbow jumpers were worth a solid seventeen or so points a game. On paper, it was the makings of an unstoppable offense—for the first time in fourteen years, there was no need for me to score twenty or thirty points a night.

On September 17, a few weeks before everyone left for training camp in Honolulu, Hawaii, we also made a trade with Seattle to get an athletic young guard named Lucius Allen, who had won NCAA championships with Lew at UCLA. We were also graced with height and rebounds and defense off the bench in Dick Cunningham, and, just as importantly, a friendly face in the form of Bob Boozer, who, in the sunset of his career, had been bouncing around the league. We also traded for McCoy McLemore.

Immediately, our defensive potential became apparent. Bob Dandridge, Greg Smith, and I were all about the same height. We were equally athletic, and we could switch any picks set on the perimeter without giving the offense any advantages. Lew had spent a good part of his rookie season adjusting to the pro game, but now he was prepared and knew what to expect. He was such a tremendous offensive player, so fluid and quick and long, that unless you did something to disrupt his rhythm, he could not be stopped. Our other offensive players used to forget what they were supposed to be doing sometimes and just stand around and watch him.

For the most part, I concerned myself with learning the plays and finding my own role. My philosophy had always been to make the weakest link stronger, and I noticed that if Greg didn't get enough touches or have someone setting him up, he disappeared from the offensive end. At the same time, when Greg and Bob got out on the fast break and provided us with scoring from the wings, you had to play them honest. The by-product was that it became harder to double-down on Lew. It also became impossible to run at me with a second defender—for the first time in my career, defenses would have to try to stop me one-on-one. If our offense hit on all cylinders, the sky was the limit.

"We're going to win it all," I told the guys. Over and over during practices, I said it.

"How do you know?" Bob Dandridge would ask.

"We just will. Watch."

Lew and I were named co-captains before the exhibition season began. Preseason games have specific purposes in the NBA; they provide time to work out the kinks and use your offense and defensive sets against live action, and they also give the guys at the end of the bench a chance to keep or lose their jobs. Not much stock goes into winning or losing these games. Nonetheless, I couldn't help but be a little encouraged when we beat Los Angeles and San Diego on consecutive nights and won our first five or six games by easy margins. Even playing limited minutes, all five of our starters were scoring in double figures.

Still, before our next game, Larry took me aside.

"I want you to take the ball to Lew more."

"What about the other guys? They're doing a great job. We've got balanced scoring and—"

"Never mind them. Get the ball to Lew more. I don't care about the others. Get it to Lew." This disturbed me. The other guys didn't like it. It didn't matter to me about the scoring, but we needed to develop a team concept and compete together. I told Larry to let me run things on the court. And that was it.

A few nights later, we played an exhibition game in Denver. Bobby Dandridge was having real problems with Costello's constant histrionics and browbeating. Wayne Embry had recently been hired as the Bucks community relations director. He and Larry called me for a meeting. They asked if I could step in and help control the team. I could see tension was simmering between the guys and Larry, and there was the possibility for serious trouble. At the same time, I was the president of the Players Association. There were all kinds of ways that getting involved with the problems between another player and the front office could adversely affect me. "Under no circumstances will I do that," I said. "You're coaching and directing this team, Larry. I play for you. You coach and direct this team. I'm one of the team."

I realized, though, that something had to be done. I learned the offense like the back of my hand and became comfortable with my teammates. Basketball is basketball. You play the right way, and good things will happen. We ended up winning all ten of our exhibition games. Lew averaged twenty-five points a game, which was what Larry wanted. He knew we had to ride our young colt's back. At the same time, Lew was just one of the *four* players in our starting lineup who averaged at least sixteen points throughout the preseason. We had a balanced, involved, and engaged starting lineup. The grumblings ceased for a while.

I also found myself taking care of other problems. For example, parking at the Milwaukee arena. There was a lot right next to the arena, but it was reserved for management and their friends. At a certain point, I wondered, why shouldn't the players park there? I went across the street to a parking lot. Listen, I said, we'd like you to save us fourteen or fifteen spots for the players; we'll take care of the cost. The guy was very nice about it. He was happy to do it. I never understood why Bucks management couldn't figure out how to do that. More importantly, it gave me some small indication of the way organizations ran things and a clue as to what they thought of players.

· Before the 1970–1971 season, the NBA had expanded yet again, with new franchises in Buffalo, Cleveland, and Portland, bringing the total number of teams to nineteen—enough that the divisions had to be split and reorganized. Where five years ago there had been nine NBA teams, 108 players, and 360 games, now there were seventeen teams, 204 players, and 697 games. Some journalists printed their worries that the franchises had been awarded only to keep ABA teams out of those cities. Others wondered about how the quality of play would be diluted.

We supported their argument by dropping three of our first seven games, which nearly sent Coach Costello off a cliff. He'd scream himself exhausted on the sidelines and then stare at the floor after games, as if wishing the boards would open up and swallow him. He didn't have to worry too long, though. Soon enough Lew was scoring easily and in the flow of the offense. Dandridge started getting out on the break and running like hell out on the wing. Then, on the heels of that little winning streak, we returned to my hometown of Cincinnati.

The crowd at the Cincinnati Gardens that night was 9,634, more than double the Royals' average that season. When my name was introduced during the starting lineups, there was a roar. Everyone in the arena rose, and the sound got louder; it extended and welled. For more than a minute I stood there. The fans kept cheering. I swallowed my feelings, raised my hand. They cheered louder. It seemed they would never stop.

On November 11, I entered Boston Garden for the first time with my new team. Bill Russell had retired from coaching by now, and Tommy Heinsohn had taken over on their bench. With Hondo Havlicek still out there, along with Dave Cowens, Jo Jo White, and a new round of dead-eye shooters, the Celtics were still loaded. The game was highly anticipated and broadcast on national television. In front of yet another record Celtics crowd, I played a complete game, scoring twenty-six points in forty-two minutes. As I led the Bucks to a 123–113 victory, we showed just how dangerous a team we could be.

"Oscar's in charge," Hondo said afterwards. "He stands out there with the ball and waits until Lew Alcindor and the corner men make their cuts, and then he hits the open man. The Bucks were tough enough to defend before Robertson got there. But now they're just about impossible."

Added our coach, "Oscar made the shots. He made the passes. He got the rebounds. He just did a hell of a job."

Our winning streak kept growing. Ten games, then twelve. During the run I not only set the pace offensively but also performed defensively with a fierceness that many critics felt was lacking during my time in Cincinnati. With Lew throwing in those hooks and me clamping down on the league's top guards, our streak reached sixteen games, and our 20–3 start was by far the NBA's best record. Next on the docket: the Bucks' kryptonite, the New York Knicks.

Consensus was that during the Knicks fabled 1970 championship run, New York had physically overwhelmed and overpowered the Bucks— especially Willis Reed. Lew had been born and raised in Brooklyn and had grown up a Knicks fan, so word was the loss was especially galling. "I wouldn't say it shook me up to lose to them last season," Lew said. "But I didn't like it one bit either. I averaged thirty-five a game, so Willis couldn't have shoved me around too much out there. I think the Knicks get higher up to play against us than anyone else, but the truth is they should have beaten us. They had the better team. This year is another story."

On November 27, inside the sold-out Mecca, New York forwards Dave DeBusschere, Bill Bradley, and Dave Stallworth badly outplayed Bob Dandridge and Greg Smith. The Knicks bench outscored ours 24–0. Still, we were up eight and had the game won, until we fell apart in the last five minutes.

After we lost to the Knicks, Lew complained to me about getting roughed up. I answered right back. "Lew, if you were not great, they wouldn't touch you." A man has to be physical out there, or else he'll be run out of the league. Basketball is concentration. It's a game where you never let up regardless of how bad you were beating somebody. You bury them so next time they would not forget. And it is a contact sport—a well-placed elbow can really help. I also told him he had to learn to pass quicker out of the pivot. He was getting double-teamed so much he needed to know where everyone else was playing.

Great as Lew was back then, it was obvious to me that he was still learning about the pro game. He needed to mature and start understanding what players were trying to achieve with the roughness. Wilt, Willis, and Nate Thurmond were the only centers who had any chance at stopping him—and their only chance revolved around beating him out of position. But the whole league had picked up on the idea. To an extent, it was working. Hard fouls could disrupt him entirely, get him off his game. "In a boring game," he once admitted, "when I look off into the rafters, Miles Davis or maybe Freddie Hubbard playing "Suite Sioux" will be going through my head. Or in a rough game, you see my face screwing up; it's because, man, I just get tired of the pushing. This isn't a contact sport. It'll never become a muscle-to-muscle situation with me, because that would defeat me. I'm not interested in tag-team wrestling; I'm a basketball player. I'm not overpoweringly strong but I'm strong enough to do my thing. I'll settle for being Sugar Ray. Let someone else be Rocky Marciano."

I saw that once Lew was able to recognize a double-team and hit the cutter, teams were going to have real problems stopping us. What we really needed, though, was a killer instinct. For many players, I knew, this came with experience—most of our guys who were getting playing time hadn't been in the league long enough to really suffer or know what it meant to want to win. They'd almost made it to the finals the previous season, and that was pretty good. But this was my eleventh year in the league, and I'd never played for a championship. Every game took a little bit out of me that I couldn't get back, and I didn't know how many chances I was going to have. I wasn't messing around out there. It was my responsibility to get this team mentally ready. From this point forward, I was more aggressive. If someone screwed up or didn't seem to want to play, we talked the situation out. People who weren't rebounding, guys who weren't playing defense, they needed to realize that we had to get the job done. "If we start getting flaky," Jon McGlocklin told reporters, "he shapes us up, quick." Lew seconded the notion, dismissing any thoughts that he might resent being told what to do. "You have to respect Oscar. You are out there playing with a legend, and he's still doing all of his job. How can you not do yours?"

Our ship righted quickly. We started another run. With Lew getting a natural and unforced thirty points a night and everyone else staying involved, we beat the hell out of a few expansion teams and then a few mid-level clubs. Our whole offense started to click. It wasn't flashy; it was just efficient and unstoppable: If you didn't double-team Lew, he scored. If you somehow did successfully double-team him in time to stop his skyhook, he could kick it back to me for the open shot. If you got to me, I might hit Bobby slashing down the middle. I might skip it across the court to Jon Mc-Glocklin for a jumper. Coach Costello sometimes told me to shoot more, but I figured I had to start our plays and make sure they were run correctly. At the same time, there was a delicate balance, because to be effective and to keep defenses from cheating too much on Lew, I had to think offensively. Where in the beginning of the season our team was feeling our way through each game, now you could see everyone trusting each other more, becoming more confident. Nobody worried about being able to get the ball up court against pressure or successfully starting the offense. Everybody knew he was going to get his share of touches and shots.

On January 8, the Knicks came back into town. They'd taken both of our regular-season meetings to this point and had beaten the Bucks in sixteen of nineteen games during Milwaukee's two seasons in the league. We knew that at some point we were going to have to beat these guys, just to prove to ourselves that we could.

Though Willis Reed had spent the previous weekend in a New York City hospital with abdominal pains and flulike symptoms, he was still in the lineup. There's no mercy in basketball, and we went after Willis immediately, feeding Lew. He had a couple of early layups, but inexplicably missed them. Time and time again he attacked Willis. Time after time, the refs called fouls on Lew. Halfway through the first quarter, our star had to go to the bench with two fouls. As we called time-out, the capacity crowd at the Mecca, which had been so crazed and hysterical during starting lineups, hushed.

Larry started scribbling on his pad.

Those Knicks were probably the best purely defensive team of that era. Red Holzman had them hustling all over the floor. In a half-court situation, they weren't flashy or tricky, but simply settled in. They made you take tough shots, and then they got the rebound when you missed. I took care of beating the press myself. In the half-court sets, with Dick Cunningham replacing Lew, our offense had to change. We switched out of a traditional low post offense. Instead of trying to establish position down low, as Lew had done, Dick came out onto the perimeter, setting picks at the elbow of the key. When I came off those picks and was open, I shot. When a man was open, I made sure to hit him.

Even with Lew sitting for half the game, the Knicks could never get ahead. We built up a double-figure lead early in the second half and down the stretch had to survive their frantic pressure. With five minutes left, they'd closed the gap to 99–95 ("a tense struggle which would have done justice to a playoff game with everything riding on the outcome," said the next day's *Milwaukee Journal*).

But where we'd folded the past two times against New York, this time a rested and determined Lew outran Willis, beating him up and down the court, disrupting their defense. I broke New York's pressure on two big possessions, hitting Bob Boozer and Greg Smith consecutively for an easy jumper and a three-point play, to salt away our 116–106 victory.

In my best performance in a Milwaukee uniform, I made eleven of nineteen shots and thirteen of fifteen free throws for a season-high thirty-five points. I also dished out thirteen assists and had nine rebounds. Bob Boozer said it was like watching me in 1961 all over again. Coach Costello said it was my best game of the year. "Oscar did it all," admitted Willis Reed. "That's his game; he runs the team. A lot of people say he's fat and out of shape, but he doesn't play like it. We could have come back, but he wouldn't let it happen."

"That win was a big part of our season," Dick Cunningham admitted, after the game. "We had to have this one. If this doesn't give us a lift, nothing will."

Our record improved to 33–7, while the Knicks' fell to 32–13. The season wasn't halfway over, but you couldn't help but start thinking. Expansion had brought another realignment with it, and if and when our teams ended up meeting each other in the playoffs this season, it wouldn't be during the conference finals, but for the NBA championship. We rode that momentum, extending what became our second major winning streak of the season to ten games.

As the all-star break arrived, we had the best record in the league. Conversations revolved around whether we could sustain this pace through the entire season, and whether the Knicks would have enough to knock us off this time.

Meanwhile at home, things had taken an equally encouraging turn.

During the first half of the season, while I was out on the road, friendships were developing between us and our neighbors. My daughters had started going next door to shoot baskets with the Preisters' girls on the hoop in their backyard. On occasions my youngest would ring their doorbell and go in and ask for cookies from the cookie jar. I hadn't known about any of this. But once Yvonne told me, I was delighted. Late one day during the fall, I'd watched as my next-door neighbor wrapped up his fruit trees. After a while I'd went over and asked what he was doing. George Preister explained the importance of and intricacies involved with protecting the fruit from rabbits during winter. George and I began to talk about basketball and other man talk. Their daughters always babysat for us. First, Janet babysat, and when she went off to college, Mary took over the job. All Yvonne had to do was give the Preisters the Bucks' season schedule.

One night after the break, our families went out for dinner together. In the summers George and I went out to Arlington in Chicago to watch the crowds and bet on a few horses. We would come back and take the girls out for dinner.

As time went by, we became completely relaxed around one another, laughing, joking, talking.

WHEN THE SEASON picked up, we found our groove. During the months of February and March, the Bucks simply did not lose. Twenty straight games—a new league record, eclipsing by two games the record New York had set the previous season. I could see our attitudes on the court evolving, watched that killer instinct developing. For the most part it was beautiful, as pure and close to the ideal of what basketball should be as anything I ever was a part of. At the same time, when I look back at it now, I also understand how much this perfection affected me. While I played the game with a serious, concentrated expression for the most part, if a teammate dogged it, I let him have it. It didn't matter how much we were up, or who we were playing. If a player started getting too out of control in our halfcourt set, he was going to hear about it. If Lew or Bob set a careless pick, that couldn't happen again. We had to get it right.

Maybe I acted this way because I saw how good a team we were becoming, maybe because I finally had a chance at a title and did not want things to go sour. Maybe part of it was because our coach had a tenuous relationship with a few of the guys, and I would rather have dealt with Bobby and other guys out there—I knew they would listen to what I said without checking, without an uproar. Basketball is a strange game. One injury can dismantle a season. One bad trade. A locker room shift in attitude. The press can create a controversy, or something can just go wrong. Little things come up, of course; that's natural during the course of the season. But the better we played, I think, the more I believed, or maybe wanted to believe. And the more I believed, the more confident I became.

"I got to be glad when time-outs were over," Lew told one interviewer, as the regular season wore down. "I couldn't believe it. Oscar would stomp around for a solid minute when things weren't going quite right, and scream at us, 'What the hell is goin' on around here?' He puts the fear of God into me. Gets on guys right on the floor. For not putting out. For acting flaky. He tells us. And that's good. Because a team has to have somebody like that. I won't do it myself. I'm a little too humanitarian. But Oscar doesn't have that problem. That's another good thing about Oscar: He wants that championship. Oscar wants it right now. Right this year. And he's got us all feeling this way."

With more than a month left in the season, we had a 53–8 record. Emphasizing execution and the simple, mechanical skills of the game gave the Bucks the best offense in the league. We were twelfth in field goals attempted and eleventh in free throws attempted, but we set a record for shooting accuracy and were the first team in NBA history to average more than fifty percent from the field for a season. We topped the league in points scored, with an average of 118 points a game. Just as importantly, by the time the regular season was nearing its end, our defense was playing as well as anybody in the league.

With six games left in the regular season, we had a 65–11 record, had won our division, and were fourteen games ahead of our nearest competition for home-court advantage. We'd dominated the league to such an extent that Coach Costello rested Lew and me and Bobby for the last six regular-season games, and yet we still finished with a 66–16 record—at the time the best in NBA history—and tied the 1964–65 Celtics for the greatest regular-season victory margin in NBA annals. If Coach Costello had decided not to rest us, the way Phil Jackson kept his 1995–96 Chicago Bulls starters in the game, there's no doubt in my mind we could have won seventy games.

Lew's thirty-one points a game led the league in scoring that season, and his sixteen rebounds per contest were fourth best. In just his second year in the league, he was the runaway winner in most valuable player voting, an award he richly deserved. But every starter on our team had an excellent year, averaging more than ten points a game (Lew— 31 points per game, Bobby Dandridge—18.3, Jon McGlocklin—15.8, Greg Smith—11.7). In fact, other than myself, Jon McGlocklin was the only starter who did not raise his scoring average from the previous season, and he actually shot a better shooting percentage than he had in either of his first two years.

During my previous ten seasons in the league, I'd averaged twenty-one shots a game. This season, that number was cut by almost a third. But after ten years in the league, I had enough statistics to last me a lifetime. If my averages didn't leap off the page anymore—19.4 points, 8.2 assists, and 5.7 rebounds—they were more than fine. More important to me was that our team had just finished the best regular season anyone had ever seen. Our starters were rested. Our reserves, Bob Boozer and Lucius Allen, were ready to go. Our team was pumping on all cylinders—that was what I cared about. I cared about the playoffs.

We won our first three games against San Francisco in the first round, dropped game four by two points, then returned to Milwaukee and finished the series in a fifty-point rout. Next came a matchup against the

Lakers. For the first time, Wilt would be squaring off against Lew in a playoff series.

Wilt was thirty-three now, and while he wasn't the dominating force he once had been, he'd still averaged twenty points and a league-leading eighteen rebounds. Wilt had befriended Lew and acted as something of a mentor during Lew's high school years, going so far as to give him his old shirts to wear. But of late they had become rivals. I think Wilt got tired about hearing that the new kid had replaced him as the top center in the league. Nobody doubted that he would be ready for Lew and would come out ready to play.

The real key to the series was Jerry West, because he had torn ligaments in his knee and wouldn't be playing. Jerry was still Mr. Clutch. Keith Erickson couldn't replace what Jerry brought to the floor.

To be honest, it wasn't much of a series. We blew out Los Angeles in each of the first two games, 106–85, and then 91–73. Before game three began, Erickson had to be rushed to the hospital for an emergency appendectomy, but Wilt still managed to carry the Lakers on his back, and he and Elgin Baylor pulled that game out, 118–107. That was Los Angeles's final stand. We crushed them in the next two games—117–94 and 116–98. Wilt always said he played some of his best basketball against Lew in that series, and after game five in Milwaukee, the fans gave him a standing ovation for his effort. Since we won the series by an average margin of nineteen-plus points, I don't think Lew cared. The win put us in the finals, so I certainly didn't. And Wilt must not have been all that broken up either, because not long after the series ended, he signed a contract to box in an exhibition against Muhammad Ali.

Wilt's fight against Muhammad never came to pass, which was too bad, because I would have paid to see it. It wasn't the only disappointment for us. While we rested and practiced, our rivals, the defending champions, the New York Knickerbockers, were in a brutal war with the Baltimore Bullets, a physical seven-game series that saw the two teams knock the living hell out of one another. Somehow Baltimore emerged from the deciding seventh game. Our locker room was stunned. All season long Lew and the guys had been looking forward to a series with the Knicks, our only real aggravation or challenge. Disappointed remarks came out of our locker room. Nobody disrespected or disparaged the Bullets, but the truth was, they weren't who we'd been gunning for. Hell, our programs for the finals were already printed—the cover featured Lew shooting a skyhook over Willis Reed and Dave DeBusschere. In a column entitled, "Knicks Will Be Missed in Final Playoff," a local columnist summed up everyone's frustration, writing, "It is as though Muhammad Ali had stumbled somewhere earlier in his comeback attempt and Joe Frazier had been forced to conduct his fight of the century against Oscar Bonavena."

We honestly didn't think Baltimore would beat the Knicks. They'd just won two consecutive series in deciding seventh games. But because of expansion and scheduling quirks, we hadn't played them in more than three months. Coach Costello and assistant coach Tom Nissalke had to lock themselves in the film room and watch tapes of the Bullets, going over each of their playoff games in order to properly scout their tendencies. Earl Monroe had been hurt against the Knicks. Gus Johnson—the player that Cincinnati had tried to trade me for—not only had chronically bad knees but also had been injured during the New York series. And Wes Unseld, their six-foot-eight, huge-shouldered rebounding machine, was walking on one leg. That's the playoffs in the NBA. Injuries.

On April 21, 1971, the top billing of the marquee outside the Milwaukee Arena listed something called "The World Championship Wonago Rodeo." About six feet below that, smaller letters announced that the Milwaukee Bucks were playing for the world championship.

I'd waited eleven seasons to get a chance at a championship.

ABC's broadcast team of Chris Schenkel and my longtime friend Jack Twyman talked about the uphill task the Bullets were facing, how they'd had less than forty-eight hours to rest since their upset over New York, and how important it was that they try to steal this first road game, shake us up, and get an advantage in the series.

Wes Unseld gave up about six inches to Lew, so of course we went inside as soon as possible. Within two minutes, Unseld had two fouls and was on the bench. To make matters worse for Baltimore, Gus Johnson's knee sidelined him (he would play sparingly through the series). Our defense attacked and pressured and tried to take Baltimore out of their half-court offense. We came up with five steals and jetted out to a 14–6 lead and, trying to go for the kill early, looked inside to Lew on consecutive trips down the floor. He was charged with two straight offensive fouls and all of a sudden, with less than five minutes gone in the first quarter, our own star had three fouls and had to take a seat for the rest of the half. The tenor of the game immediately changed. Baltimore closed to within two. Their next trip up the court, I was caught on a pick and switched onto Fred Carter. He shouted to teammates, "Get me the ball. I've got Oscar on me."

I scored the next six points, a run that extended our lead to ten and, just as importantly, calmed down our guys.

We led 50–42 at halftime. Lew came out in the start of the third quarter, and we immediately fed him the ball. Wes Unseld was wide as a city block and was a crafty, physical defender. While he couldn't see over Lew's shoulder, he was able to push him out of position at times and make Lew start his skyhook farther away from the basket than he wanted. Denying him the ball from one side on one trip down the floor, Wes might overplay the opposite side the next time down, then spin around and knock the ball away from Lew's other hand. He did the best job he could, but too often he was left one-on-one in the post with Lew—and all his tricks weren't enough. Lew scored eighteen in the third quarter, and we built a 79–62 lead. The Bullets went on midway through the fourth quarter and closed to within six when I sat down for a rest. But I came back to the game and again settled our guys. With three minutes and twenty-four seconds left, we pushed our lead to thirteen and Baltimore couldn't do anything.

Lew ended the night with thirty-one points and seventeen rebounds in thirty-three minutes as we took the opener 98–88. I had twenty-two points, seven rebounds, and seven assists. Fred Carter (six points on 3–11 shooting) did not have a good game.

Afterwards, I tried to downplay expectations and not get too excited. "The championship is what every player hopes for, and I am no different."

In game one, Baltimore's Earl Monroe was well on his way with twenty-six points. Four nights later in Baltimore, after a 19–9 run in the second quarter gave us a working margin, the Pearl hit four straight times and assisted on another basket, igniting the crowd with his flash and flair, bringing Baltimore right back. Meanwhile, Wes Unseld and Lew were attacking one another without mercy—Unseld scored eleven points and grabbed seventeen rebounds in the first half; Lew answered with fourteen points and fourteen boards. When defenders sagged in on him, McGlocklin nailed open jump shots. I finished the half with twelve points.

We led 50–48 at halftime, during which free-form rock dancer and Bullets' fan Marvin Cooper proved himself to be Baltimore's best performer. Cooper had started dancing in the aisles during the first round, when Baltimore had taken down Philadelphia in seven games. As we were warming up for the second half, he sauntered down near our bench and wiggled his fingers and hips at us, as if he were casting a spell. You had to give the guy credit: He was far more entertaining than Steve Swedish's Polish Sausage Band, which had played at halftime in Milwaukee.

In the second half, I set my sights on Earl Monroe, muscling him through his famed spins, battling him for position down low and refusing to let him post me up. On the other end of the court, Baltimore's coaching staff had decided that Bobby Dandridge and I were hurting them too much from outside, and ordered Kevin Loughery, Fred Carter, and company to stop sagging on Lew. Big mistake. Lew exploded while we played swarming defense, going on a 19–2 run which gave us a 70–51 advantage, a lead that stretched to 84–63 early in the fourth quarter.

"They stopped us from getting any layups," Baltimore's Jack Marin said, shaking his head. "You look up there and see that Afro up by the rim, and you just don't figure out what to do about it. They gave me the lane to the basket all night. I took it once, I took it again, then I said forget about it. It's like taking a golf shot through a tree; it's supposed to be ninety percent air, but you always seem to hit a twig. They figure you can't beat them with twenty-foot jumpers and they're right."

With two minutes left, we were up by twenty-four and started clearing the bench in a 102–83 blowout. Frustration set in for the Bullets.

Lew amassed thirteen points and ten rebounds in the second half and totaled twenty-seven points and twenty-four rebounds for the game. A good game for Lew. I had done pretty well and was one of four of our starters in double figures. As for the Pearl, he finished with just one point in the second half and had eleven points for the night, on four of eighteen shooting, with all four of his baskets coming during in that single second-quarter run.

"Oscar has helped us on defense as much as on offense," Coach Costello told reporters afterwards. "He plays even better defense than Walt Frazier of the Knicks. He's stronger than Frazier, and nobody is going to take him inside and get six-foot shots. You didn't see Earl Monroe get the ball in low against him like he did against the Knicks."

Added Bullets coach Gene Shue: "Oscar should have been on the all-defensive team. He got my vote. He played better defense than any guard in the league this year. When a man is a great offensive player and as smart as Oscar is, he knows what the other offensive players are going to do. Oscar is as smart as they come." Shue smiled. "And he holds a little too."

Through the rest of the series, the *Milwaukee Journal* called me "Counsel for the Defense." Broadcasters and columnists wondered if any glimmer of flamboyance, or so much as a peep of exuberance, would escape from our locker room when we finally won the title.

That was how it was discussed now. When, not if. There was no way around it. The 102–83 win put us firmly in control of the series. A championship was ours to take or lose. We knew this, but we also knew that a loss in game three in front of our home crowd would have given Baltimore the home-court advantage for the rest of the series, putting them right back in the thick of things.

The Pearl came out on fire to start game three, scoring Baltimore's first nine points. Eventually, we were able to cool him off, and our offensive machine started its efficient churn. We led by eight after the first quarter and had a commanding 68–52 lead at halftime. When I was called for my fourth personal foul early in the third quarter and had to go to the sidelines, Baltimore's starters chipped at our lead and worked the gap down to 70–68. Coach Costello's eyes met mine; I took off my warmup jacket, and we shut them down. We closed the third quarter with a 9–1 run, then opened the fourth with eight of the next twelve.

Bobby Dandridge's twenty-nine points led all scoring, and our fans gave us an extended standing ovation at the end of the 107–99 win. We were at the threshold.

Conventional wisdom says that a three-game lead in a best-of-seven series is insurmountable. At the same time, the last thing you want to give a down team is hope. If they win one game, suddenly they're back in their place with a chance—now all they have to do is win that game to get into game six. Once you're there, the momentum shifts. Now all the pressure is off the underdog. After game three, Earl Monroe and Jack Marin admitted to being "emotionally spent." The last thing we wanted was to give them a chance to reload.

Players' wives didn't travel back then, not even during the playoffs. Throughout the playoffs, all of our wives had ritually met at someone's house to watch the games on television. For game four, everyone came over to our house. They watched an unknown actor named Tom Selleck hawk shaving cream on commercials before the game. They heard Jack Twyman talk about the desperate energy of the Baltimore Civic Center. Once again Baltimore came out strong early and took a 15–10 lead midway through the first period.

The game was seven minutes old when Earl Monroe was called for a foul. On the next possession Jack Marin and Bobby Dandridge traded elbows and then exchanged punches. Gus Johnson pulled Dandridge away. Jon McGlocklin calmed down Marin. A double technical foul was called, and both sides cooled down. During the last six minutes of that first quarter, our offense slowly awoke, and we outscored the Bullets 21–7 and took control of the game, 31–22.

I saw that we had them when they walked over to their bench at the end of the quarter. I told the guys not to let up and we didn't, stretching the lead to nineteen in the second quarter.

Wes Unseld was on his way to a triple-double that night, and Baltimore managed to close the gap to 64–53, with ten minutes remaining in the third quarter. And that's when the Big O made another appearance.

Lew forced a Baltimore player to miss a wild reverse layup, got the rebound, and fired me an outlet pass. I caught the ball at around half-court and centered the ball, basically bringing the ball to the middle of the court. On videotape it looks like I am moving at less than full speed. Players seem to be whizzing past me to the left and the right. Two defenders are back for Baltimore, defending the basket. As I approached the top of the key, I suddenly changed pace, speeding up a bit, veering off at a sharp right angle. The two defenders reacted, coming toward me. Immediately, I threw a blind bullet of a pass to Greg Smith, who was cutting down the left side of the court, and hit him at full gallop for the uncontested layup.

From there I hit Jon McGlocklin for an open jumper. McGlocklin knocked down another on his own. Our lead mushroomed to 82–64, with 89–77 going into the final period.

That last quarter of basketball I remember as being as close to perfect as the game of basketball can be. I remember Lew getting a defensive rebound under the basket, and that I ran up to him and got the ball and told him to post up. He jogged ahead, and we went into a spread offense. I took my time bringing the ball up, waiting for everyone to get good and wide. From nearly half-court, I threw a hard pass into the middle of the lane, where Lew had gotten position on Wes Unseld. Lew caught the ball and in one motion leaped and turned and dunked right over a stationary Unseld.

Lew hit another majestic, one-handed, over-the-shoulder dunk, his body extended entirely, his arm bent and head inches from the rim.

Another fast break; this time I hit a streaking Bobby Dandridge for the assist.

I cut past Lew now, getting the pass on the perfect give-and-go, which I finish with a double-pumping layup.

I am alone against Kevin Loughery on the right side of the court, posting him up from about fifteen feet, with my back to the basket. I square up, take one hard dribble left, and drain the jumper.

Fred Carter is guarding me on the right side of the court. I have him isolated, without any help. Using my height and strength, I dribble toward the baseline. Fred is hand-checking me, pushing at me, and I am using my hip to ward him off. I half-turn and give him a little bump and half-spin off him toward the baseline. While he shouts to the referee, I take a fifteen-foot fadeaway that hits nothing but the bottom of the net.

"I played over four years with him at Cincy and Milwaukee, and the four-straight championship sweep with Baltimore was the most perfectly orchestrated performance I ever saw," Bob Boozer told reporters. "Oscar was so great that once in a while, when I was in the ball game, I'd have to shake myself into the realization that I was out there too. I'd get entranced watching him."

With two minutes and fifty-four seconds left to play, we were ahead by seventeen, and Coach Costello was still diagramming new plays on his yellow pad. He started substituting, a starter at a time. It was my 886th game in the National Basketball Association, and finally I was going to be a champion. I remember the seconds counting down. Hugging guys on the sideline and our celebration spilling over onto the court, the Baltimore fans collectively standing and cheering out of respect.

When I got into the locker room, the first person I saw was Jack Twyman, waiting to interview me. I hugged him. "Finally," I said.

Champagne popped all over the place. People were screaming. "Finally," I repeated. "It's been a long time, Jack. A long time coming."

I was exhausted, elated. I raised a number one finger to the camera. Lew came into the locker room, and I hugged him. "Big fella!"

It had been sixteen years since I had won the Indiana state high school championship with Crispus Attucks. After that game, they'd given us soda pops.

It had been eleven years since I'd won a gold medal at the Olympics. I don't remember what I'd had after that win.

Finally, I was an NBA champion. I grabbed a bottle of champagne and a paper cup. Of all the champagne I'd drunk in my life, this was the sweetest. Amid the insanity, I congratulated each team member. I'm supposed to be stone-faced, but I was jubilant and kept repeating, "Finally. We finally did it."

The celebration continued, and so did the hugs. Waves of relief and emotion crested and ebbed, crashing over one another and intermingling. I wished I could have hugged Ray Crowe. Tom Sleet, Al Spurlock, George

Smith, J. W., Austin, and every teammate and anyone who had ever helped me on and off the court were there. Most important, I wished my family would have been there. I slipped away from the ruckus. Lew was sitting quietly in a corner, drinking a Coke and chewing gum. He'd now won national titles at high school, college, and the professional level. After a few moments to himself, he admitted to a reporter that he was glad the ordeal was over and said he wanted to get some rest. He got up, took a paper cup, and drank some victory champagne. I passed by him and found a phone.

Yvonne picked up on the first ring. I could sense her tears and happiness through the phone static.

"Hi Yvonne," I said. "We finally did it."

In the press conference afterwards, someone asked Bullets coach Gene Shue who he thought should have won the most valuable player award. "Oscar," he answered. "Oscar was their leader, he controlled their offense, he hit the open man, and he played tremendous defense. I said when they got him they would be the best team in basketball." The majority of voters felt otherwise. Averaging twenty-seven points a game, Lew was named the series MVP, and for his efforts received a new car. I was happy for Lew.

Now I had a championship. It was a heavy load off my shoulders.

In the deciding game of the series, I'd played some of my finest basketball, scoring a team-high thirty points (on eleven of fifteen shooting), while amassing nine assists and three rebounds. There couldn't be any greater vindication for all the hell I went through in Cincinnati. When a reporter mentioned how easily I could have ended up being in the other locker room right now, I answered, "Yes. I know how close it was. And I'm glad I wound up in Milwaukee." I didn't say I was glad I didn't go to Baltimore. I just said I was glad I came to Milwaukee.

I've always felt that the 1970–71 Milwaukee Bucks were one of the great teams in basketball history. Including the ten preseason and fourteen playoff games, our overall record was 88–18. We were the second team in league history to sweep the championship series (the 1959 Celtics had been the other). Moreover, we lost fewer playoff games (two) and won by a higher average margin of victory (14.5) than any previous champion—to this day only Moses Malone's 1982–83 Philadelphia 76ers have ever beaten our playoff record (12–2). Sure, some people said that competition was diluted by the ABA and league expansion. But I disagree. For one thing, the reserve clause, along with the lack of any salary cap, ensured that teams had a depth that is unimaginable in today's game. As for the expansion issue, Michael Jordan's 1995–96 Bulls won their seventy-two games right after the league expanded. There's no question that competition that season was watered down, and expansion allowed the better teams to pad their win total (Seattle also won sixty-five games that season, for one of the ten best regular-season records of all time). Yet nobody questions the Bulls' status as an all-time team.

Teams around the league regarded 1970 as the year to beat us. Lew and Bobby Dandridge and Lucius Allen were all coming into their own. By all rights, we had the makings of a dynasty.

The next afternoon we flew back to Milwaukee. A cheering crowd was waiting for us at Mitchell Field. I drove back into Kenboern. Turning into the cul-de-sac, I saw out in front of my house that a sign had been tacked up. It was maybe thirty feet long and three feet wide, with huge, spray-painted letters:

CONGRATULATIONS O.

CHAPTER FOURTEEN

Do Not Go Gently
1971–1974

GREAT PLAYERS WIN CHAMPIONSHIPS. It's a common remark among sports experts and talk-show people. The idea is that unless a player carries a team to a title, individual achievements don't quite measure up. As if one guy, playing a team sport, can make up for his team's front-office mistakes, coaching blunders, and small-market payrolls. As if all by himself he can overwhelm other teams that not only have talented players but also might be run by smart coaches, with a front office that just maybe scouts and picks well at the draft, negotiates good trades, or has the payroll and kind of market that allows them to attract the best players.

Michael Jordan happened to be an unbelievable individual player. He also was fortunate enough to play on a team that recognized major talent, especially Scottie Pippen's potential, drafting him out of Central Arkansas. The duo was fortunate enough to play together for many years and grow as players and teammates. They may not have been happy with all of the decisions that their general manager, Jerry Krause, made, but few would disagree that the man successfully constructed teams around the pair that were geared toward and complimented their individual abilities. Add to that Michael's indomitable will, and you get a stunning total of six titles. A testament to Michael's desire and talent, yes. Still, I can't imagine anybody claiming that Michael's will alone won those titles.

Ted Williams never won a World Series. Neither did Ernie Banks. Gale Sayers never won an NFL championship, and Dan Marino never won a Super Bowl. Charles Barkley never won an NBA title. Connie Hawkins, Karl Malone, Sidney Moncrief, Darrell Griffith—none of them won championships. The list goes on and on. Does it mean any of them weren't great players? Don't they deserve consideration when people talk about all-time greats?

Having said this, man, was I glad to win that title.

Losing weighs on you, no doubt about it. A title *was* a validation.

Our team split $212,000 in playoff money. For some reason I never understood, Milwaukee's front office let the play-by-play announcer pick the ring design instead of giving the players a say. Everybody got rings. The players, all the minority owners and investors, every secretary in the office. Everybody except one guy, the equipment manager. We used to call him Goody, and he'd taken care of the equipment for the team since their inception and, man, he wanted one of those rings. I never understood why he didn't get one.

Soon my attention turned back to union responsibilities and our lawsuit. *Robertson v. NBA* had resulted in a preliminary injunction against any merger between the National and American Basketball Leagues. However, the court left a window of opportunity to NBA and ABA representatives to file for a Sherman waiver—a move that would have allowed for an exemption from antitrust status. (Baseball and football had received similar waivers; in the case of the NFL, this had cleared the way for a merger with the AFL.)

The ranking member of the Senate Judiciary Committee was a Republican law-and-order senator from Nebraska, Roman L. Hruska. In September 1971, he introduced a bill (S237) to the Senate that would grant the NBA a Sherman waiver. A subsection of the Committee on the Judiciary, the Senate Subcommittee on Antitrust and Monopoly, considered whether to grant the waiver and clear the way for a merger.

The stakes could not get any higher than this.

Hearings were held. Hruska was a principal advocate of the merger. Former California state senator Thomas Kuchel spoke on behalf of the NBA, saying that the salary wars for untested college stars "will inexorably end in ruin."

There was but one senator who spoke out against S237. He was the longtime Republican senator from North Carolina, Sam Ervin. Ervin was a strict constructionist, interpreting the Constitution literally. During the 1960s, Ervin had been known as something of an independent. To the delight of liberals, he supported civil liberties, opposed "no knock" search laws, data banks, and lie-detector tests as invasions of privacy. In 1966, he helped defeat a constitutional amendment that would have allowed prayer in school. At the same time, Ervin also opposed almost all civil rights legislation, in part on the grounds that a civil rights law took rights away from others (whites, for example: the right to hire whom they wanted, to sell their homes to whom they wanted, to go to school where they wanted).

Sam Ervin would go on to become the chairman of the Senate Select Committee to Investigate Campaign Practices—popularly referred to as the "Ervin Committee" or the "Watergate Committee." With eyebrows arching and references to Shakespeare and Bible-themed speeches of moral indignation, Ervin was a major figure in the Watergate investigation and Richard Nixon's eventual presidential downfall. (One choice line: "The President seems to extend executive privilege way out past the atmosphere. What he says is executive privilege is nothing but executive poppycock.")

However, before his Watergate heroics landed his face on counter-cultural tee shirts, the strict constructionist helped determine the fate of professional basketball.

Witnesses from each side of the argument came, testified, and answered questions in front of the imposing half-circle of committee members. As with all political issues, certain senators already had made up their minds to advocate one side or another, and the slant of their questions be-trayed this advocacy. Often, Ervin ended up squaring off with Senator Hruska and others.

John Havlicek and I were the only two players to testify. During the weeks when I should have been getting ready for training camp, a great deal of my time was spent in offices working with Larry Fleisher in preparation for my appearance. We didn't go over testimony, per se, because we didn't know what questions were going to be asked. We reviewed various sce-narios; we wanted to make sure that I let the senators know exactly what the Players Association was trying to do as an organization.

On September 22, 1971, accompanied by Larry, I testified:

> I speak here today on behalf of the players in the National Basketball Association. Our opposition to the proposed merger (of the two leagues) is total. Every player supports our stand and the positions as indicated by our counsel in prior testimony. The players recognize the unfairness of a system of professional basketball which allows them to negotiate with only one team. They have gone through the experience of no competition prior to the ABA's existence and of great competition since 1967. They understand that every player has been dramatically helped by the competitive aspects of a second league. All of their salaries have increased, from the last man of the team to the superstars.
>
> I have personally seen the hardships that were wrought upon many players in the NBA during the early 1960s—the men who played for five thousand or six thou-sand dollars a year, the men who were not able to bargain ef-fectively for increases, the men who retired and were finished with their careers at age thirty without any benefits. We, the so-called superstars, really do not need to fight the merger. I have a long-term contract. I will probably retire at the end of my contract. I do not stand to benefit financially by having the leagues continue to compete for my services,

but I do stand to benefit by seeing that the four-hundred-some-odd ballplayers in professional basketball have an opportunity to be treated as other people in American life; that they can truly negotiate for their services; that they can escape from the ghettos or leave the suburbs, knowing full well that they have a right to earn an income commensurate with their skills and commensurate with the risks involved in the shortness of their careers.

All of our players stand behind me in this position.

The questions proceeded. Senator Ervin began by asking about a player's brief career window and the idea of players receiving the same chance to work in a free market as everyone else. Other senators asked about how I felt about being traded and the right to choose my workplace. Soon Senator Hruska became involved.

SENATOR HRUSKA: Mr. Robertson, there are some people who believe that a draft of some kind is necessary for organized league sports, that without some discipline of that kind, it would not be possible over the long run for league sports in this type of team sports to do their most effective work or perhaps over the long run to perform in the fashion and the way that the American public is willing to support. Have you given that proposition any thought on your own?

OR: Yes, I have. Quite a bit.

SENATOR HRUSKA: Would you mind sharing with us some of the conclusions you have reached in that regard?

OR: Well, this will be my twelfth year in professional basketball, and I have seen some of the ills brought on the ballplayers when I first started playing basketball, and I think it is terribly wrong for anyone to limit anyone's ability to earn money no matter where it may be, whether it is in business or in sports. I think any time you limit a person as to where he can go, such as the case was prior to the two leagues, I think it is terribly wrong.

SENATOR HRUSKA: It is wrong to limit the amount of money a man can earn?

OR: I think in America it is.

SENATOR HRUSKA: Does the draft system do that?

OR: I think if you only had one league, that is true. As long as you have two leagues, there is no telling what a person can earn.

SENATOR HRUSKA: You seem to have done pretty well. Do you think you are worth more than the one hundred thousand dollars you are getting?

Immediately, Larry Fleisher leaned over toward me. We'd known each other for years now, and he knew what my immediate reaction might be: "There may be those who wonder if you are worth the money you are getting from the taxpayers." Larry whispered in my ear. I thought about his advice, paused, took a drink of water.

OR: To be honest and frank, I think so.

There was some laughter from the committee and the gallery. I waited for it to end.

As the hearings proceeded, an independent report by the Brookings Institute found that clubs in both basketball leagues suffered not from salary inflation, but from insufficient revenues due to playing in arenas too small to support them. According to the report, only the sharing of home-game receipts with visiting clubs, plus the end of compulsory option clauses, could save the leagues. When the findings were brought in front of the committee, NBA commissioner responded with the opinion that these provisions "wrecked the chance of merger." Witnesses continued to be heard. The committee went into deliberations. By this time, training camp was about to start.

From the first day of practice, the Bucks were seen as the new Celtic dynasty in the making, with a repeat championship in the future. But there were some minor changes to our team, and none were particularly positive. For one thing, our owner, Wesley Pavalon, was up to his neck in the red ink of a crumbling empire. He became neurotic, jittery, and this has an effect on the franchise, trickling down through management and the coaching staff. On the court, Bob Boozer had retired, and we'd gotten rid of Greg Smith and Dick Cunningham in a trade that hamstrung our ability to defend on the perimeter. And while newcomer Curtis Perry was an athletic power forward, he was a limited offensive player, and he had problems adjusting to Coach Costello's histrionics. The pressure to repeat, along with the ownership problems, affected Coach Costello, I think, because he started applying the whip more and more in practice, treating thirty-year-old men like they were college freshmen. The team was bitching about it.

Racial overtones bubbled beneath the city's breweries and bratwurst halls, and this affected things as well. While Milwaukee may have been a bigger city than Cincinnati, it wasn't particularly more progressive on the racial front. (In 1977, after he'd left the Bucks for Washington, Bob Dandridge told an interviewer, "Coming to Wisconsin was one of the biggest adjustments of my life. I had never experienced true racism until I came to Wisconsin.") The tensions came to the forefront with the news that Lew Alcindor had gone to court and changed his name.

Before his senior season at UCLA, Lew had converted to the Islamic faith. At the time of his conversion, he had been given the new name of Kareem Abdul-Jabbar (he'll be referred to as Kareem from this point on). Though the court filing did nothing more than legally change his name, there was a significant public backlash, just as there had been years earlier, when Cassius Clay had become Muhammad Ali. I think it affected Kareem. He'd never been too keen on the city, and the backlash only furthered his sensitivity. And while it did not matter too much on the court—Kareem would lead the league with 34.8 points a game, as well as 16.6 rebounds, good enough to earn him MVP honors for the second consecutive year—the chill was noticeable in the locker room.

I was thirty-three years old during the 1972 season, and the Bucks were on their way to a 63–19 record and a second consecutive conference title. But the season was marred by a major injury. In early February, I suffered sciatica. I could not feel my feet, and I missed eighteen games. By the time we met the Warriors in the opening round of the playoffs, I still couldn't run at full speed. Somehow, I managed to average twenty points, ten rebounds, and eight assists in the first three games of the series.

We advanced into the conference finals for a highly anticipated rematch against the Los Angeles Lakers. Where last season we had been the record-setting juggernaut and the Los Angeles Lakers had been the walking wounded, now the Lakers were the team at full strength. They had had a record-setting winning streak (thirty-three games—starting with a win over us on November 5, 1971; ending forty-three days later, on January 7, 1972, with a loss to us, on national television). They had the record for most wins in a regular season (sixty-nine, breaking our mark by three games). Hobbled by my injury, I played just seven minutes in game six. Going into that must-win game, we got in foul trouble early, and Coach Costello gambled, keeping both Curtis Perry and Bobby Dandridge in the game early in the second half. Both eventually fouled out. The Lakers beat us 104–100, to take the series four games to two, and Jerry West went on to win his first title.

The next season was just as frustrating. On October 6, Kareem and Lucius Allen were arrested for suspicion of marijuana possession in Denver. Although they were released on bond and never charged due to lack of evidence, the event was a horrible overture for the regular season. I was playing about forty minutes a night. At least until January 7, I was. I injured my right hamstring at practice and sat out the next four games. We went on the road, and I stayed with the team and kept traveling. During games, I did rehab by jogging underneath the stands. Well, we were in Phoenix and the game got underway, and, lo and behold, they went up fifteen in the first quarter. Soon the trainer was chasing me. "Oscar, you have to go into the game."

"What?"

"Larry wants it."

"Man, there's a reason I'm not playing. I'm hurt."

"What can I tell you?"

So I went out there, aching like a bitch, and dragged myself up and down the floor, and wouldn't you know it, I ended up breaking a finger in that game. For the next two months I played like that, limping, my thigh wrapped up like a mummy, unable to extend my leg to a certain angle or get it into certain positions.

With about two months left in the season, the situation went from irritating to downright scary and surreal. Gunmen involved with the Black Muslims movement murdered seven people at a mosque in Washington, D.C. Kareem knew all seven victims and had helped finance the mosque in which they were killed. Speculation was, there was a contract on Kareem's life as well, and he played the remainder of the regular season and playoffs with armed bodyguards around him. Somehow though, with the constant tension dogging us and the media asking questions, with me hobbled and Kareem distracted and looking over his shoulder, we still were able win sixty games for the third consecutive regular season—becoming the first team in NBA history to do so.

We met the Golden State Warriors in the opening round of the Western finals again. (The San Francisco team had moved to Oakland the previous season.) But this time Nate Thurmond and the Warrior defense played aggressively, seriously outrebounding us and overplaying all the passing lanes. We blew the Warriors out twice, winning in twenty-point runaways, but lost three games playing catch-up. I was playing well and scoring at will, and if we could start rebounding, I was sure we had a chance to pull out the series. We fell behind early in game five, but had pulled within striking distance with eight minutes left when, all of a sudden, an enormous pain shot into my leg. I was carried to the sideline and was diagnosed with a ruptured Achilles tendon. We lost game five and were soundly trounced in the sixth and deciding game. Once again, our season was over.

We had been the city's darlings during our championship season, but sports is a fickle game—yesterday's headlines carpet today's birdcages. So it didn't matter that the best teams of that era—the Bucks, Lakers, Knicks, and Celtics—were among the elite of all time. It didn't matter that the championship teams from 1970 to 1973 still hold an almost mythic place in the record books and NBA lore. Our successes during the regular season also didn't matter. The bottom line in professional sports is the championship.

And for the second straight season, we hadn't gotten the job done. And for the second straight season, I'd frequently been on the sidelines, watching.

———

ON SEPTEMBER 8, 1972, the Senate Subcommittee on Antitrust and Monopoly officially approved the merger of the American and National Basketball Associations. On the surface, the ruling looked to be a defeat for our union. But even a cursory reading of the opinion found otherwise. For while the committee declared that a merger of the two leagues would not violate antitrust laws, they also decided that the reserve clause was illegal and could not be part of the merger agreement. Along these lines, the Senate subcommittee also announced the preparation of a bill that would strike down the reserve clause and replace it with an option clause, allowing a player to switch to another team a year after the end of his contract without the original team retaining his rights. In addition, the subcommittee ruled that the ABA teams did not have to pay $1.25 million to get into the NBA and that players should all be signed to one-year contracts with an option for a second season. Following that, they'd become free agents.

Just as importantly, the subcommittee declared that without any verdict or settlement in the Players Association's lawsuit against the NBA, the injunction preventing the two leagues from merging would stay in place.

It was a landmark victory. We'd gotten rid of that reserve clause and successfully suspended the merger. Not everyone in the union was pleased with the results of the option clause, but we'd definitely won, giving even more momentum to our lawsuit against the league. After years of being mistreated and taken for granted, our struggle had been validated.

Almost immediately, club owners returned to the negotiating table. After meeting with Larry, the league signed a bargaining agreement with the union, the first in NBA history. It was a three-year deal, and under its terms, players received a minimum set salary of $20,000. Moreover, beginning at age fifty, former players were to receive an annual pension for each year of service.

Eight years and eight months after players voted to boycott the all-star game over the pension issue, we got what we wanted.

Change may have been slow, but it wasn't impossible. The same month as the labor settlement, my old roomie, Wayne Embry, was promoted to become the general manager of the Milwaukee Bucks. Wayne became first African-American in professional sports to hold such a title. It was another unbelievable step, a sign of how far things had come—one that even now is too rarely taken. But it couldn't have happened to a more deserving guy.

Still, history would show that professional basketball was entering a difficult period. Wilt retired at the end of the 1973 season, signaling the end of an era. And while the American Basketball Association had some of the most exciting players in the game in Julius Erving, David Thompson, Artis Gilmore, George McGinnis, and George Gervin, the ownership did not have the financial strength to sustain their league as a viable rival league to the NBA. Except for a few solid franchises like the Indiana Pacers and Denver Nuggets, the great majority of their clubs was relying on the hope of a merger in lieu of self-sufficiency.

In order to generate interest in a merger, interleague exhibition games started. While the NBA dominated the early meetings, by the mid-1970s, the wins had evened out. The general public remained unmoved. Television ratings for basketball had been slumping for some time. ABC's executives were unhappy with all sorts of things—the NBA's recent expansions, the glut of basketball, and the changing face of the game. Memos circulated that the game was becoming "too black." When the NBA's contract came up in 1973, ABC refused to meet its terms, and the league switched networks, joining CBS. Executives at ABC countered with a slap in the face, a low-budget show called "The Superstars," where athletes and stars competed against each other in outdoor events, such as swimming and the obstacle course. The slap became a sting over the course of the next few years. The NBA Game of the Week routinely got clobbered in the ratings by infamous spectacles, not the least of which was the sight of Joe Frazier needing help to reach shore while competing in a swim contest.

286 ★ OSCAR ROBERTSON

As far as my own career was concerned, there was, at first, a similar floundering.

My three-year contract with Milwaukee had ended with the loss to Golden State, and when I told a newspaper reporter that I had to assess things before making any decisions about my future, speculation began that I might retire. The reality was that I just wanted to think about what I wanted to do. I knew I wanted to play another season, and Wayne Embry had already indicated that he wanted me to come back.

If I was going to have one final run, I wanted to go out at my best, and I spent that off-season rehabilitating my body, watching my diet, and working out. By the time training camp came around, I weighed a trim 217 pounds. But even as we started negotiating the terms of a new contract, I told Embry that pretty soon he was going to have to start looking for another guard.

"Don't say that now," he told me.

"Wayne, I am serious." I said.

We'd known each other for a long time. This wasn't management and player giving each other smooth talk. "Between you and me," I said, "I'm hanging it up."

Soon we'd reached an agreement on a one-year contract for $250,000; when we announced the deal to the press, I made sure to say I didn't have the patience to coach, never wanted to coach, and anything else that I thought might bury the worries in Larry Costello's head. (Larry needn't have worried, black athletes weren't getting too many opportunities to coach back then.) I also said that this would definitely be my final season in the National Basketball Association. For his part, Larry told reporters that if I did not play more than thirty minutes a game, my body wouldn't run down. "Thirty minutes a game is all we need from Oscar. We want to run all the time, and with four experienced guards, we should be able to do it."

With Kareem, Bob Dandridge, and myself, we had a solid core. Lucius Allen had come into his own as a starter. He became athletic enough to run the wing and score on the fast break, solid enough a ball-handler to take pressure off me in the backcourt, and good enough as an outside shooter to make you pay for ignoring him. Jon McGlocklin could nail a jumper at any opportunity, and Cornell Warner and Curtis Perry contributed ruggedness and athleticism, respectively, in the frontcourt. We also picked up Ron "Fritz" Williams, the prototypical hustler who could not shoot at all, and a twenty-three-year-old, six-foot-seven forward from the ABA named Mickey Davis. While I was concerned about our ability to rebound, as long as the core took care of business, I thought we had a chance to compete for another title.

We came out blazing in the regular season, winning fourteen of our first fifteen games, including a run of thirteen straight. After I scored thirty-four in an early-season showdown against the Bullets, my old nemesis K. C. Jones, who had taken over as Baltimore's coach, marveled. "He still does it all. Nobody in the world can stop him when he's ready to put the ball up. He pulled the whole game out of his bag tonight." Phil Chenier, who'd scored a season low of eight points, agreed. "He's like Super Quarterback. He knows where everybody is going, and he scans the play and makes a decision before making a move. He's too much." Kareem was also back to his usual dominant self, scoring thirty a night, even if he had shaved his beard and muttonchops ("Nothing happened, I just felt like shaving"). By all accounts, we were the team to beat.

Our only early slip came in a 105–90 loss in Boston. After winning sixty-eight games during the 1973 regular season, the Celtics had reached the conference final, only to lose to the Knicks in game seven—in Boston Garden, of all places. Then they'd had to watch Willis Reed pull his infamous game-seven heroics, as he led New York over the Lakers for the championship. That Celtics squad obviously was one of basketball's elite teams. With Jo Jo White racing around at point guard, Don Chaney hounding you to death on defense, and John Havlicek still running through screens, shooting the hell out of the ball, and hustling all over the place—Boston was loaded in the backcourt. Their frontcourt was just as good: Don Nelson had an ugly but almost automatic jumper and was sly as hell on the boards. At center, Dave Cowens, who may have been only six nine but had long arms, was a great post defender. He caused all kinds of matchup problems on offense because he could run, handle the ball, was relentless on drives and running hooks, and also loved to drift outside and light up your post guy from out there. Tom Heinsohn topped the roster off by bringing in Paul Silas, an off-season acquisition from Phoenix who grabbed every rebound in sight, and Paul Westphal from the bench, providing the Celtics with rebounding options as well as the depth to press and trap and fast break. It was almost as if Bob Cousy and Bill Russell were still out there, wearing the green and white.

Jo Jo White had scored twenty in Boston's early victory over us. On December 1, we played them again, and we shut him down. Jo Jo scored two early baskets, but accomplished little else in the first half. If you took away their fast break, Boston was a fairly average team. We jammed their outlet passes in the frontcourt, made sure to have men back to defend against their running game, and also took care of the ball, denying them the advantage of any turnovers. Boston sagged in on Kareem, and in the second half we capitalized by swinging the ball across the court, where Hondo Havlicek was left alone to deal with Bobby Dandridge. Bob scored fifteen in the fourth quarter to blow the game open, and we won going away.

My durability was great, according to the *Milwaukee Journal.* "His remarkable forty-five-minute performance was probably the biggest single factor in the 117–93 rout that ended the Celtics' twelve-game winning streak. The thirty-four-year-old campaigner did it all. He collected twenty points, ten assists and six rebounds; sank nine of fifteen shots; ran the offense with his usual aplomb; and perhaps most important of all, made a nonfactor of Jo Jo White by holding the fleet Boston guard to eight points."

Bobby led us in scoring that night, with twenty-seven points, and also held Havlicek to 6–20 shooting. We improved to 21–4, while the Celtics fell to 16–9. I remember thinking that it was a good win for us, because it showed that we could, man for man, shut down Boston. This boded well for the future.

At a practice, however, pain shot through my lower extremities. I was taken to Milwaukee Lutheran Hospital and diagnosed with a flaring sciatic nerve. I stayed overnight, underwent diathermy, and was literally stretched.

Milwaukee's team doctor, Thomas Flatley, expected me to be out of action for about ten days. I ended up missing eleven games.

I remember that the Lakers came to town, and Jerry West was on the sidelines too, out with the same abdominal injury that had crippled me the previous season. Sitting there, watching the action, I recognized how strange it was: these teams playing, with Wilt retired, and neither Jerry nor I on the court. Some things you can't ignore, you know? Soon I told Larry Fleisher that next season he was going to have to find someone else to run the association. For at least the second time, I told Wayne Embry that the team should really start to look for another guard. He told me Lucius could handle the responsibilities.

"Maybe he can," I said. "But think about getting another guard in to handle the ball."

I still didn't think I was finished, mind you, and the last thing I was going to do was give up on the season. Without me on the floor, Lucius Allen moved over to the point and Jon McGlocklin replaced him as the shooting guard, and while they kept the team above water, it wasn't natural. We slumped a little and slipped in the standings, but we were still a playoff team. I was determined to get back in time for the postseason. Herman Cowan approached me. He said the front office wanted to know what I thought about the team having a day in my honor. It wasn't the easiest moment. It was my fourth year, and I'd talked to Wayne, so I knew and they knew I wasn't going to be with the team anymore. At the same time, hearing Herman ask that question really brought things home.

Suddenly, it was apparent to me that the Bucks weren't planning on my coming back either. Whether I was planning to leave or not, I wanted the Bucks to be honest with the fans.

"If this is a retirement party, just say so," I answered. Then I thought about it. And I told Herman, "Sure."

By the start of March, my back was feeling better. Returning to the lineup, I made six of nine shots and scored fifteen points as we beat the Pistons by twenty-three at home. Coach Costello called it an encouraging sign, and Lucius Allen told reporters that I played like I did when he came into the league. Two nights later, I played fifty minutes in an overtime victory over Houston. Then we headed to San Francisco. I scored a season-high thirty-four points, and we rolled to another rout. "Even when he isn't scoring, he's getting the ball to somebody else for a basket," Warriors coach Al Attles said. "This is the best I've seen him play in several years." Kareem remembered that night in his autobiography, writing: "Oscar just dominated the floor. He crushed everyone who opposed him on the court; threw hard, precise passes that demanded to be converted, rebounded with a passion, made seventy percent of his shots and scored thirty-four points before he was lifted. Total mastery. I envy the guys who played with him in his prime. Playing with Oscar was like working with Thomas Edison."

We'd won four straight and were on a roll. Then on March 15, we were in Detroit. Lucius Allen was chasing a ball out-of-bounds when he skidded on a warmup jacket and grabbed his knee. Nobody wanted to believe it was a serious injury, but the x-rays showed ripped ligaments. He was done for both the season and the playoffs.

It was a huge loss. In thirty-three minutes a night, Lucius was good for more than seventeen points, five assists, and four rebounds. He gave us about six running strides on our fast breaks, was an excellent penetrator off the dribble, a strong second ball-handler and decision-maker, and in all ways took all kinds of pressure off me in the backcourt.

If a team tried to trap me and take the ball out of my hands, for example, Lucius would free himself up, attack the back end of their press, and turn their pressure into our own fast-break opportunities. Without him, we not only lost that ability to attack, but were more susceptible to backcourt pressure. We also lost a second distributor. And by inserting Jon McGlocklin into the lineup, we lost any backcourt depth we might have had.

Those Milwaukee teams I played on were structured in a very specific manner. I'd say Kareem and I were all-around basketball players, but otherwise our guys had defined and more specific roles. Running the team meant knowing exactly what each guy could and could not do. For example, it meant knowing that Bobby Dandridge was an excellent finisher on the break, had a knack for being in the right place at the right time, and was dangerous in half-court situations where he could strike quickly, while also being aware that if Bobby had the ball too much, he tended to get out of control. It meant knowing that Cornell Warner might be able to rebound and score off a lot of garbage and second-chance efforts, but that his jumper was unreliable from beyond eight feet. That Jon McGlocklin was a great shot but not a point guard.

Where at the start of the season, Coach Costello had wanted to play me thirty minutes a night and keep me fresh, now, healing back or no, I was going to have to be out there constantly, shouldering the ball-handling responsibilities. I didn't complain. In fact, I understood immediately what had to happen. My back wasn't bothering me any longer, and my legs were fine. Larry got to drawing on his pad and simplified our offense even further, so that we concentrated even more on feeding Kareem, then letting everything else build off the big fella. The four-game winning streak became six, then seven.

On February 24, 1974, Herman Cowan hosted a "Day for Oscar." The mayor of Milwaukee was there, as were assorted senators and governors, the mayor of Cincinnati, my parents and brothers, Yvonne and our daughters, and close friends like the Browns and Tillotsons. Bill Cosby was supposed to emcee, but it turned out that he had a scheduling conflict and was replaced by another comedian, Arte Johnson. Senator Richard Lugar gave me a key to Indianapolis. The mayor of Milwaukee read a proclamation declaring Oscar Robertson Day, and a pair of scholarships was awarded to two underprivileged African-American youths. I was presented with a thoughtful gift: two pieces of art done by prominent African-American artists. It was a lovely evening, equaled two nights later, at a sold-out game against, yes, my old team—now relocated and renamed the Kansas City–Omaha Kings. The Bucks officially honored me with a halftime ceremony, during which they announced a scholarship in my name to be set up at the University of Wisconsin–Milwaukee, plus a second scholarship for a Nigerian basketball coach.

It was a wonderful night. Friends from high school and college came. The fans were wonderful, as they always were to me. We won the game and ended the season riding a fourteen-game winning streak, including eight on the road. Where a month ago we'd been struggling, now we'd tied for the best record in basketball, Kareem was on his way to being named the league's most valuable player for the third time in four years, and we were cresting into the playoffs on waves of momentum.

Some time after the ceremony, I was talking with J. W. Eventually, the subject of my contract came up, and somehow or another we ended up wondering just when, exactly, the thing would expire. When I got home, I took a look at my copy and, wouldn't you know, it had expired. Ended with the regular season. The next day I called them and said, "I don't know if you knew this, but I don't have a contract with you guys."

"We'll work something out," they said.

"No," I said. "You can't work out anything. We both know I'm not coming back. I just want you to know I don't have a contract."

It was a very unprofessional situation. If I'd have hurt myself during one of those games, the team wouldn't have been responsible for my rehab, because I wasn't an official employee of the Bucks. Without a contract, I shouldn't have been allowed to play in the postseason, let alone to receive my players' share of the revenue. Hell, I should have had to buy a ticket to the games. But I was going to play. Our team had worked too hard. And there was no way I was sitting out.

Kareem and Bobby Dandridge combined for about sixty a night on our way to a four-game sweep over Chicago in the first round. In the conference finals, I provided some key leadership, and we stormed over the Lakers in five. Our half-court offense was operating about as well as I'd ever seen it, and Bulls coach Dick Motta said I was playing as well as he'd ever seen me. Bobby Dandridge told reporters not to pay attention to my stats, I was holding the team together. Wayne Embry said the same thing.

I was back in the finals. And who better to go out against than my old nemesis?

The Boston Celtics were back in the finals for the first time since 1969 and were making their franchise's first appearance there without Bill Russell. I couldn't think of anything nicer than taking that victory cigar from Red Auerbach's mouth and puffing on it myself.

On paper, it was a textbook matchup of opposite styles, with Boston's blistering fast break, pressure defense, motion offense, and outside prowess going up against our disciplined half-court machine and Kareem's dominance in the post. If we had Lucius and had been at full strength, I think we would have been huge favorites, because we could have attacked them all night. As it was, no less an expert than Bill Russell himself predicted that we'd ride Kareem to the title, calling him the greatest player in the game.

The Celtics were playing inspired basketball. At thirty-five, John Havlicek was probably having the best playoffs of a career that had been built on playoff excellence. Dave Cowens and Paul Silas made life miserable for us in the post. And their backcourt of Jo Jo White and Don Chaney was just a bitch to deal with.

Boston had led the league in rebounding and assists during the regular season. Before the series started, Tommy Heinsohn announced that he was going to let Dave Cowens guard Kareem one-on-one. Harkening back to the strategy that his mentor Red Auerbach had used against Wilt, Tom said he'd give Kareem his points and try to shut everyone else down. Kareem didn't seem to mind too much. Presented with his MVP award before the game, the big fella came out and hit three skyhooks, a bank shot, and a free throw, scoring nine of our first fourteen points. The score was knotted at eleven when his counterpart, Cowens, came right back—first with a driving one-handed shot over Kareem's fingertips, then two jumpers from the top of the key. Then he converted a slick pass from Jo Jo White into a layup.

He was going to be a problem throughout the series. At six nine, Cowens had no problem popping outside—he was a deadly shooter from out there, and Kareem wasn't that eager to venture away from the basket. At the same time, Dave was mobile and long and could take the ball to the basket. Really, he was a combination of power and small forward, and he caused all sorts of matchup problems for us.

Even more daunting for us was the matter of the Celtics' defense. Boston's defense relied on pressuring the ball every time it came up court, using Jo Jo's speed and Don's physical approach to frazzle and wear you down. If your forwards and centers were still in the backcourt, their men would leave them and jump the ball. The second Boston scored, they started pressing us; we turned the ball over six times in the first quarter. Our spacing was horrible, and guys who should not have had the ball were forced to make decisions, and they just couldn't do it. Boston pounded us, racing out to a 35–19 lead. And though we closed to within ten at halftime, Jo Jo White came out and scored eleven of Boston's first fifteen points. From there we got no closer than six. The Boston Garden celebrated as we were blown out, 98–83—and only three garbage jumpers in the last minute got us over eighty.

While Kareem had forced Cowens into an 8–25 shooting night, Dave finished the game with nineteen points and seventeen rebounds. Jo Jo White added nineteen points and seven assists. Kareem led our squad with thirty-five, and Bob Dandridge and Mickey Davis had twelve each.

If the loss wasn't bad enough, Jon McGlocklin—who had replaced Lucius in the starting lineup—pulled a calf muscle late in the first half on a jump shot and was going to be out indefinitely.

The series was barely underway, and already the pressure was firmly on our shoulders. We couldn't afford to fall behind 2–0, and now were basically crippled in the backcourt. Jon wasn't the best ball-handler in the world, but he saw the court and understood the game. He knew where the gaps were in a defense and how to head into those weak areas, or pass ahead and break pressure. Without him, we had to rely on guys who weren't as strong with the ball, or who didn't understand the importance of spreading the court to create passing lanes. Fritz Williams was a competitor and hustled like a madman, but he was our third-string guard.

We flew back home and had a day off. On April 30, we came out and attacked their press the right way, fed Kareem for one basket after another, and led by sixteen halfway into the third quarter. But here came Hondo Havlicek. And here came the pressure. And there went our offense. Our backup guard, Williams, turned the ball over three times. Kareem missed nine of eleven shots in the fourth quarter, and the rest of us stood around like zombies. While we netted just thirteen in the frame, Hondo went nuts, scoring ten of his eighteen points. With fifty-eight seconds left, he hit a jumper to bring them completely back and tie the game at ninety. With six seconds left, I had the ball and tried to drive on him. He hacked and stripped me. No call. His running fifteen-footer at the buzzer wasn't close. I went back to the sidelines before overtime, screaming at the ref.

Overtime started and Havlicek hit another jumper. Kareem matched it with a dunk. I hit a baseline jumper. Jo Jo White scored on a backdoor layup off a beautiful bounce pass from Dave Cowens. The game was tied with two minutes left when Kareem hit another turnaround bank shot. On the next possession Dave Cowens came down the lane. Kareem rejected his shot, and the ball bounced to the right corner, into the hands of Fritz Williams.

Fritz took off into the open court and, going in for a layup, was fouled by Don Chaney. He hit two free throws, and we were up four.

After a Jo Jo White jumper made it a two-point game, with forty-six seconds left we called time-out. Cornell Warner got the inbounds pass at halfcourt. He was supposed to find a guard and hand off the ball, but Paul Silas was on him, pressuring and overplaying.

"I just wheeled and took off for the hoop," Cornell said.

It was the biggest play of his life. Cornell was six nine. He was athletic and a good role player and had decent skills. He drove the down that lane and took off and dunked right over Dave Cowens, who was called for his sixth and eliminating foul.

Our crowd went insane. Cornell went to the line and finished off the three-point play, giving us a five-point lead with thirty-four seconds left.

When Boston missed, Cornell got another uncontested dunk and from there it was all celebration. 105–96. The series was tied.

Cornell and Fritz may have been two of our less-heralded performers, but they scored our final nine points. Cornell was one of the game's real stars, finishing with eleven points and thirteen rebounds. His work on the boards helped us to a controlling 55–38 rebounding edge. Of course, Kareem was his usual dominating self inside, scoring thirty-six points and fifteen rebounds. And Bobby Dandridge broke from his slump, scoring twenty-four. As for me, most of my efforts were devoted to getting us through the pressure. Playing fifty-two of fifty-three possible minutes, I had ten points on four of ten shooting, nine assists, and seven rebounds.

Afterwards, talking with reporters, the Celtics backcourt felt the game boded well. "When it comes to dribbling the ball up and passing, Oscar's as good as ever," Don Chaney said. "He hasn't lost that much. But he doesn't have the endurance he did several years ago." Jo Jo White agreed, saying the pressure would eventually wear me and the Bucks down.

And so the stage was set. Boston came out at home in game three and forced us into eleven turnovers. They rushed out to a 32–11 lead. We chipped at it before halftime, but Havlicek and Cowens outscored us by themselves in the quarter, and the game was never in doubt. Cowens had thirty points and six rebounds. Havlicek had twenty-eight and seven assists. Even a reserve center named Hank Finkel gave them a lift with six points and three rebounds. "Their defense is their offense, and we've got to do something about it," Coach Costello told reporters. "We can't play the whole game in the backcourt."

In forty-two minutes, I'd scored twelve points and had five assists, but a good chunk of the turnovers came when guys were trying to get me the ball. That had to change. And it did. Larry changed our starting lineup for game five, starting Mickey Davis instead of Fritz Williams, who'd turned the ball over three times in game three and drained all of Larry's confidence.

Mickey Davis was twenty-three years old and had left Duquesne after his junior year of college to sign with the Pittsburgh Condors in the ABA. At six seven, Mickey wasn't well known around the league. He was something of a defensive liability—no matter how hard he tried, he couldn't guard outside. A natural forward, he also had never played in the backcourt. But Mickey could score. Given the biggest opportunity of his young career, he came out on fire in game five, scoring eight of our first sixteen points. When Boston pressed, he and everybody else cleared out and let me bring the ball up myself. We spread the court and took away their double-team, making it impossible for them to trap. For the first time we were consistently able to beat their pressure and execute the way we were supposed to, and on top of that, Jon McGlocklin came back from his injury. Even though he was favoring his leg, Jon was still an excellent outside threat. With him in there, Boston couldn't sag on Kareem. Jon also knew how to find the open man and get back on defense, which had been a problem for us—especially when we had Mickey out there.

For what seemed like the first time, we weren't playing catch-up all night. It was 28–27 after the first quarter. Whenever the Celtics tried to double me, I hit Davis or Dandridge streaming down the court.

Once again Kareem led our scorers with thirty-four points, fourteen rebounds, and six assists. Bobby Dandridge scored twenty-one, including eight in the fourth quarter to stifle a Celtics run. As for me, playing forty-five of forty-eight minutes, I had ten points (five of ten shooting), and nine assists. More importantly, we had only eleven turnovers. Our 97–89 win tied the series once more.

Still Tommy Heinsohn kept the company line for the Celtics. "Starting Mickey Davis out of the backcourt was no major move. All it means is that Oscar is going to have to do more work."

It was a best-of-three series now, with two games in Milwaukee.

We made only six of twenty-four shots in the first quarter of game five and fell behind early. But then I started finding my range. I kept us in the game in the second quarter, scoring twelve points; Kareem had nine, and we trailed by just one, 45–44, at the half.

The second half wasn't as pretty. A three-second violation. A twenty-four-second clock violation. Offensive fouls. Bad passes. Traveling. We had only fourteen turnovers that night, but seven came during the first nine minutes of the third quarter. Jo Jo White abused our youngster Davis, and Hondo scored eight points in the quarter. With three minutes left in the third, Boston opened an eighteen-point lead. Kareem tried to lead us back; he had thirty-seven on the night, with eleven coming in the fourth. I added twenty-three points on nine of thirteen shooting, defused the great majority of Boston's pressure, and also had six assists. But for the first time, Bobby Dandridge's gun came up empty. Though he was our only other player in double figures, with ten points, he couldn't hit a damn thing all night and·shot just four of seventeen from the field.

A day later, we went back to Boston facing a do-or-die situation. Either we won and forced a final game, or we watched the Celtics celebrate. That was the last thing in the world I wanted to do, especially on the parquet of Boston Garden. We scored eight straight in the opening quarter and were firmly in control, stretching our lead to 43–31 halfway through the second quarter.

Boston made a run in the third. But Kareem kept Cowens in foul trouble, and Bobby Dandridge was back on track, moving well without the ball and torching the Celtics whenever they sagged into the paint. With two minutes and thirty-five seconds left in the game, Kareem's skyhook made it 84–78. Boston came back. Cowens drove past Kareem for a bucket. Don Chaney hit two free throws.

I was fouled on a drive and hit two free throws with a minute fifty-three left to give us a 86–82 lead. But those would be our last points in regulation. Hondo got free for an eighteen-footer, and then Cowens followed it up with a twenty-footer. With a minute left, the game was tied.

We held for the last shot. The clock was running down, and I was behind the top of the key, dribbling, about to run a pick and roll with Kareem. Suddenly, Dave Cowens hedged out and knocked the ball loose. Dave and I dove for the ball, and one ref called for a jump ball. Then backup referee Don Murphy ran into the fray.

He said the twenty-four-second clock had expired. Celtics' ball. Our bench screamed for a foul. Boston's fans went wild.

Jo Jo White missed a jumper. Don Chaney got the rebound and passed to Cowens, and he missed. We had a shot at the buzzer, but it was a wild rush. We were going to overtime.

After the game, John Havlicek said that the first overtime session featured some of the best defense he'd ever seen. Each team could score only four points. After a Curtis Perry tip gave us a 90–88 lead with twenty-eight seconds left, Kareem won a jump ball from Cowens, but Bobby Dandridge was pressured into a bad pass. Hondo dribbled the length of the floor, missed a foul-line jumper, but then followed up his miss. His bank shot with five seconds left tied the game.

The place shook with applause. We were going to double overtime.

I was tired, but at that point adrenaline carries you. It was without a doubt the most dramatic game I ever played in, and the stakes couldn't have been any higher. After Havlicek started the second overtime with a jump shot from the right side, we struggled back and forth, with the lead flipping an incredible ten times in last three minutes and twenty-three seconds. Hondo all but carried their team, scoring nine of the Celtics' eleven points in that session. With a minute and a half left, Dave Cowens fouled out. Trailing by one, the Celtics had to rely on Havlicek alone. Hondo got the ball off a pick and sped toward the lane with twelve seconds left, launching a fifteen-footer over Kareem for his thirty-fifth and thirty-sixth points, putting the Celtics up 101–100.

Eight seconds left. We called time-out. In the huddle, Larry diagrammed a play for Jon McGlocklin. Guys were confused because Jon had been hurt for most of the series, and had only five points in the game. But that was the play, and the horn sounded. I went to my position on the sideline to inbound the ball. Everyone broke for their moves, but Jon was covered. I saw that Kareem was free on the right side and threw a hard pass that couldn't be intercepted.

Kareem turned into the lane for a moment, hoping to see McGlocklin cutting for the hoop. But Jon was still blanketed. Kareem spun toward the right baseline, took two dribbles and, on the run, some fifteen feet from the basket, from almost behind the basket really, went into the motion for his famous skyhook, shooting over the outstretched arms of Cowens's replacement, Hank Finkel.

With three seconds left, Boston Garden went into a collective gasp, then a shocked silence, as the ball settled through the hoop and into the net.

"Man, I was happy to see that thing go in," Kareem said.

A desperate shot at the buzzer by Boston wasn't close, and with an epic 102–101 victory, we were heading home for a deciding game seven. We ran onto the court, celebrating while the shocked crowd revolted. Suddenly stunned by the turn of events, they started cursing us and throwing bottles as we made our way back to the locker room.

As he'd been the entire series, Kareem was truly heroic that night, with thirty-six points; Bobby Dandridge had twenty, and I had eighteen. At this point Larry was using his starters exclusively. I think each of us played the entire game, logging fifty-eight minutes apiece.

The game ended in the small hours of Saturday morning. We had less than forty-eight hours to travel and rest before game seven. Six games and three overtime periods translate into 303 minutes of active basketball. I had played in 291 of them. While I'd been a calming force and on-court general for our offense, the truth was I hadn't shot well. Throughout the series, it seems we had been simultaneously trying to catch up to Boston and to hold them off. We were shorthanded and twice had given away the home-court advantage that we'd worked all season for. Yet somehow we'd hung in and weathered the storms and pressure. We had made it to the deciding game, and it would be played in front of our fans. After all of the shouting and excitement, here we were, forty-eight minutes away from a championship.

The final game of my career was played on Sunday, May 12, 1974. The Milwaukee arena was filled beyond its capacity of 10,746. I went out on the floor and warmed up.

The Celtics stole the opening tap, and Don Nelson scored on a layup. When I was bringing the ball inbounds, Don Chaney literally stood out-of-bounds with me and pressured me, tipping the pass. Havlicek scored on a jumper seconds later. The game was fifteen seconds old, and we were down 4–0.

Against Chaney's pressure, I brought the ball up court, yelled out instructions, and got everyone settled. Immediately, we looked inside for the big guy. But for the first time in the series, Tom Heinsohn had switched his defense. Instead of having Cowens simply play Kareem one-on-one, he had his power forward—first Don Nelson and then Paul Silas—heading toward Kareem as well. A basketball maxim holds that you don't want a team's best player to beat you. Since Cornell Warner, our starting power forward, was not a good shot, Tom Heinsohn decided he'd leave him open in order to double Kareem. As if this wasn't enough, whenever Kareem touched the ball, a third player, either Havlicek or Don Chaney or Jo Jo, depending on the situation, might also come down.

It was the right strategy. We'd seen the same things from each other for six games. With the whole ball of wax on the line, you've got to try to do something different. It didn't mean that they surprised us—teams had been doubling Kareem his entire career. It didn't mean we didn't know what to do.

In a perfect world, Cornell Warner would have been able to make them pay. But Cornell wasn't strong enough offensively to be given that kind of responsibility in a deciding game.

Kareem remained our first priority. We spread out our half-court offense so that nobody could cover the distance to Kareem in time to double him. Matched up against Cowens alone, Kareem hit a bank shot, then a follow-up, then two skyhooks. We kept pounding the ball inside, and our MVP was all but unstoppable, scoring fourteen points in the first quarter. A twenty-five-footer by Cowens at the buzzer broke the tie, but at 22–20, we were well within striking distance.

Immediately, Hondo stole the second-quarter tap and nailed a jumper off it, increasing their lead to four. Kareem answered by recognizing a double-team and hitting an open Curtis Perry for a dunk.

Coach Costello tried a few things to take the pressure off. He wanted guys to pass the ball up whenever possible and then attack the Celtics' back line. It was a good idea in some ways. I was busting my ass on defense, following Jo Jo White through thickets of screens. Any break from the pressure would only help carry me into the second half and allow me to preserve some energy for crunch time. There was only one problem. When we went after the Celtics' pressure this way, the ball went into the hands of guys who weren't equipped to make ball-handling decisions. Things got ragged, and we got out of our half-court offense, and this only made the Celtics apply more pressure. Instead of Kareem getting the ball in the post, we started settling for long jump shots, which triggered the Celtics own running game. Even the few jumpers we made were akin to fool's gold, because they kept us away from working the ball inside, where our money really was. Cowens popped outside and nailed another jumper. Paul Silas hit a jumper. And John Havlicek was abusing poor Mickey Davis. Mickey was holding his own offensively, but he simply had no experience guarding guys out there. Boston got the ball in so low against him that they were almost in position to shoot layups before they started their offense.

On one occasion, we beat their pressure, and I pushed the ball up and had a wide-open eight-foot pull-up jumper—I probably didn't miss that shot ten times in my career; I probably could make that shot right now.

It bounced off the back of the rim.

The next time I had the chance, I penetrated again, and at the last moment hit Kareem for a dunk. It marked the last points he'd have for almost eighteen minutes. Boston began to pull away. Bobby Dandridge, along with Mickey Davis and his substitute Jon McGlocklin, were scoring for us, but we'd gotten too far away from our game plan. The Celtics defense was relentless. We went into the locker room down 53–40. I wouldn't say we were panicked. But something had to happen. Either we were going to get back on track, or we were going to lose.

In the locker room, Larry Costello didn't have any changes or special defenses for us. At this point, there wasn't anything else we could do. Kareem and Bobby and I had played the entire first two quarters, and we were going to have to go the whole distance. We didn't have the energy or personnel for any tricks or changes at that point. Two days earlier might have been the time. Or at some point during the year, when I'd told management we needed another guard, might have been the time. Or if we'd have drafted anyone decent in the four years I'd been there. But it was too late to worry about any of this stuff. It was too late to complain about being exhausted. There are all kinds of reasons why things happen, but at this point there were no excuses.

In basketball, if you are going to lose, you want to go out with your guns blazing. You want your best players to have the ball.

We had to get back to our game. We had to stop taking bad shots and run our offense and try to pound them inside. It was as simple as that.

Midway through the third quarter, with the score 65–50, we started a run. Kareem ended up with a breakaway dunk off a loose ball. Following a strong defensive series, we slowed down, spread the court, and Mickey Davis fed Kareem for a skyhook across the lane. Another outside miss from Boston, and we grabbed the defensive board and walked it up. I caught Mickey coming off a screen. He pumped Hondo out of position and drained the shot, and it was a game again, 65–58; Boston had to call time-out.

A loose ball, a scrum on the floor. Havlicek stole the tip again, and once more our defense tightened and forced another Celtics' miss from outside. We fed the big fella again. Despite a protest from Havlicek that was played on highlight shows for years to come, Hondo was called for a foul, and Kareem returned to the line. The action went back and forth. Kareem missed a skyhook, but Bobby Dandridge was fouled and went to the line.

Finally, Boston broke the slump when Havlicek made a marvelous driving reverse layup. After Kareem was fouled and hit one of two free throws, Dave Cowens answered with a tough fifteen-footer over Kareem.

When Curtis Perry rattled home a foul-line jumper, we'd cut the lead to 71–68. There were eleven minutes to play.

We would get no closer.

There were about ten minutes left when Dave Cowens hit another running hook shot. Coming back down the court, no answer. My jumper bounced long off the front rim. Boston got the rebound and headed the other way. I was caught in a gray area and couldn't get back in time. Jo Jo White scored on the transition layup, and the lead was back to seven. Boston would score eight straight points on us, pushing the cushion back to double figures.

Though we managed another run to bring the deficit to 87–79 with four minutes, thirty-five seconds to play, it was cosmetic. Hondo scored six straight. Cowens had four. Paul Westphal added a free throw. I remember watching and not being able to stop or do anything about any of it. I remember the fans in the same sort of daze. With two minutes to go and the score 98–79, Red Auerbach was on the other sideline, lighting up his cigar. Larry called time-out.

In the huddle he told us to be proud of ourselves, and pulled the starting lineup.

I played forty-six minutes that night, scored six points on two of thirteen shooting, and did not have a field goal in the second half, though I did add six assists and three rebounds. It wasn't the way I would have chosen to end the series, let alone my career, but I have no regrets. There wasn't a second when I wasn't doing everything I could out there.

The final buzzer sounded, and the Celtics celebrated the 102–87 victory and their twelfth title in eighteen seasons.

I went into the Celtics locker room afterwards. Amid all the champagne and bedlam, I sought out John Havlicek. He was telling reporters that of the six titles he'd been involved in, this one meant the most to him. I put my hand on his shoulder.

"Congratulations," I said. "You deserved it."

CHAPTER FIFTEEN

Endings
1974–1976

AND SO I WAS RETIRED—or was I? The Bucks kept me on their active roster through the summer and asked me not to announce my retirement. It was curious. Since I hadn't had a contract through the play-offs, I wasn't sure that, if I decided that I wanted to play again, the Bucks still even owned my rights. Rather than answer them, or even think about this stuff, I spent time with Yvonne and the kids and worked on a pair of real estate projects that would bring housing to low-income people in Cincinnati. My physical condition was fine, I stayed in shape, but I didn't have plans to play or coach.

Eventually, Wayne Embry and Bucks president Bill Alverson called me in for a meeting. Wayne wanted me to come back and let it ride for a final run. His only caveat was about my contract. The NBA rules declared that for them to re-sign me, my new contract would have to contain the same clauses and the same monetary value as my old one. This not only meant paying me a minimum salary of $250,000, it also meant no-cut and no-trade clauses.

The NBA already had plans to add two more teams at the end of the 1976 season. This meant that at the end of the season, established clubs would lose two players each to an expansion draft. If a player had a no-cut clause, he had to be listed on his team's roster for purposes of the expansion draft. Moreover, if he had a no-trade clause, he had to be protected from such a draft. I fell into both of these categories.

The Bucks wanted me back, Wayne said. But they also wanted to get me signed without the no-cut and no-trade provisions, so as to protect their younger players. The only way they could do this was to not send me a contract by August 1. This would make me a free agent. Then we could renegotiate from scratch.

Bill Alverson mentioned the possibility of getting involved with building some housing in and around Milwaukee. They hadn't done that for anybody, but they said they'd help me.

I said, "Are you telling me that's it?"

Alverson said, "Well, we thought this was the best thing for you."

I told them that if I was going to come back, I had to have the no-trade and no-cut clauses. The Bucks president said he couldn't approve it. Considering my age and my injuries . . .

I answered that John Havlicek had those clauses, and he was my age.

It was a matter of economics, Wayne responded.

When you've played and worked a long time in sports, you get accustomed to people and their dealings. The meeting ended. August first came and went. I officially became a free agent. From my end, that was pretty much the end of things between the Milwaukee Bucks and me. While I wished them nothing but success, the moment they relinquished their rights to me, I stopped being interested in what they did.

The only problem with this was that as of August 15, 1974, Milwaukee still had me listed on their official roster. So while they may not have wanted me back, they sure didn't want anyone else to know I was available. Maybe they figured I might come back at a cut rate. Or that I could be an insurance policy if someone else got hurt. I don't really know.

By now training camp was less than a month away. Word was starting to get out. The ABA's the Spirits of St. Louis had gotten into the act and obtained their own version of negotiating rights for me. They had just moved from North Carolina, renamed the franchise, and almost disbanded their whole team. I wasn't heading there. I was not going to the ABA under any circumstances.

Around this time, a representative from CBS called. They'd fired Elgin Baylor from the analyst's position halfway through the season. Rick Barry—who had to sit out a year between jumping leagues—had been hired as his replacement and finished the season and the playoffs. Now Rick was heading back onto the court. Did I have any interest in being a television analyst?

It was an odd possibility. Most of my career had been spent deflecting the media or giving them whatever information our union needed to get out. I'd never really thought about working on the other side of the microphone. I gave it a little thought and immediately saw advantages. I'd still be around basketball. I'd be able to travel on the weekends to broadcast games, while during the week, I'd be at home with my family.

I didn't know anything about broadcasting, but I knew basketball. I didn't give the network an answer, but said I was willing to listen.

ON AUGUST 28, 1974, *The New York Times* reported my retirement after fourteen years of professional basketball. I retired as a twelve-time all-pro, the all-time leader in assists, second only to Wilt Chamberlain in points scored. On the same page, a smaller story detailed the signing of recent high school graduate Moses Malone to a contract with the Utah Stars of the American Basketball Association. The eighteen-year-old was the first player to enter professional basketball immediately after finishing high school. Within a year, Bill Willoughby and Darryl Dawkins would follow.

Six days later, CBS sports director Bob Wussler announced I had signed a multiyear deal and would be joining the network as a color commentator. Ex-football star Johnny Unitas also would be joining CBS, as a football analyst. Afterwards, at a cocktail reception, NBA commissioner Walter Kennedy approached me and shook my hand.

But not everyone was excited about my hiring.

Going back to the summer before my final season with the Bucks, Paul Snyder, the owner of the expansion franchise Buffalo Braves, had been concerned about the direction of television coverage. Snyder had been writing the commissioner letters that would be uncovered later, during the discovery and deposition process of our union's suit against the league. He wrote: "It was my understanding that we are most interested in trying to change the image of our league, and certainly we all must realize the importance of attracting more white association and identification with the NBA game."

The day after CBS hired me, Snyder kept at it, sending this telex off to the commissioner and each of the other owners:

Sept. 5, 1974

In view of the Oscar Robertson lawsuit against the NBA, I feel that all NBA owners should have been advised before the NBA mutually agreed with CBS that Oscar Robertson will be doing the NBA games during this coming season.

It is my opinion that Robertson is presently an adversary of the NBA and should be treated accordingly.

I would like to know if our NBA Television Committee agreed with the selection of Robertson and, in fact, if they have been involved at all in Robertson's selection.

Paul L. Snyder
Buffalo Braves

That same day, Walter Kennedy replied, disavowing any and all participation in my hiring as a broadcaster: "I had no involvement nor participation nor knowledge of CBS intent to engage the services of Oscar Robertson until 5:00 P.M. Tuesday, September 3, when CBS telephoned me to advise me that they were announcing at 6:30 P.M. that they were engaging Robertson as a narrator."

Thank goodness I did not know about any of this. With less than a month before the regular season, I was too busy undergoing a crash course in Sports Broadcasting 101. CBS hired a voice coach named Lillian Wilder to work with me. I'm from Tennessee, and I had a speech pattern they didn't like. In short, I didn't talk white enough. "I am Oscar Robertson," I told them. "This is the way I talk." We worked on other things. How you hold still for the camera and smile; making sure you were sure of yourself when you hit the camera; waiting to get your comments in, then striking quickly, getting in and getting out—"This is Oscar Robertson here in the locker room talking to Rick Barry. Rick, you just won the championship, Tell me how you feel about it and what is going through your mind right now." Most aspects weren't hard to pick up; they were just presence and timing. A big part of what Lillian impressed upon me was that I didn't have to worry about being a commercial-type guy. If I knew what I was talking about, it would come through. That was important, because I did know what I was talking about.

My partner was another network rookie, Brent Musburger. He had been announcing triple-A baseball when Bob Wussler had discovered him. Impressed by Brent's never-ending well of enthusiasm and what viewers would come to recognize as his constant machine-gun patter, Wussler brought Musburger to CBS.

I was, without a doubt, a rookie announcer. We were all rookies. Musburger and I didn't meld well in the beginning. His rapid-fire delivery and my careful analysis were sometimes at odds. Moreover, some people didn't like my natural enthusiasm for the game. So be it.

But these were correctable problems—by the second half of the season, I'd toned down the excitement and learned to make my points more incisive. But other concerns might have been more institutional. Different members of the print media like to complain about something they've labeled "the Jockocracy"—former athletes who are hired to announce games on television. One of their constant gripes about the Jock-ocracy is that former players are too hamstrung by their friendships and aren't critical of other players. Part of this might be true, simply because as a player you know how hard the game is. You also know how it feels to be criticized. At the same time, honesty is part of being a commentator. When someone messes up, the fans deserve to hear about it. While I've always been known to answer questions and talk straight, I never publicly pointed fingers at teammates. Even during my worst days in Cincinnati, I never got involved with mudslinging. There's a separation point, obviously, between criticizing a player and pointing out a mistake.

One columnist decided that because he'd never heard me speak ex-pansively in a locker room after game, I couldn't be a competent an-nouncer. Plenty of cheap shots were taken. Having said this, no matter how snide they got, even my worst critics said that I could pull through if someone would give me direction.

No one did. I don't think the NBA wanted black announcers. Pe-riod. I loved being around the game, and I could see what was going to happen out there before half of the players—let alone a production truck guy or sports columnist—could. And because of who I was, I could get post-game interviews from players who barely nodded to other announcers. But as the season progressed, the producers tried to muzzle my honesty. When-ever I criticized officials, I was told to be quiet. It got ridiculous: everyone in the stadium would be booing a call; we'd show it on instant replay, and the call would be obviously wrong. Then they'd tell me not to say anything. I started to feel that the people in the production truck just wanted a rubber stamp of approval for anything the officials did. No way. When I was out there on the court, I told a ref if he missed a call. If I'm supposed to be an-nouncing a game for people, the last thing I was going to do was keep quiet and let a blown call go unremarked.

I remember one time, near the end of the regular season, we were cov-ering a game between Los Angeles and Portland. Tradition held that after the game, you interviewed the star from the winning team. Well, they wanted me to interview Bill Walton. Walton hadn't played well that night, and Kareem, who was now with L.A., had killed him. Los Angeles won easily.

But the producers told me to interview Bill Walton because he was white.

"Wait a minute," I said. "Doesn't the star come from the winning team? If you want me to do Walton, I can do Walton also."

They told me no. Interview Walton.

I told them I wouldn't do it.

I knew then I was going to be leaving. My instincts were confirmed during a game when Brent literally kept his face right on the television monitor we had set up in front of us. He had his hands blocking the sides and his face in front of the screen the whole game. Nobody from the truck said a thing to him. My fate had been decided, and Brent was well aware of it. The season wound down, and I could live with what was happening. The last thing I was going to do was let any of those critics or whoever know they got to me.

At the same time, ratings that season were up in comparison to previous years. And by the time the playoffs arrived, my commentary improved dramatically. None of it mattered.

On June 4, CBS president Bob Wussler was asked for a comment on my future. He answered: "I haven't thought about it yet. But I recognize that it is something that . . ." His voice trailed off.

It wasn't any secret. Meanwhile, when I was fired, different reporters each gave different reasons for my release.

Look. I had a long way to go before I was slick. I knew that. And it wouldn't have bothered me too much if the league and CBS had just simply told me I was inadequate and given me the gate. That's life. But I also know that giving someone a chance means giving someone a chance. It doesn't mean putting someone on the air, then saying he's no good and hanging him out to dry. But blacks in broadcasting didn't get much of a real chance. I'm still not sure why they offered me the job in the first place. That said, I am still happy about my ratings.

The real reason I was released, I think, can be discerned in the unpleasant opinions of Paul Snyder and the lingering enmity from the Oscar Robertson suit. And racism. Pure and simple.

If you want to play devil's advocate, or be charitable, you might say that Paul Snyder was a lone wolf among the owners. I've been through too much to be so naïve. Paul Snyder was on the competition committee and had clout with the television committees. When I was hired as a commentator, the players union was still embroiled in our lawsuit with the NBA. I'm sure that the last thing Paul Snyder and other owners wanted was to have an enemy of the league in a position to spout opinions and influence the general public on basketball matters.

To add insult to injury, here came a black man—a popular, proud, and successful black man—announcing the games for a predominantly white audience. Commercial sponsors were jittery already because of how many black men were running up and down the court. Putting a black face and a black voice in front of the action only made things worse.

If I hadn't had secret negotiations with and through the network, I wouldn't have been hired in the first place. But once I was on board, the powers that be were upset. While they couldn't fire me or directly pull me off the air during the season, after the season was over was a different matter.

When it came time for the network to either let me grow into the job or cut me loose, I believe that ownerships' opinions, influenced by the NBA, helped CBS make their decision.

By now I've accepted all of this. I realize that at that time, given the way things were, there simply was no way a black man was going to stay on the air as the voice of the sport. But the indiscretion of the whole thing has always irritated me. It's irritated me that over the years, so many great black players have been hired, given one or two years as a commentator, and then either moved over into the ineffectual position as studio host or fired. (Off the top of my head: Elgin, Jim Brown, Magic, Isiah, Julius Erving. Most recently, during the 2003 NCAA basketball tournament, you could see the process happening to Kareem Abdul-Jabbar). So many people on the air today are nothing more than front men who don't know anything about the sport. I can't tell you how often I watch a game and just turn it off.

WHETHER IT WAS A coincidence or not, without me the Milwaukee Bucks fell apart. In 1974, after being poked in the eye by Don

Nelson during an exhibition game, Kareem Abdul-Jabbar punched the basketball standard in frustration, broke his hand, and missed the first sixteen games of the 1974–1975 season. The Bucks ran through those games at 3–13. When Kareem came back, he was constantly double-teamed. Save for my departure, the Bucks had retained essentially the same roster, but they only won thirty-eight games and finished last in the Midwest Division. Near the end of the season, Kareem tired of being double-teamed and worked a trade to the Los Angeles Lakers. He would not return to the NBA finals or have another chance at a championship until the start of the next decade, when the Lakers drafted a young, oversized guard named Earvin "Magic" Johnson.

After the 1975 basketball season ended, Yvonne and I packed up the kids and moved back to Cincinnati. Yvonne's family was there and so were my mother and brothers Henry and Bailey. We had lots of friends nearby—Austin and Gladys Tillotson, Art Hull, J. W. Brown, Adrian and Paula Smith . . .

On July 29, 1975, Tim Sullivan of *The Cincinnati Enquirer* wrote about the occasion as follows:

> Pro basketball returned to Cincinnati Monday. It was not in the form of a franchise granted by one of the two pay-for-play leagues, but in the six-foot-five frame of Oscar Robertson, who left town on April 21, 1970, shortly before the Cincinnati Royals did.
>
> The loss of one may have signaled the loss of the other. Local fans harbor no bitterness for Big O, who is settling back in the Queen City, after a four-year "exile" in Milwaukee. Monday, the city honored him, still possessed with impressive energy, as "O" was carted from one site to another.

That day I visited the Hirsch Community Center for retarded children and paraplegics. I was honored at a Fountain Square luncheon, where, just as Seton Hall's coach had done so many years ago during my inaugural game at Madison Square Garden, a city councilman referred to me as Oscar

Robinson. That night I returned to the University of Cincinnati and walked the campus. I passed through the same fieldhouse I'd played in so many years ago; now a huge painting of me hung in the corridor and a bronze tablet listed my various accomplishments.

It was nice to be back.

ON VALENTINE'S DAY, 1975, federal judge Robert Carter of the Southern District of New York denied a motion by the National and American Basketball Associations to dismiss charges that they conspired to restrain competition for players' services. The judge's seventy-one-page ruling expressed sympathy for the players' position and denied a bid by the league to dissolve the preliminary injunction issued as part of *Robertson v. NBA*. It was a stunning setback for the powers of professional basketball. Both leagues were at a point where they needed each other. Two ABA teams went so far as to independently apply for entry into the NBA. Because of dismal ratings, the NBA and CBS began plans to replace a national game of the week with regional coverage.

If professional basketball was going to survive, its house needed to be unified. The judge's ruling meant that even if the leagues reached a deal on a merger, our union could have prevented the merger through legal action. Our aim had always been to get fair treatment for the players and create a competitive marketplace for their services. We didn't want to see professional basketball die. This was our moment to obtain everything that we had been fighting for while still ensuring the future of basketball.

Finally, on February 3, 1976, after six years of litigation, and millions of dollars in legal fees, the National Basketball Association settled the Oscar Robertson lawsuit. Jim McMillan of Buffalo, John Havlicek and Paul Silas of Boston, and Jeff Mullins of Golden State served as player representatives during the negotiations. I represented the retired players. The settlement profoundly changed the business of basketball and produced a fair and just working environment for its practitioners. We eliminated the option clause, which bound a player to his original team for a year after his contract expired. A player selected in the college draft would only be bound for one year to the team that drafted him. If he had not signed by the end of that year, he was free to reenter the draft. Underclassmen and high school graduates were permitted to enter the draft. We negotiated that NBA teams would pay a total of $4.3 million in restitution to the players. Four hundred seventy-nine players ended up receiving money; the amounts were based on how long they had played professional basketball prior to the agreement. (The most any player received was upwards of $32,000.) In short, we had brought free agency to basketball.

Years of struggle were justified, generations of players vindicated. Not only had we sent a message that we had been treated wrongly, but we'd also put an end to the unfair treatment. I can't put into words how it felt afterwards—the sense of relief and accomplishment and jubilation. After eleven years, pro basketball players were, like any other members of the workforce, allowed to go and play anywhere they chose, so long as they obeyed the rules and clauses of their contract.

Though modified many times, this settlement remains the backbone of the relationship between the NBA and its players. And the guideline removing compensation for teams who lost free agents has become known as the Oscar Robertson rule.

Whenever I look back, I am so proud of what we accomplished. In 1965, when I took over as the association's president, the average player salary was about $18,000. In 1975, when I stepped down, it was around $110,000. The union won the fight for a pension plan—where all players, upon reaching age fifty, receive a yearly salary for the rest of their lifetime; we fought for and established a severance plan independent of the pension; we'd also won the right to a disability program in which any player whose career is ended due to injury gets paid for five years after the end of his career. Of all our victories, free agency was the topper.

Larry Fleisher was an instrumental part of this. He was there every step of the way. During the quarter century that Larry served as our general counsel, he did so without a salary. Larry was instrumental in establishing an antidrug program whose model other leagues came to emulate; he helped cut the draft to two rounds, and later, negotiated the agreement that established the NBA salary-cap system. He managed to do all these things without calling for a players' strike. With the help of John Havlicek, Dave DeBusschere, and Wes Unseld, Larry ushered in appropriate per diems, decent travel, and reasonable accommodations. It's always bothered me that Larry was not admitted into the Basketball Hall of Fame until 1991, two years after his passing. Without him, I don't know how our struggles would have turned out.

As it was, once the Robertson suit was out of the picture, the road was clear for a merger. On June 17, 1976, after nine years and some fifty million dollars in losses, the American Basketball Association officially came to an end, with the Indiana Pacers, New York Nets, San Antonio Spurs, and Denver Nuggets being accepted as the newest members of the National Basketball Association.

The Oscar Robertson suit was officially resolved on August 2, 1976, when Judge Carter officially approved the settlement. When the merger was complete, the NBA had twenty-two teams. By this time, I was approaching my thirty-eighth birthday and had been out of the game for almost two years.

Epilogue

You can still visit Bellsburg, Tennessee, and walk the farmlands where my great-grandfather Marshall Collier and my maternal grandfather Papa Bell worked and toiled. On his deathbed, Papa Bell told my mother to keep his land and never sell it.

In most cases, though, change is constant. While the run-down area of Indianapolis where I grew up is still called Lockefield Gardens, that's where the resemblance ends. Half of Lockefield's original twenty-four buildings were demolished during the early 1980s. The blacks were put out. Most of the remaining buildings were converted to upscale apartment complexes, replete with manicured lawns, fountains at the entranceways, and swimming pools where yuppies lounge and college kids flirt. Need I say it is predominantly white now? There's a waiting list for apartments. As for the Dust Bowl, it was dismantled during the renovations. I don't think that should have happened. Indiana is supposed to be a state that cares about basketball. But if urban basketball had mattered at all to the city planners, if the politicians cared one bit about what the community thought or considered the significance of those courts to the history of the game and the city, the Dust Bowl would have been landmarked. Now it's too late.

Crispus Attucks High School also was a casualty of progress. Once Attucks won its second state basketball title, white high schools started admitting and attracting black athletes. When the athletes diffused into other schools, more and more of the Attucks student body followed. By the mid-1960s, Crispus Attucks no longer served as the educational, social, and cultural backbone of black Indianapolis. Some of the more radical activists in Indianapolis wanted to tear down the school because of the supposed memories of prejudice it evoked. Those activists were on the wrong track. When they looked at the school, they saw a symbol of the white man's prejudice. But if you attended Attucks, you didn't experience prejudice within its walls. I remember Crispus Attucks as a haven where I learned much of what helped me become a success. I was truly happy at Crispus Attucks. The prejudice I encountered was in the white sections of town.

In the 1970s and 1980s Crispus Attucks was integrated. Enrollment kept shrinking. In 1986, the school was converted to a junior high.

Yvonne and I had moved back to Cincinnati in 1975. Including the years I spent here during college and the pros, I've called the city home for well over forty years. My Ohio license plate reads, simply, 'OR4', and it is not unusual, even now, for cabbies or pedestrians to crane their necks as they greet me. Restaurant maître d's are happy to rush me to a good table, and every once in a while a teenager or child recognizes me from television. My wife takes me to cultural events and has helped me to enjoy social occasions. I like to smoke an occasional cigar and drink a beer. I own businesses here. I raised my children in Cincinnati, and I'm comfortable here.

I am a part of Cincinnati life.

And yet . . .

Though the racial divisions that were so prevalent when I first moved here have been closed in many ways, in too many other ways things are worse than ever. There were acts of vandalism through the streets last year. The political leadership needs improvement. The city's school and library systems are having financial trouble. Banks should certainly lend more to minority-owned businesses for them to be successful. A local talk-radio station broadcasts such racially charged invectives that it's hard for me, in good conscience, to go onto my friend Andy Fuhrman's radio show, because it's on the same station. The city's still not the best sports town for blacks. Coming off a 2002 season as the NFL's laughingstock, the Bengals responded by hiring Marvin Lewis as their head coach. Lewis has been one of the best defensive coordinators in the league for years. I hope he starts winning fast. The window of opportunity does not stay open long.

For decades I've done whatever I could to help the University of Cincinnati's basketball program. Whenever I could help in recruiting, I would. At the same time, I also let the school know it would be wrong for me to tell some young man to come to the university if I didn't think he could do the academics or wasn't a good enough ballplayer. I support the school, but without sacrificing my own personal integrity. This never went so far as to create a rift between the University of Cincinnati and me. But I have to admit, for a time relations between us were a bit chilled. We're on better terms now, the university and I. In 1989, Bob Huggins was hired to try and rejuvenate the men's basketball program. While I wasn't going to impose myself or go anywhere I wasn't wanted, I wanted to welcome him to town. Soon he, George Smith, and I went out to lunch and talked about the program, where it had been, where it was going. At my daughter's urging, I have six season tickets. I stop by practices once a week or so, talk to the players about basketball.

In 1993, before J. W. Brown passed away, he did one final wonderful thing for me.

I remember when Rod Noll first mentioned to the idea of having a statue of me constructed. It was a nice gesture, but I thought it was kind of crazy. I actually told him no, that I appreciated the thought but didn't want any statues put up for me. But J. W.'s son, Robert, said that J. W. wanted it.

Then he told me he was dying.

The Myrl Shoemaker Center is the hub of the University of Cincinnati's athletic facilities, a 13,176-seat, ultramodern basketball and volleyball arena, with private executive suites, a restaurant and lounge, and an expansive video scoreboard. Among his final activities, J. W. arranged to have a statue of me put out in front of the center's main entranceway. Not only that, but he found the artist—Blair Buswell of Highland, Utah. As if this was not enough, he also financed the statue's construction and installation.

I remember the press conference when the university announced the statue's placement. I couldn't help but think back to when I was seventeen years old and J. W. took me under his wing, invited me to his home for the first time. I couldn't help but remember how tough things were for me at school and on the road.

So much time had passed, so much had happened.

The sculpture is larger than life. It shines, impervious to time and the elements.

I look at it and see a bronze version of myself—young and lithe, in motion, racing up court, looking up, my body ready to spring, the basketball connected firmly to my hand.

I told everyone that I was going to drive downtown and come around at 5:30 in the morning when nobody was here, just to look at it sometimes.

Finally, when it was time to unveil the statue, I took to the podium, first making a joke about college students, then about how the statue takes twenty pounds and twenty years away from me. When it was time to get serious, I once again was flooded with memories—of black cats in locker rooms and the Klan and also all the friends who'd stood by me.

"Time is slipping by," I said.

"This statue is for Oscar Robertson," I said. "But it's also for you. And you. *And you.*"

As I pointed into the crowd and as my voice rose, it also tremored and cracked, and I started crying. I couldn't help it. This was the catharsis, the happy ending, the hero riding off into the sunset. It was wonderful.

And yet . . .

It was rumored that either my wife or me would be asked to be on the University of Cincinnati board of trustees. When my name came up,

I've been told, the idea was dismissed, with the excuse, "Oh, he'll want to hire black professors." Never mind that it's a public university now, so by law it should be diverse. Never mind that the issue has nothing to do with me; if there aren't enough black professors, then some should be hired. It's just a matter of right and wrong. Never mind that seeing how many Jewish people have helped me in my life, I might want to hire Jewish professors, I might want to hire Martians, but neither Yvonne nor I are going to be given the chance to so much as express our respective views in preliminary interviews. Never mind that if I hadn't integrated the basketball team, it might be getting around to admitting its first black student right about now.

So long as I am a statue or a symbol, everything is fine. It's when I express views and ideas that doors close. Is this what it means to be an immortal?

My old uniform from Crispus Attucks sits safely on display in a glass case in the Basketball Hall of Fame, in Springfield, Massachusetts. My Cincinnati Bearcats jersey hangs from the rafters of Shoemaker Center, and my bronzed likeness stands in front of their arena. The Milwaukee Bucks have retired my number. I've received every honor that a basketball player can get, ranging from being named player of the century to gracing the NBA's roster of the fifty greatest players of all time. The United States Basketball Writers of America even renamed their college player of the year award in my honor. I'm honored and more than happy they named such a prestigious award after me.

Doing things the right way always has been important to me. It remains so. For example, on February 16, 2003, a week or so after the 2003 all-star break and some thirty-three years after my career with the Cincinnati Royals ended, the Sacramento Kings retired my jersey during halftime of a nationally televised game against the San Antonio Spurs. During the game, the Kings wore retro jerseys. Some of this was done in conjunction with an NBA program called Hardwood Classic Nights.

Since 1999, when Joe and Gavin Maloof became the majority owners of the Sacramento Kings, they've turned that moribund franchise around, transforming it from one of the NBA's graveyards into a crown jewel. The Kings are a title contender for the first time, really, since Jerry Lucas and I had our chances ruined by that stupid trade that got rid of Bob Boozer.

The Maloofs invited me and some others from the franchise's history out for the weekend. They didn't have to have a ceremony, didn't have to acknowledge the Kings' roots in Cincinnati, didn't have to do any of this, NBA program or not. But they not only hosted the weekend, they treated everyone very well. It was one of the most professional situations I've been involved in, in my life.

That was a wonderful gesture, let me tell you. While in Sacramento, my wife and I had some talks with their superstar forward, Chris Webber. My wife spoke to him about African art.

So other than my Olympic and all-star jerseys, every number I've ever worn has been retired. I guess I am a regular living legend.

Until Michael Jordan came onto the scene, most basketball experts considered me the greatest all-around player who ever lived. Even now the question rages. Phil Jackson played against me as a member of the New York Knicks and also coached Michael to all of his championships. He's always answered the "Who's better?" questions diplomatically, talking about the impossibility and unfairness of comparing players from different eras, especially considering how different Michael and I were on the court. (Michael was a scoring machine; I was a player who could assume that role, but I was first and foremost a floor general.) Kareem Abdul-Jabbar played with Magic and against Michael, and he's always been generous, saying that he played with me first and that made his time with me special.

I think Hubie Brown has a unique perspective on matters. Hubie was an assistant on our championship Milwaukee team. After a stint as head coach of the Knicks in the early 1980s, Hubie retired to the announcing booth until just this past year, when Jerry West asked him to take over as coach and teacher of the Memphis Grizzlies.

"When they pick the top ten players of all time, they are always going to pick the same four guards," Hubie says. "Oscar Robertson, Michael Jordan, Jerry West, and Magic Johnson. Oscar will always be one of the top ten players to ever play. And then when people say Michael Jordan was the greatest player in the history of the game, well, the guy he had to top was Oscar Robertson."

Again, a generous answer. The truth is, I get the question a lot: How would I stack up against Michael Jordan? I'll tell you the question that really should be asked: How would players like Michael Jordan or any of the players playing today stack up against Oscar Robertson? How would they do against Jerry West or Wilt Chamberlain?

Michael is truly a once-in-a-lifetime player. He always seemed to understand what his team needed from him. But in the context of playing the game, no, I don't think anyone was any better than I was. As I said before, people don't realize what's asked of you when you play with a team that's not very good. You have to get other players in control; you can't freelance. If I would have—if I could have—shot the ball thirty times a game (18.9 field-goal attempts per game was my career average), I would have scored a lot more, I guarantee that.

Does it bother me that people today tend to think everyone who plays now is better? No. Because I know no one in basketball could achieve what I could achieve if I were in my prime and playing now. No one could do now what Bill Russell could do. No one could do what Wilt could do. And that's the end of it.

Of course, speculation is beside the point. You can't alter history or change time. We live in the here and now; a new generation of players is maturing and becoming the game's leaders, Iverson and Webber, McGrady, Kevin Garnett, and Vince Carter among them. They're all very good, even great, players, but if there's anything missing from their games, it's this: Some of these great basketball players do hardly anything to help the team or the other players on the team. I always thought that my role was to get the team going, get other players involved. You don't see that a lot anymore.

Of today's generation of players, I think Kobe Bryant is the best. Kobe has a tremendous game. Everyone wants to compare him to Michael Jordan. Kobe is so far ahead of Michael Jordan at this point in his career, it's unbelievable. Kobe Bryant is the heart and soul of the Lakers. Lots of people say it's Shaq. Shaq is great, no doubt about that. If you look at the games that have been won by Los Angeles, and you look at the most important parts of the game, yes, Shaq is very important. He is an outstanding big man inside, especially if he stays close to the basket, but Kobe Bryant makes the plays. He makes the pass, the block, gets the rebound, gets out and gets the tempo up. He has the size and speed to go to I don't know what heights.

The business of basketball has changed a lot in the past twenty years. At the beginning of the 1980s, the NBA finals were being televised late at night, on a tape-delay basis, because ratings were so awful. Magic and Bird changed that and began a cult of personality that Michael Jordan then took to previously uncharted dimensions. At the same time, the free-agency clause that I went to court to obtain ushered in a new level of salaries, with players signing contracts for unheard-of amounts of money and agents exerting as much control on a team's roster as general managers. In 1998, it reached a boiling point: A labor stoppage seriously hurt the game, damaging owners as well as the image of players and the union (especially when player meetings were held in Atlantic City, and one guard joked, to *The New York Times*, "If this strike goes another week, I may have to sell one of my cars").

Thankfully, the game has emerged from the wreckage. Revenue sharing allows all teams, be they small- or large-market, to pay top salaries. There's free agency and player movement and salary caps, not only for rookies, but for all levels of veterans, dependent on how long each player has been in the league. During the 1980s, Michael Jordan opened the gates to endorsement millions for Charles Barkley, Patrick Ewing, and untold others, but there are not that many great endorsement deals off the court anymore. Those days are gone. They had their run, and the players enjoyed it.

I am not privy to what's going on between the union and the owners today, negotiation-wise. I watch the game as a fan. And I know that right now the game is not as competitive as it could be. Maybe four or five teams could win a championship—that's the extent of it. Other than that, the league has become a marketing tool that is used by the NBA and its licensees to sell products. Caps. Socks. Jackets. Headbands. Everything that kids want. Even the history of the game is being marketed as fashion. The league is more than willing to license three-hundred-dollar "retro" jerseys styled after the uniforms of the 1960s, 1970s, and 1980s. But does this do anything besides sell the image? What about the actual history of the game? *NBA 2Night* is a nightly show on ESPN. There's a weekly show, *Inside Stuff*, which the NBA produces, that runs on ABC, and an ESPN2 program that follows teams around. There are those pre- and post-game shows on all these networks: ABC, ESPN, ESPN2, ESPN Classic, TNT, TNN. They're affiliated with the NBA, they cover the NBA, and none of them capitalizes, utilizes, or even pays attention to the history of the league. Nothing matters to the press beside tonight's highlights, this week's wackiest plays, and dunks, dunks, dunks.

Meanwhile, the fans are saying something else. Retro jerseys featuring the names and numbers of the all-time greats are selling out. I'm pleased to report that some things have changed: The retired wing of the Players Association is totally involved with this.

ONCE I RETIRED and came home to Cincinnati, I felt I would be able to capitalize on my career and popularity here. J. W. Brown and his son Robert helped me make the transition to the private sector. I still took time out to conduct youth basketball clinics—both throughout the nation and internationally. I was hired as a consultant for Specs International, a sportswear business, and even spent a few years working part-time as a television analyst for the Metro-7 league, a forerunner of what has become the Great American Conference. But my primary professional focus was the business world.

If my years of union struggles taught me one thing, it was that when you want to get something done in this country, you've got to have an economic and political power base to work from. Without that, you have no leverage. Without financing, even the greatest idea and project comes out to nothing.

Too many people are content to live in their little shells, their suburbs, their homes, to plan vacations and pull down the shades on what's happening around them in business, their communities, and governments.

Not me. I learned that all this world owes you is the opportunity to do something for yourself.

Black people in this country have a problem though, in that we don't produce or manufacture enough. When the average college-trained black man comes out with his degree in engineering or one of the sciences, where does he go? I observed that there were hundreds of people in the post offices who are not working in their chosen fields or up to their God-given capacities. I saw firsthand that blacks didn't own enough companies to help themselves. When you work for other people, you can be fired for any number of reasons, relevant or otherwise. Sometimes, you can be affected by unforeseen variables that have nothing to do with you. It's gotten to the point where the factor of true ability may be the last thing to keep a guy on a job.

By the time I ended my professional basketball career, I knew I wanted to build a solid foundation for a viable company. I wanted to grow a company that would create opportunities for hiring young black prospects out of the University of Cincinnati or Northeastern Louisiana, or wherever.

Maybe it was a pipe dream, but I intended to give it a thorough effort.

I didn't exactly receive an open-armed reception from the business community. Banks did not want to lend me capital. When I tried to spearhead plans to bring two different franchises to Cincinnati—Coors and auto dealerships—I lost out. These experiences were disappointing, certainly. But when I stopped and thought about it, they weren't all that different from what I'd gone through with the players union. Indeed, they only reaffirmed every idea I'd had about the business world, every notion concerning equality and competition.

Like with anything else in my life, I knew that the one thing I wanted was a chance. This meant I was going to have to accomplish certain things in spite of people. Back in my old hometown of Indianapolis, I soon became involved with the White River Canal Project, a redevelopment effort near my old neighborhood and the ghetto home where I'd been raised. In Indianapolis, I spearheaded a project that developed affordable housing in Oxford Terrace and helped families with the down payment, creating a financing arrangement that was a first for the city. I've never been able to put my childhood conditions behind me, and these projects were steps to make sure that others wouldn't have to be raised in similar climates. But they weren't the extent of my dealings.

They were the beginning.

I now own and am the CEO of Orchem Inc., a manufacturer of chemicals used in industrial cleaning and the nation's largest minority-owned chemical manufacturing company. And I am the president, CEO, and majority shareholder in Orpack-Stone, a company that produces corrugated packaging, and I am starting the Oscar Robertson meat company. In addition, I have a hand in a general contracting and development company, a document management service, a trucking company, and a media ventures group. I also serve on the boards of a number of national and local charities. I am a member of so many boards of directors and/or trustees that I have to get out my résumé to track them all. These days, my principal motivation is to make sure my companies are sound for my daughters. Shana works for Orchem, and Tia works for Orpack. (Mari, my youngest, works for a company that provides low-, moderate-, and middle-income families with the financial services to purchase homes.)

No father has adequate words for the love he feels for his children. Whenever anyone asked me if I wanted a boy, I said, "I never really thought about it." And I didn't. I just hoped my children would be healthy. My daughters loved sports when they were growing up, and all of them were excellent athletes. Yvonne says that they always tried to be their father's boys. I guess it's true. I used to play football with them. And whenever neighborhood boys knocked on the door and asked to shoot baskets, I always answered that if they could beat my daughters, then I'd be happy to come out. They were always able to talk sports with me, and still do. They have always been my pride, my joy.

In late 1989, Tia was twenty-five years old and working for the National Association of Securities Dealers in New York. She wanted the experience and she was happy. But one day she noticed there were strange marks, like stars, or little cracks, on her fingertips. It looked like her fingers were drying up. She didn't think much of it at first, but it didn't go away. She visited doctors in Cincinnati, but none of them knew what it was. Aches followed in her joints. I flew out to take her to a specialist. Before the appointment, Tia got scared in my hotel room. We called Yvonne, and Tia started crying, asking, "Mom, am I really sick?" The question hit me really hard. Worse still, I didn't have an answer. I started crying too. Tia was diagnosed with lupus, a disease that causes the body's immune system to attack tissues and vital organs. She moved back to Cincinnati and went to work at Orpack. Gradually, the disease took its toll. Her joints constantly ached. Soon she had to cut back on her physical activities.

In 1994, doctors determined the disease was causing her kidneys to fail. She moved back in with us. By November 1996, she began dialysis at our home; a machine cleaned her blood for seven and eight hours a night.

If she was going to have any semblance of a regular life, it became apparent that she would need a transplant. While Tia went on a waiting list for a kidney from a cadaver, our family started undergoing tests to see if one of us was a compatible as a donor.

Shana and I turned out to be good candidates. Shana had her own child, and I wouldn't put her at risk. I didn't even want her to have a chance to make the decision. I never thought twice about it. When you see a family member suffer and you know there's a way out, you'll do almost anything to help. That's just part the territory that comes with being a dad.

The surgery took six hours and left an eighteen-inch scar down my side and back. Doctors at the university said the kidney was one of the largest they'd ever seen. The first thing I said when I regained consciousness was, "How's Tia?"

The doctor said she was doing fine.

It wasn't something that any of us wanted publicity for. But somehow news got out anyway, and there was a media blitz. Tia refused all interview offers, but *People* still ran a four-page spread, calling it the Big O's biggest assist. Soon after, Oprah Winfrey offered praise on her Father's Day show. Our family received hundreds of cards and letters from throughout the country. A basket of them sits on a display case I built, next to a basketball from the 1960 Olympics.

These days, Tia is taking medication, of course, like many transplant patients, and I think she is doing great. I tell anyone who asks that I'm no hero. Just a father. I have to believe that any dad worth his salt would do the same. The reason I tell the story anymore is because now I'm a spokesman for the National Kidney Foundation, as well as for organ donation.

In so many ways my life has worked out perfectly. I have a lovely wife who I've been fortunate enough to love and spend my entire adult life with. I have three healthy grown children, am a happy grandfather, a successful businessman. Mine is a dear and wondrous life. And basketball has been a huge part of it.

The game has done more for me than I could ever begin to repay. Basketball has opened a lot of doors for African-Americans. Every day it continues to help bridge the gaps between whites and blacks that exist to this day in this country. I was fortunate enough to play an important part in the sport's development, to have been able to stand up and fight to achieve better working conditions for the men who played the game. Throughout, no matter what I was going through, no matter how I felt about some of the things that happened to me, no matter what kind of people I had to deal with, basketball itself never stopped being fun for me; I've never felt anything for the game except love.

Once I heard someone say that in order to write love songs, you have to have been through some bad times. To write a love song, you have to have had your heart broken.

If that's the case, I can state right here and now that I could write the greatest songs in the world.

I have viewed the game as a spectator for the past twenty-eight years, less an outsider than a Moses figure, unable to enter the Promised Land. Where the men I helped build the league with—Jerry West, Bill Russell, Elgin Baylor, and Willis Reed, among others—received offers to coach teams or were general managers, I was passed over. Did I really want that experience? We'll never know. I can't say whether my union involvement had anything to do with this, or if it happened, in part, because of my struggles with various front offices, or because I had a reputation as being difficult. Maybe other factors were involved as well.

I've been told that I could never have survived as a coach, that I'm too much of a perfectionist, too blunt. Even my wife thinks I would have had problems dealing with players who weren't as dedicated as I used to be.

There might be some truth to this. Magic Johnson and Larry Bird each had chances to coach teams, and this very problem drove each of them from the bench. Maybe it would have gotten to me as well. I can't speculate on how I might or might not have responded. I just know that I played professional basketball for fourteen years, played in a lot of big games, shouldered a lot of pressure. I always noticed who should be in a game in certain situations and who shouldn't. I know how to evaluate talent. I know players. And I doubt there have been ten people who understood the game as well as I did. But you must play the cards you are dealt.

I also know this: When I left basketball in 1975, Wayne Embry was the only black man involved on a management level. Wayne remained general manager of the Bucks until 1977, when he "accepted" a less active role with the organization. In 1985, he left Milwaukee and became general manager of the Cleveland Cavaliers, assembling a team that could never get past Michael Jordan in the playoffs. Aside from Wayne, it's almost impossible to come up with a black man who had a serious career in NBA front offices during that period. I am not talking about being hired as a community relations officer, mind you; I am talking about a significant position.

If you look at the history of the league, it wasn't until the late 1980s and early 1990s that African-Americans began being hired as general managers, and even then strings were attached. But things are changing. Elgin Baylor has been the general manager of the Los Angeles Clippers for some time now. Willis Reed spent time as the general manager of the New Jersey Nets and is now an executive.

The league has publicly spearheaded a push for diversity—in ownership, in management, in coaching, in announcing. Right now, Magic Johnson and Michael Jordan each own parts of various franchises. The Nuggets, for a time, were owned by a group of minority businessmen, and the expansion Charlotte franchise is owned by Robert Johnson. Throughout the league, you can find African-Americans coaching and behind the microphones. But I also know that to this day, coaching jobs have too often arrived in the middle of the season, only after the old head coach has gotten the axe and the team has fallen apart. That's when a black assistant gets bumped up to the head job. I know that too often the announcers have nothing to say or are put in milquetoast positions such as a studio anchor.

I can't tell you how much it dismays me that in the storied history of the New York Knicks, just one African-American has ever been involved with their front office. In a diverse city like the Big Apple, just as there are untold good soldiers who will do as they are ordered, there are untold good prospects, men and who could work for teams and someday become strong general managers.

But of course, some of us are generals.

I know that it is more than possible that the present-day corporate NBA has less of an issue with race than it does with outspokenness. Whatever problems still exist in the game today, no matter how much I may feel that nonwhites are still underrepresented in front offices around the league, in fact the NBA *has* taken extraordinary steps forward. In this struggle any victory, by anyone, is a victory for us all.

I also think it's important to acknowledge the role of history.

It's important that there be some record of how the game of basketball got here. How we got here. It's important that my grandchildren know. That their children know.

Because too often I tell people what happened to me and am met with disbelief. I'm told that I am just being bitter.

I'll never forget the time a young reporter interviewed me. He listened for a little while and then said, "You're opinionated." I answered, "Young man, I'm not opinionated, because these things happened, they happened to me. You're opinionated because nothing's happened to you. You've decided you are a writer, but you don't have any firsthand experience in the world of basketball. But somehow you've decided who is and isn't opinionated. That's what being opinionated is. Whether you like it or not, this is what happened to me."

I do wish I could look back on my time in basketball and how I left and feel that it was all done cleanly.

My solace has been the knowledge that what I achieved in the game of basketball was unparalleled both on and off the court. It is the knowledge that whatever people may have thought of my methods, I fought the good fight. In retrospect, maybe it could have been fought in a different manner, but what the hell, it was a good run. I can see now the price was high—higher than I could have ever known. But I was more than willing to pay it.

I would never want anyone to think I was the only person who suffered, because I was not. My life was just one piece in a much larger puzzle. There were players in each and every sport who suffered just as I did, whose accomplishments have been forgotten. Even more could have set records and created history but never received the chance. Those players have faded away. It is as if they never existed.

As I write this, basketball has entered a strange new century. The game has become international; it has become computerized and wireless and fiber-optic. Nobody knows what the next five years will look like, what heights players will be capable of reaching, how brightly they will shine. Whatever happens to the sport, I hope that the men who gave their blood, sweat, and tears to build the league will be remembered. I hope that people will never forget that when any man reaches for previously unattainable heights, he does so only because he stands on shoulders of those who came before.

If you forget the contributions and accomplishments of Oscar Robertson, then how will you understand about Bill Russell's role?

Without the context of history, the accomplishments of Wilt Chamberlain and Jerry West and Kareem Abdul-Jabbar mean nothing.

Without understanding the struggles of the players who came before, the highlights of Magic and Bird and even Michael Jordan might as well never have existed—because one day they, too, will be dust.

Add Tim Duncan to the list. Add Shaq.

This sport has had to fight and scratch for its place on the landscape. It has come so far. It has so far to go.

This country has had to fight and scratch for the slightest bit of understanding between blacks and whites. We have come so far. We still have so far to go.

Credits

The article on page 82 entitled "Cincinnati to Meet Seton Hall Tonight," which appeared in the January 9, 1958, issue of *The New York Times*, is excerpted with permission of the publisher.

The excerpt on page 85 from Jimmy Cannon's column, which appeared in the *New York Post* on January 10, 1958, is reprinted with permission of the publisher.

The article on page 103 entitled "How to Stop 'Big O,'" which appeared in the January 19, 1959, issue of *Newsweek* magazine, is excerpted with permission of the publisher.

The excerpt on page 146 from the article entitled "The Graceful Giants," which appeared in the February 17, 1961, issue of *Time* magazine, is reprinted with permission of the publisher. © 1961 Time Inc.

The excerpt on page 156 from the book *Giant Steps* by Kareem Abdul-Jabbar, © 1989 Bantam Books, is reprinted with permission of the author.

The excerpt on page 222 from the book *Miracle on 33rd Street: The New York Knickerbockers' Championship Season* by Phil Berger, © 2001 McGraw-Hill, is reprinted with permission of the publisher.

The excerpt on page 230 from the article entitled "The Big O's Hardest Time" by Milt Gross, which appeared in the January 22, 1970, issue of the *New York Post*, is reprinted with permission of the publisher.

Index